The Future of
Financial Privacy

The Future of Financial Privacy

private choices versus political rules

ISBN 1-889865-03-6

Printed in the United States of America.

COMPETITIVE ENTERPRISE INSTITUTE
1001 Connecticut Avenue, NW
Suite 1250
Washington, DC 20036

COMPETITIVE ENTERPRISE INSTITUTE

Cover design by Marja Walker
Layout by Dyann Collins

The Future of Financial Privacy: Private Choices Versus Political Rules arose from a conference on financial-privacy issues held by the Competitive Enterprise Institute in late 1999. Many of the contributors to this volume participated at that event. The editing chores were undertaken by several CEI staff members involved in the Financial Privacy Project, most notably Vice President James Gattuso; Director of Economic Studies Tom Miller (now at the Cato Institute); Editorial Director Max Schulz; and Assistant Editor Dyann Collins.

CEI launched the Financial Privacy Project in early 1999, with the aim of reframing the terms of the debate by delving into the questions of private versus political regulation of individuals' private financial information. The Project's mission is to develop and promote pro-consumer and free-market approaches to questions of financial privacy.

The Competitive Enterprise Institute is a public policy organization committed to advancing the principles of free enterprise and limited government. Founded in 1984 by Fred L. Smith, Jr., CEI promotes pro-market policies and the institutions of liberty through analysis, education, coalition building, advocacy, and litigation. A nonprofit, tax-exempt organization under Section 501(c)(3) of the Internal Revenue Code, CEI relies entirely on donations from corporations, foundations, and private individuals. All contributions are tax deductible to the extent the law will allow.

For more information, please contact:

Competitive Enterprise Institute
1001 Connecticut Avenue, NW
Suite 1250
Washington, DC 20036
Phone: (202) 331-1010
Fax: (202) 331-0640
E-mail: info@cei.org
Web site: http://www.cei.org

Contents

Introduction

Fred L. Smith, Jr.

"Privacy will be to the information economy what consumer protection and product safety were to the industrial age." *Marc Rotenberg, Electronic Privacy Information Center**

We love the fruits of an information-intensive society, and in no area is this more evident than financial services: the ability to engage in transactions around the world, quick access to credit from a deluge of sources, competition among numerous producers jostling to underbid each other. Moreover, entrepreneurs recognize the value of inexpensive data, which enable them to identify potential suppliers and customers and to learn quickly whether the person at the other end of the wire is a solid citizen or a deadbeat.

Nevertheless, there is something disturbing about this "brighter" world we now inhabit. It's not so much that we have something to hide, but rather few of us relish the idea that a stranger, or, perhaps worse, a neighbor or a co-worker, might with the touch of a button download a list of all our financial transactions over the past year, or discover we bounced a check two years ago, or even that we bought six boxes of sugared cereal at the local supermarket last month.

Still less do we like the possibility that this information, with perhaps our credit-card numbers tossed in, might circulate freely over the Internet. Consumers ask: Is my money safe? Who has access to my spending habits and credit files? Are companies selling my personal information to third parties, and for what purposes? What are the risks of aggregating all my accounts on one web site?

---

*Quoted by Nina Bernstein, "Lives on File: The Erosion of Privacy—A special report; Personal Files Via Computer Offer Money and Pose Threat," *The New York Times*, June 12, 1997.

Perhaps most troubling is the thought of all the information the technological revolution is making available to governments. Consumers worry about the relentless and ever more intrusive demand for information by law-enforcement agencies, tax authorities, and others.

Because of these and other concerns, privacy has become a popular issue among politicians. They have found that privacy resonates with the public, and thus provides them with opportunities to introduce legislation, hold hearings, and get favorable media coverage. And the privacy issue at first glance appears to be very simple—after all, who can possibly oppose protecting privacy? As indicated by the quote at the beginning of this introduction, privacy may become an all-purpose rationale for all manner of government action, whether justified or not.

Likewise, regulators are busy recommending new laws, competing for broader enforcement authority, and refining their interpretations of existing rules and guidelines. The legal profession views the privacy debate as an opportunity to expand litigation and the courts' influence on social policy. For the media, individualized privacy "horror stories" provide an endless supply of saleable copy.

This is not a purely American phenomenon; privacy has become as big or bigger an issue elsewhere, notably Europe. The totalitarian history, fascist and communist alike, of many European countries has created awareness of the dangers government databases might pose to the individual. Secret police, dossiers, concentration camps—all were the products of a Big Brother society.

The memory of these abuses led Europe to impose stringent restrictions on information collection, restrictions that later were applied to the collection of information on a voluntary basis by private firms. That such collection was voluntary, that firms often provided offsetting benefits in return for the information, none of these differences seem to have been fully appreciated by European privacy advocates.

The contradictory desires and concerns of individuals facing new technology, the incentives of policymakers and media, and the history of privacy abuse are driving today's debate over privacy. However, unless terms are clarified, that debate will continue to be confused, resulting in hasty legal solutions that will almost certainly worsen the problems.

At the same time, we should be aware that the ultimate answer to consumers' privacy concerns may come from the private sector, not government. Sophisticated companies recognize that protecting customer privacy is a necessary part of establishing trust, which is essential to mutually beneficial long-term relationships. Moreover, for some companies, concerns over privacy provide opportunities to create new products and services to help consumers protect themselves.

Ultimately, we may come to view privacy as less of a "right" than a valued feature of cooperative information sharing. Privacy is ensured when the individual voluntarily decides his or her personal level of information sharing. If one has voluntarily shared information, privacy has been protected. One may remain "private" by remaining secluded—and some famous people have done exactly that.

Whatever the answer, it is sure to take time. The opportunities presented by new technologies come with major disruptions to social and economic conventions and practices. An economic frontier by its nature is unexplored; mistakes are more likely, customs are less established. Errors are likely, but these errors create the very incentives to develop new rules suitable for the expanded scope made possible by the frontier itself.

Over time, we'll become accustomed to the greater "transparency" of the modern world and learn to "dress" appropriately. In the transition period, embarrassing mistakes will be made. As with all frontier sectors in an economy, there is currently great confusion. The ground rules have not yet been established, the terrain is largely unknown, and the institutions that will eventually emerge to structure the area have not yet fully developed.

There are still many questions to be resolved: Should privacy advocates be worried more about "Big Business" or "Big Brother"? What do we mean by "voluntary"? What, if anything, should be done about the serious (if isolated) mistakes, stupidities, and fraudulent behavior sometimes found in unsettled frontier areas of the economy? Does globalization require harmonization of policies, or do differing national policies create a beneficial state of competition?

This book, based upon a conference hosted by the Competitive Enterprise Institute in the fall of 1999, explores these and other questions. It presents a variety of perspectives, from academics to business, from America to Europe, on one key aspect of the privacy debate—privacy in financial services.

* * *

In the first chapter, "United States Privacy Law and Policy," Robert Belair and Kevin Coy provide a comprehensive overview of the current environment, and future outlook, for privacy protection, noting that there already exists a large body of "privacy" laws and regulations which must be considered by reformers. Belair and Coy illustrate the ever-widening scope of federal and state privacy laws and regulations, and focus on the significance of major privacy laws, such as the Fair Credit Reporting Act and the Gramm-Leach-Bliley Act.

Much of the rationale for protecting consumer privacy is based on myth, not reality. Duncan MacDonald dispels these misperceptions in Chapter 2, "Myths in the Privacy Debate." MacDonald maintains that existing US privacy laws are not deficient, and that we do not need *more* laws to protect privacy. Despite popular perceptions, MacDonald argues that privacy is not becoming extinct, and that most businesses do not use the personal information they collect to manipulate consumers. Moreover, unlike many privacy advocates, MacDonald does not believe that mandating consumer opt-in requirements would kill business marketing efforts.

Peter Gray argues in Chapter 3, "Privacy Concerns: Perception Versus Reality," that closer scrutiny is needed of the commonly held assumptions about privacy before further action is taken. He argues that existing privacy laws and regulations should be enforced before any new ones are introduced. Gray believes concerned consumers are increasingly taking steps to protect their privacy. He also notes that as new privacy concerns emerge, business entities find it profitable to develop inexpensive, easy-to-use privacy-protection methods for their patrons. Thus, businesses and individuals may well be solving voluntarily the problems now receiving so much negative publicity.

Chapter 4 by Fred Cate, "Public Policy and the Privacy Avalanche," highlights the significance of open data flows to the functioning of our modern information society. He discusses how increased privacy regulations would affect information exchanges between consumers and producers, how costs and prices would be affected, and whether such policies would encourage or slow the development of products and services. Cate discusses what exactly is meant by "harm" in the privacy area, and reviews the necessary balance between greater information access and potential harm. He also points out the irony of the dual role of governments as intruders on privacy even as they claim the mantle of its protectors, and notes that laws and regulations designed to protect privacy may actually weaken it by ignoring, and even interfering with, the power of new technologies to protect privacy. Businesses must take privacy concerns seriously, says Cate, but they must still defend the importance of open information flows and the right to provide information.

Marty Abrams picks up the theme of open information flows in Chapter 5, "The Economic Benefits of Balanced Information Use." He discusses the practical benefits of information and its contribution to our economy, pointing to tangible savings that consumers obtain from the free flow of information; he also warns of backlash from misuse of customer information. Abrams believes concerns over privacy reflect three factors: consumers today are largely unaware of the value they obtain from their sharing of information with business; consumers have a mistrust of those businesses which collect and use such information; and users lack an understanding of the limits on personal financial information use. Abrams argues that companies need to strike a balance between consumer trust and business information use.

In Chapter 6, "The Future of Money and Financial Privacy," Richard Rahn focuses on the significant changes in the nature of money and international capital flows made possible by the electronic revolution. He comments on the changes in the nature of money, from paper and coins to electronic signals, and the implications of digital money for financial privacy. Since funds can be electronically transferred in encrypted format, they can more readily be kept private and secure from both criminal and government intrusion. However, such anonymity is opposed by those enforcing America's money-laundering laws. Recent efforts (largely by the United States) to prevent encryption technology from reaching the public, and the more recent retreat from that policy, suggest that major changes are occuring in this area of financial privacy.

Jerry Loeser, in Chapter 7, "Some Practical and Theoretical Thoughts about Privacy and Banking," provides a banker's perspective on privacy protection. He discusses his bank's experience with allowing individual customers to opt out of information sharing with affiliates and third parties. He balances that discussion with a review of the significant consumer benefits that flow from allowing the sharing of such financial information, and with a theoretical discussion of the constitutional basis for privacy found in the First and Fifth Amendments. Loeser notes that banks have an interest in protecting the privacy of their customers. He also touches on proposed privacy regulations that have received much attention in past years, especially those mandating disclosure of personal financial data. Support for such provisions largely originated from those who use such disclosure policies to strengthen tax, drug prohibition, and "deadbeat dad" laws. However, forcing banks to comply with such regulations and report on their customers' financial activities undermines the ability of the banks to develop stronger privacy programs for their customers.

In Chapter 8, "Credit Information Reporting, Social Accountability, and Consumer Opportunity," Daniel Klein provides a case study in the social utility of shared information. He examines the origin and history of credit bureaus, pointing out that exchange opportunities depend critically upon the ability of two parties to trust one another—and that modern informational databases (for example, consumer-credit databases) facilitate the development of that trust. Klein critiques the view that privacy is threatened by requirements for information disclosure as a condition for exchange. As noted earlier, a world in which individuals refuse to share information is a world in which parties are likely to remain strangers and thus forego the opportunities and concrete benefits of that exchange. Klein sees financial information sharing as a way of facilitating trust—of becoming "intimate" commercial friends.

Lawrence Lindsey, in Chapter 9, "The Money-Laundering Conundrum: Mugging Privacy in the Assault on Crime?" addresses many of the same questions as Mr. Loeser but from a different perspective. He emphasizes the need for balance between protecting individual privacy and strengthening the ability of government to enforce its laws. He addresses the national-security interest in dealing with threats of terrorism, money laundering, and drug cartels. Lindsey likewise notes the tensions which exist between the laws requiring banks to report any "suspicious" financial transaction to the government, and the banks' desire to protect customer privacy. He also critiques some of the more aggressive marketing practices of financial institutions, with the view that these practices simply encourage further government intervention into private transactions.

In Chapter 10, "Personalization, Privacy, and the First Amendment," Eugene Volokh expands on Mr. Cate's concerns about the impact of privacy protection on freedom of speech and open information flows. He argues rules on privacy may have unintended consequences. Chief among these risks to the free flow of information are government restrictions on various forms of communication. Volokh argues that the protection of consumer privacy on the Internet does not justify weakening First Amendment rights, and he rejects the widely held belief that added privacy restrictions are needed to attract consumers to the Internet.

In "Privacy and Human Rights: Comparing the United States to Europe," Chapter 11, Solveig Singleton compares privacy and human rights in the US and Europe. She challenges the notion that European privacy laws are more protective of privacy than US ones. She also warns that federal regulatory controls on information flows will dampen innovation and reduce overall consumer welfare. Her work also reviews the basis for the difference in perspective between these two regions.

The European perspective is then outlined in the two remaining chapters. Franz Blankart, Jean Bonna, and Michel Dérobert offer a Swiss-specific view in Chapter 12, "Swiss Views on Financial Privacy." Switzerland constitutes an interesting intermediate position between other European nations and the United States. Her banking rules traditionally have conveyed greater privacy protection to customers, placing her banks into potential conflict with the United States and even Europe.

Finally, a more technical discussion of the nature of European privacy law is provided by Alfred Büllesbach in Chapter 13, "Financial Privacy and Data Protection in Europe." His work focuses particularly on some policies now extant in Germany but relevant to the broader European situation.

* * *

Change, both technological and institutional, has dramatically altered the information-economy landscape. Like much change over the last several centuries, the impact has generally been favorable to consumers and the economy. Economist Joseph Schumpeter might well have invented the phrase "creative destruction" to describe the information revolution.

Privacy concerns are just one example of the tensions created by this revolution, of the new issues that we must confront as policymakers, consumers, producers, and individuals. Our challenge is to ensure that privacy concerns are not captured by those who would use them to impede the positive value of broader, voluntary information sharing in commercial spheres. Only trust makes it possible to trade and exchange. Such trust requires that we know more about each other, that we share information, but that such sharing is voluntary, not mandatory.

The privacy environment is in flux. The issues, arguments, and policies raised by privacy advocates are both legitimate and complex. Those who care about economic growth and economic liberty must meet this challenge. We must develop an intellectual and moral understanding that will make it possible for policymakers to resist the political temptation to rush in and "solve" transient problems that consumers and information firms are well on their way to solving. If we fail, we risk transforming temporary problems into permanent rigidities, creating permanent obstacles to the discovery process of the market.

As this volume and the ongoing work of the Competitive Enterprise Institute demonstrate, tensions between businesses and consumers encourage innovations that reduce such tensions. The market is rapidly finding ways to protect consumer privacy while still allowing the information sharing necessary to attain the benefits of an information-rich society.

CEI is proud to present this volume. We hope and expect that our work over the coming years will move privacy policy in this more positive direction.

September 2000
Fred L. Smith, Jr.
President, Competitive Enterprise Institute

United States Privacy Law and Policy

Robert R. Belair and Kevin Coy

INTRODUCTION

Privacy has "arrived" as a major policy issue in the United States. In recent months, privacy has received front-page and editorial coverage in major newspapers, been featured on the cover of magazines, and been discussed on television talk shows and newscasts. Thousands of legislative proposals with privacy components have been introduced at the federal and state levels, and scores have been enacted. The public is increasingly concerned about privacy and increasingly willing to act on that concern.[1]

For privacy, this is an extraordinary time. While it is true that there was significant privacy activity in the 1970s—the so-called early days of modern information-privacy protection in the United States—including the adoption of the Privacy Act, the addition of very important privacy language to the Freedom of Information Act, and the creation of the Privacy Protection Study Commission, the level of activity then was nothing like what we have today; nothing like the level of state activity today, nothing like the level of media penetration today, nothing like the level of activity in the Congress today. And just to go back to the 1970s again for a moment, in 1979, 67 percent of the American public said it was concerned about privacy; today it is 94 percent. Such an extraordinary level of attention and activity confirms that a sea change is underway.

Privacy's new traction as an issue is further illustrated by the following statistics:

- A *Wall Street Journal*/NBC News survey found that the potential loss of personal privacy is the issue of most concern to Americans entering the new millennium. Concerns about personal privacy finished ahead of concerns about issues such as terrorism, overpopulation, world war, and global warming.

- An October, 1999, public-opinion survey for IBM conducted by Harris Interactive and Dr. Alan F. Westin[2] found that 80 percent of respondents believe that consumers have "lost all control over how personal information about them is circulated and used by companies."
- There has also been a major increase in privacy-asserting behaviors by US consumers. According to the IBM survey, the percentage of people who say they have refused to give information to a business or company because they thought it wasn't needed or was too personal has risen from 52 percent in 1990 to 78 percent in 1999. Also in 1999, 53 percent of respondents said that they have asked a company not to sell or give their name and address to another company, and 54 percent said they had decided not to use or purchase something from a company because they weren't sure how their personal information would be used.
- During the 105th Congress, over 150 bills addressing privacy were introduced and more than 40 days of congressional hearings were devoted to privacy issues. The 106th Congress is on track to match or exceed those levels.
- Privacy issues also received considerable attention at the state level. During 1999, over 7,300 privacy bills were introduced, an increase of over 3,000 bills from the previous year.

Amid this frenetic privacy activity, it is sometimes said that privacy protections in the United States are an uneven and inadequate patchwork. True, the United States lacks the sort of comprehensive privacy legislation found in many European countries. It is also true there are areas of US privacy law that might be strengthened. However, let's be very clear. It is wrong to dismiss US privacy protections as inadequate. As this article will detail, the US privacy environment presents a diverse, interwoven array of *de jure* and *de facto* protections, which, despite the occasional loose end, provides considerable protection.

The article begins with a brief examination of the history of information privacy, the democratic interests served by information privacy, and the growing public concern over information privacy. The article examines the legal and self-regulatory privacy protections that exist in the United States, including protections arising from US constitutional law, common law, federal statutory law, and state constitutional and statutory law, as well as informal, *de facto* privacy protections, such as media scrutiny, the actions of advocacy organizations, and corporate self-regulatory efforts. Finally, the article identifies key trends in privacy law playing out over the next few years.

UNITED STATES INFORMATION-PRIVACY ENVIRONMENT
WHAT IS INFORMATION PRIVACY?

"Information privacy" is certainly the focus of intense public, legislative, and media attention, but what does it mean? The term "information privacy" does not have a universally accepted definition. Customarily, the term is used to refer to standards for the collection, maintenance, use, and disclosure of personally identifiable information. The ability of an individual to control the use of information about that individual provides the individual with "information privacy."

Information privacy is frequently distinguished from other clusters of personal interests that are nourished by the privacy doctrine, including surveillance privacy—the interest in being free from governmental and other organized surveillance of individual activities under circumstances where one has a reasonable expectation of privacy; and behavioral privacy—the right to engage in certain intimate and sensitive behaviors (such as behaviors relating to reproductive rights) free from governmental or other control.[3]

The principal focus of surveillance privacy and behavioral privacy, in particular, is the protection of the privacy of citizens from governmental intrusion. The desire to protect citizens' privacy from governmental intrusion has deep roots in American law, most notably in the Fourth Amendment's constitutional limitations on the government's ability to conduct unreasonable searches and seizures. The public's perception of the government as the principal threat to personal privacy was refreshed by Watergate and events of the late 1960s and early 1970s, resulting in new laws, some of which, such as the Privacy Act,[4] also protect information-privacy values by limiting the government's ability to collect and use information about individuals.

The concept of information privacy as a distinct branch of privacy is relatively new, emerging in the late 1960s amidst rising concerns about computers and growing disenchantment with government. Alan Westin's 1967 book, *Privacy and Freedom*,[5] made a seminal contribution to the nation's thinking about information privacy. Later iterations in the US Department of Health, Education and Welfare 1973 Fair Information Practice Report[6] and the 1972 National Academy of Science's Report, *Databanks in a Free Society*, developed a basic code of fair information practice.[7]

The Report of the Privacy Protection Study Commission published in July, 1977, provided further development for the concept of information privacy and its application to specific record-keeping relationships.[8] Five information-privacy strategies enunciated in the Privacy Commission report continue, to this day, to characterize the United States' approach to information-privacy law:

- Record-keeping standards should be mostly industry specific, not omnibus.
- The protection of information privacy must depend primarily upon subject participation rights (such as the subject's right of access and correction and the right to bring a civil action for privacy violations).
- Record keepers should retain discretion to set standards for the type and amount of personal information which they collect.
- Record keepers should retain discretion to set standards for the management and use of personal information within their organizations.
- Record subjects should have an expectation that their personal information will be kept confidential—subject to specific expectations appropriate for the record-keeping relationship, the sensitivity of the personal information, and whether the information could be used to make decisions about the indi-

vidual (*i.e.* administrative uses) or is to be used only for non-decision-making purposes, such as marketing or research.

INTERESTS SERVED BY INFORMATION PRIVACY

Protection of information privacy is widely seen as serving at least four interests that are critical to the vitality of democracy:

- an interest in insuring that society (both public and private sectors) makes decisions about individuals in a way that comports with notions of due process and fairness;
- an interest in protecting individual dignity—when individuals endure stigma, embarrassment, and humiliation arising from the uncontrolled use and disclosure of information about them, they lose the sense of dignity and integrity that is essential for effective participation in a free and democratic society;
- an interest in promoting a sense of trust in institutions—when individuals lose the ability to selectively disclose their sensitive personal information, they lose trust in the institutions, both public and private, which collect, hold, use, and disclose this personal information (public-opinion surveys for *Privacy & American Business* indicate that the public's "distrust index," *i.e.* the extent to which the public distrusts the government, is at all-time-high levels of approximately 80 percent); and
- an interest in promoting the viability of relationships that are critical to the effective functioning of a democratic society—numerous relationships, such as the lawyer-client relationship or even the news-media-and-confidential-source relationship, depend upon promises of confidentiality in order to promote the candid sharing of personal information and trust within the relationship.

CONCERN ABOUT INFORMATION PRIVACY IS PERSISTENT AND GROWING

Why all the attention to privacy? New advances in information technology and, particularly, advances associated with the Internet; public concern over identity fraud; a belief by many consumers that their privacy is being invaded; new business models reflecting a seemingly ever-growing "urge to merge"; international privacy developments; an apparently never-ending succession of media reports of "tin ear" business and governmental initiatives aimed at selling government-employee information; "deputizing" financial institutions to watch their customers; creating "Star Trek"-type surveillance systems and databases; and combining data about online and offline behaviors and preferences without adequate notice or permission have all combined to make the public more privacy-conscious than at any time in our history:

- The explosive growth of the Internet is having a profound impact on privacy. What began as a research tool for a small cadre of scientific and academic users has exploded into a mass-communication medium that has caught the imagination of the public, the media, and policymakers. Increasingly, anything impacting on the Internet, including privacy, is a ground for media, and potentially legislative, attention. Privacy concerns in the online environment are receiving particular attention because of the public's high level of concern over privacy, and because the Internet makes it far easier to obtain, collect, and redisseminate personal information. There is a widespread perception that if consumer privacy concerns are not addressed, electronic commerce will falter.
- Concern over information privacy is also being fueled by concerns over identity fraud. Many believe the ready availability of personal information makes it easier for criminals to assume the identities of innocent consumers, with potentially disastrous results for the consumers that are victimized.
- The privacy issue is also growing in importance because an increasing segment of the public believes their privacy is being invaded. As a result, privacy has increasingly become a tangible issue for people rather than a "wonk" issue that is of concern to few other than a cadre of academics and advocates.
- Corporate restructuring is creating larger, more diverse conglomerates that increasingly use personal information for a wide

array of purposes. Mergers, such as that of Citibank and Traveler's Insurance, have created new companies that collect information on consumers in a wide variety of contexts, creating consumer fears that their health, financial, and insurance information will be shared within these new companies in a way that will detrimentally impact their ability to obtain employment, insurance, health care, or other benefits or services.

- The European Data Protection Directive, with its restrictions on the transfer of data to countries outside the EU that lack "adequate" data-protection safeguards, is a driving force behind the growing globalization of information privacy as an issue. The directive has increased the pressure on the United States to strengthen its privacy laws. The directive and the safe harbor discussions between the EU and the US have generated considerable press coverage, further raising the profile of privacy issues in the United States. In addition, some privacy advocates have argued that the draft safe harbor agreement would result in two sets of privacy protections in the United States, one for information pertaining to citizens of the EU and a second, lower, standard for Americans.

- The media has also fanned the flames of the public's privacy discontent by highlighting privacy practices that reporters find to be questionable. Once these practices become well-known, the ensuing firestorm of public pressure has frequently forced private- and public-sector entities to modify or terminate the offensive practices.

- Business is working to allay consumer privacy concerns through self-regulatory activity. Many individual companies and major industry associations have developed and adopted privacy guidelines. These typically draw on fair-information-practices principles and similar core expressions published over the past 30 years. The industry-association policies call upon the association's members to apply these principles to their particular organizations and operations; and—increasingly—promise to monitor member compliance and take enforcement actions against noncompliers.

INFORMATION-PRIVACY LEGAL STANDARDS

The United States does not have an omnibus privacy law or a nationwide enforcement mechanism for the protection of privacy interests. The US, however, does embrace a particularly wide array of privacy protections, including:

- Federal constitutional law recognizes a right to privacy in a variety of contexts.
- The common law provides a number of privacy protections including actions for the public disclosure of private facts, actions under the misappropriation theory, and breach of implied contract actions.
- Federal statutory law provides the bulk of federal privacy protections. Specifically, over two dozen federal statutes address privacy concerns in both the public and private sectors. Of those measures regulating the private sector, the Fair Credit Reporting Act represents what is perhaps the most comprehensive approach.
- State law also provides privacy protections which are either independent of, or designed to supplement, federal privacy protections. These measures vary by state, although "uniform state laws" help to bring some degree of uniformity in some areas.
- In addition to legal protections, many other factors provide informal and *de facto* privacy protections. Chief among these factors is the "watchdog" effort of the media and consumer and privacy advocacy groups, as well as numerous self-regulatory efforts by business, including the Online Privacy Alliance, the Individual Reference Services Group, BBB*Online*, and TRUSTe.

a. Constitutional Law

It is often emphasized that the federal Constitution does not include an express privacy provision. The Supreme Court, however, has read behavioral- and surveillance-privacy protections into several of the amendments to the Constitution, including, in particular, the First, Fourth, Fifth, and Ninth Amendments. For example, the Fourth Amendment protects citizens from "unreasonable searches and seizures" and has been interpreted, through an extensive body of case law, to mean that individuals may enjoy a reasonable expectation of privacy from improper governmental searches and seizures.[9] By contrast, the Supreme Court has had relatively little to say about the extent to which, and the way in which, the Constitution provides information-privacy protections.

In *Paul v. Davis*,[10] the Court rejected a constitutional claim aimed at a local sheriff who had released the plaintiff's name on a police flier containing the names of individuals who had been arrested (but not convicted). The Court dismissed the constitutional privacy claim, suggesting that constitutional privacy protections apply only to freedom of action in spheres thought to be private, and not to the government's disclosure of personal information. In *United States v. Miller*,[11] the Court ruled that the Fourth Amendment does not protect the confidentiality of personal information held by institutional record keepers (in that case, a bank).

In *Whalen v. Roe*,[12] however, the Court acknowledged that "the accumulation of vast amounts of personal information in computerized databanks or other massive government files" could constitute an unacceptable invasion of constitutional privacy rights, depending upon the government's purpose and its controls on redisclosure. While the Court upheld the New York statute at issue, which required physicians and pharmacists to report all prescriptions for specified controlled substances to the state, it suggested that there could be circumstances where the Constitution may limit "the unwarranted disclosure of accumulated private data, whether intentional or unintentional or by a system that did not contain comparable security provisions."[13]

Several Supreme Court decisions involving not the Constitution, but federal statutes, suggest that the present Court is sensitive to information-privacy claims and perhaps, when presented with the right case, would be willing to read information-privacy protections more directly and emphatically into the Constitution. In *Reporter's Committee for Freedom of the Press v. Department of Justice*,[14] the Court held that the compilation of public-record information and its automation in a comprehensive, name-accessible database of criminal-history information created a record which, if disclosed under the Freedom of Information Act, would create an unwarranted invasion of personal privacy. A few years later, in 1994, the Court again interpreted statutory privacy provisions to hold that individuals have a "far from insignificant" privacy interest in their home address information.[15]

In 1995, the Supreme Court once again took notice of the importance of privacy in the computer age. In *Arizona v. Evans*,[16] the Court found that the "exclusionary rule" does not require suppression of evidence seized incident to an arrest resulting from an inaccurate computer record. In a concurring opinion, Justice O'Conner wrote that

> the advent of powerful, computer-based recordkeeping systems...facilitate[s] arrests in ways that have never before been possible. The police...are entitled to enjoy the substantial advantages this technology confers. They may not, however, rely on it blindly. With the benefits of more efficient law enforcement mechanisms comes the burden of corresponding constitutional responsibilities.[17]

Justice Ginsburg, in dissent, also expressed concern over the impact of modern technology on privacy:

> Widespread reliance on computers to store and convey information generates, along with manifold benefits, new possibilities of error, due to both computer malfunctions and operator mistakes....[C]omputerization greatly amplifies an error's effect, and correspondingly intensifies the need for prompt correction; for inaccurate data can infect not only one agency, but the many agencies that share access to the database.[18]

During the 1999-2000 term, the Supreme Court handed down two decisions regarding controls on access to public-record information, which, while not decided on privacy grounds, are likely to encourage stronger privacy initiatives.

The first case, *United Reporting Publishing Corp. v. California Highway Patrol*,[19] arose from a 1996 change in California law to limit the release of arrestee and victim address information to those who certify the request is made for scholarly, journalistic, political, or governmental purposes, or for investigative purposes by a licensed private investigator. The law specifically prohibits the use of such information "directly or indirectly to sell a product or service to any individual or group of individuals."[20]

United Reporting Publishing Corp., a private publishing service that had been providing arrestee address information to clients under the old statute, filed suit, alleging that the statute was an unconstitutional violation of its First Amendment commercial-speech rights. The 9th Circuit, while finding that arrestees have a substantial privacy interest in the information at issue, nevertheless concluded (as did the district court) that the law was an unconstitutional infringement on United Reporting's First Amendment commercial-speech rights because the "myriad of exceptions...precludes the statute from directly and materially advancing the government's purported privacy interest."[21]

On December 7, 1999, in a decision that was somewhat of a surprise to many in the information industry, the Supreme Court voted seven to two to reverse, reinstating the California statute.[22] In its opinion, the majority characterized this as a case dealing with access to government records rather than restrictions on free speech.[23] The Supreme Court also characterized the case as a challenge to the "facial validity" of the California statute and not a challenge based upon its implementation or actual experience with the statute.[24]

In the second case, *Reno v. Condon*,[25] the Supreme Court unanimously reversed the 4th Circuit Court of Appeals, rejecting a 10th Amendment[26] challenge by the state of South Carolina to the constitutionality of the Driver's Privacy Protection Act of 1994 (DPPA).[27] The DPPA provides that state departments of motor vehicles (DMV) "shall not knowingly disclose or otherwise make available to any person or entity personal information about any individual obtained by the department in connection with a motor vehicle record."[28] The DPPA does contain 14 exceptions pursuant to which states may elect to disclose DMV records in certain instances, such as with the consent of the licensee.[29] Violation of the DPPA may result in criminal fines and a civil cause of action against a person who knowingly violates the statute.[30] While the Court's brief opinion was based on 10th Amendment rather than privacy grounds, the decision potentially opens the door for further federal regulation of access to state records on privacy grounds.[31]

b. Common Law

Common-law information-privacy principles also have an impact on the private sector's handling of personal information. Outright false and malicious statements about an individual, of course, may constitute defamation or slander. Falsity, however, is not the key to common-law privacy protections for personal information. Common-law theories that may be used to protect the privacy of personal information include "public disclosure of private facts," "misappropriation of name or likeness," and a breach of implied contract or fiduciary duty.

Public disclosure of private facts. Where a party publishes or makes widespread disclosure of sensitive personal information without authorization, resulting in harm to the individual, the individual, in most states, will have a cause of action in tort for public disclosure of private facts.[32] According to the Restatement (Second) of Torts, the tort of public disclosure of private facts or "Publicity Given to Private Life" is described as follows:

> One who gives publicity to a matter concerning the private life of another is subject to liability to the other for invasion of his privacy, if the matter publicized is a kind that: (a) would be highly offensive to a reasonable person [if disclosed], and (b) is not of legitimate concern to the public.[33]

There are, of course, hurdles. In order to mount a claim of public disclosure of private facts, for instance, a plaintiff must demonstrate widespread disclosure of the private facts. In addition, public-record information (*e.g.* criminal-history records) is usually not considered to be private. On the other hand, private facts would typically include personal health information, financial records, and educational records.

In order for there to be publicity, most courts require "communication of the information to the public at large, or to so many persons that the matter must be regarded as substantially certain to become one of public knowledge."[34] Some states have adopted a more relaxed definition, permitting recovery based upon publicity to "a particular public" that has a special relationship to the plaintiff, such as coworkers, family, or neighbors.[35]

This tort may prove to be of particular and growing utility to protect privacy in the Internet environment, where everyone with e-mail capability has the potential to become a "publisher."

Misappropriation. The tort of misappropriation of name or likeness creates a cause of action when an individual's name, portrait, or photograph is used for commercial benefit, without the prior consent of the individual. Although the tort is not available to protect against the use of an individual name on a mailing list, the tort does protect very public uses of a name or likeness in a commercial setting.

Breach of implied contract. When record keepers in confidential and fiduciary relationships disclose personal information without authorization, some courts have provided victims of the disclosure with a cause of action for breach of an implied promise of confidentiality. Both physicians and bankers, for example, have been held liable for unauthorized disclosures of personal information about their patients and customers, based on breach of contract theories.[36]

Indeed, some courts have held that an implied contract of confidentiality between a doctor and a patient arises more or less automatically from the doctor-patient relationship. In a New

York case, for example, a psychiatrist who included patient communications *verbatim* in a book without obtaining the patient's consent was found to have breached an implied contract with the patient.[37] Similarly, in *Hammonds v. Aetna Casualty and Surety*,[38] a physician's disclosure of medical information to a hospital insurer was held to constitute a breach of an implied contract between the physician and the patient.[39]

c. Existing Federal Statutory Law

Many existing laws address privacy. Most information-privacy protections are provided by statute and address particular record-keeping relationships or types of records. Literally dozens of federal laws are in place. Examples include:

- Census Confidentiality (PL 87-813) limits the disclosure of identifiable data except to officers and employees of the Census Bureau, and prohibits the use of census data for purposes other than the purpose for which it has been gathered.
- The Equal Employment Opportunity Act of 1964 (PL 88-352) limits the collection and use of information to discriminate in employment on the basis of categories such as race, sex, religion, and national origin.
- The Freedom of Information Act (FOIA) (PL 90-23) requires that federal-agency records must be made available to the public unless one of the enumerated exemptions applies. The FOIA explicitly exempts from public disclosure "personnel and medical files and similar files the disclosure of which would constitute a clearly unwarranted invasion of personal privacy," 5 U.S.C. § 552(b)(6) (1996).
- The Fair Housing Act of 1968 (PL 90-284) limits the collection and use of information to discriminate in housing on the basis of categories such as race, sex, religion, and national origin.
- Title III of the Omnibus Crime Control and Safe Streets Act of 1968 (PL 90-351) protects the privacy of wire and oral communications by prohibiting wiretapping and eavesdropping except for surveillance done pursuant to a court order.
- The Postal Reorganization Act of 1970 (PL 91-375) prohibits

the opening of an individual's mail, with limited exceptions such as pursuant to a search warrant or the consent of the addressee.

- The Fair Credit Reporting Act of 1970 (PL 91-508) provides the subjects of consumer reports with rights of access and correction, as well as placing substantial restrictions on the disclosure and use of consumer reports.

- The Federal Youth Correction Act (PL 93-415) requires that juvenile records shall be safeguarded from disclosure to unauthorized persons. The act also sets forth the circumstances under which records may be released.

- The Privacy Act of 1974 (PL 93-579) gives individuals a right of access and correction to their personal information held by federal agencies; imposes data-quality standards on federal agencies; and places limits on the collection, use, and disclosure of personally identifiable information. Under the Privacy Act, information contained in "systems of records" may not be disclosed by federal agencies without the prior written consent of the record subject, except under certain circumstances.[40] Federal agencies must also keep an accounting of records disclosed under the Privacy Act.[41]

- The Family Educational Rights and Privacy Act of 1974 (PL 93-380), sometimes called the Buckley Amendment, requires educational institutions to grant students or parents access to student records and establishes limits on disclosure to third parties.

- The Equal Credit Opportunity Act (PL 93-495) regulates the use of information by creditors in making decisions regarding extensions of credit and requires the retention of certain documents relating to credit transactions. It also requires notice if credit is denied or revoked and guarantees the opportunity for the individual to learn the reason for the denial or revocation.

- The Tax Reform Act of 1976 (PL 94-455) requires notice to taxpayers and an opportunity for taxpayers to challenge information requests before the Internal Revenue Service can obtain certain records. It also strictly limits the disclosure of tax returns and tax-return information by the agency.

- The Fair Debt Collection Practices Act of 1977 (PL 95-109) restricts the communications by debt-collection agencies concerning debtors from whom they are attempting to collect.
- The Right to Financial Privacy Act of 1978 (PL 95-630) provides customers of banks and certain other financial institutions with a right of notice and an opportunity to contest access when federal agencies seek to obtain their financial records.
- The Privacy Protection Act of 1980 (PL 96-440) prohibits government agencies from unannounced searches of press offices and files unless there is a reasonable basis for suspicion that a crime has been committed.
- The Paperwork Reduction Act of 1980 (PL 96-511) prevents federal agencies from collecting information from the public if the Office of Management and Budget does not believe the agency needs or can make use of it, or if another agency has already collected the information. The act also requires agencies to give notice why the information is collected, how it is used, and whether a response by the individual is required.
- The Cable Communications Privacy Act of 1984 (PL 98-549) requires cable companies to inform subscribers about the cable companies' information practices including collection, use, and disclosure, as well as providing subject-access rights.
- The Electronic Communications Privacy Act of 1986 (PL 99-508) extends Title III protections and requirements to digital voice data and video communications, including cellular phones, electronic mail, and computer transmissions.
- The Computer Matching and Privacy Protection Act of 1988 (PL 100-503) requires agencies to formulate procedures before exchanging computerized records for purposes of searching or comparing those records.
- The Employee Polygraph Protection Act of 1988 (PL 100-347) prohibits most private-sector uses of lie-detector tests for employment purposes.
- The Video Privacy Protection Act of 1988 (PL 100-618) prohibits video stores from disclosing their customers' names and addresses and the identification of the video tapes rented or bought by customers, except in certain circumstances.

- The Americans with Disabilities Act of 1990 (PL 101-336) prohibits the collection and use of information to discriminate in employment and accommodation on the basis of a disability.
- The Telemarketing Protection Act of 1991 (PL 102-243) and the Telephone Consumer Privacy Protection Act of 1992 (PL 102-556) restrict telemarketing calls, including those made by autodialers.
- The ADAMHA Reorganization Act of 1992 (PL 102-321) prohibits the unauthorized disclosure of information relating to the treatment of individuals for alcohol and substance abuse in federally supported facilities.
- The Driver's Privacy Protection Act of 1994 (PL 103-322, as amended by PL 106-69) restricts the disclosure of identification and certain other personal information held by departments of motor vehicles for marketing and other purposes.
- The Telecommunications Reform Act of 1995 (PL 104-104) places restrictions on the disclosure by telecommunications carriers of customer proprietary network information (information about the pattern and use of consumer telephones and other telecommunications equipment, but not the content of calls).
- The Health Insurance Portability and Accountability Act of 1996 (PL 104-191) requires the Secretary of Health and Human Services to issue health-information privacy regulations for transactions electronically transmitted in connection with standard health-care transactions due to congressional failure to enact legislation by August 21, 1999.[42]
- The Taxpayer Browsing Act of 1997 (PL 105-35) prohibits unauthorized browsing through tax-return information by IRS employees.
- The Wireless Telephone Protection Act of 1998 (PL 105-172) prohibits the use of scanners to capture cellular-phone conversations.
- The Children's Online Privacy Protection Act of 1998 (PL 105-208) regulates the collection and use of personal information over the Internet from children under the age of 13.

- The Gramm-Leach-Bliley (Financial Modernization) Act (PL 106-102), enacted in November 1999, requires financial institutions to provide certain privacy protections for consumers' nonpublic personal information and permits consumers to opt out of disclosures of nonpublic personal information to non-affiliated third parties under certain circumstances.

A closer look at the Fair Credit Reporting Act. Of all of the statutes cited above, the Fair Credit Reporting Act (FCRA), as amended, is one of the earliest and, perhaps, most comprehensive measures regulating the privacy of personal information in the private sector in the United States.[43] The purpose of the FCRA is to promote the accuracy, fairness, and privacy of personal information held and distributed by consumer-reporting agencies.[44] Consumer-reporting agencies are organizations which, for a fee or on a cooperative, nonprofit basis, are in the practice of assembling or evaluating personally identifiable information obtained from third parties and bearing upon a consumer's credit worthiness, credit standing, credit capacity, character, reputation, personal characteristics, or mode of living.

Under the FCRA, a consumer-reporting agency may only provide a report to a party when the agency has reason to believe the party will use the report to make a determination on credit, employment, insurance underwriting, or otherwise in connection with a legitimate business need in a transaction involving the consumer or pursuant to written instructions of the consumer. Reports can also be provided in connection with firm offers of credit or insurance.

The FCRA includes all of the safeguards expected in a comprehensive, fair-information-practice/privacy statute, including notice to consumers; choice, including opportunities for opt-in/opt-out; accuracy, relevance, and timeliness standards; confidentiality and use safeguards; security expectations; consumer-access and correction rights; content restrictions; and remedies, including administrative sanctions and private rights of action. More specifically, the FCRA provides consumers with the following privacy rights:

- A consumer must be notified when information in his or her credit file is used to take an action against him or her, such as the denial of a credit application. In such cases, the party denying the benefit must provide the consumer with information on how to contact the consumer-reporting agency that provided the information.

- Consumer-reporting agencies must, upon request, provide a consumer with a copy of that consumer's credit file, as well as a listing of everyone who has requested it recently. The cost to the consumer of obtaining the report can not exceed $8.50, and may be free if requested in connection with a recent denial of benefits or other specified circumstances.

- Consumers are permitted to request a correction of information they believe to be inaccurate. The consumer-reporting agency must investigate unless the dispute is frivolous. The consumer-reporting agency must send a written investigation report to the individual and a copy of the revised credit report, if changes were made. The consumer may also request that corrected reports be sent to recent recipients. If the dispute is not resolved in the consumer's favor, the consumer has the option of including a brief statement in the consumer's file, typically for distribution with future reports.

- Consumer-reporting agencies must remove from their files, or correct, unverified or inaccurate information typically within 30 days after the consumer disputes the information.

- If a consumer disputes an item with a creditor, the creditor may not forward the disputed information to a consumer-reporting agency without noting that the item is in dispute.

- In most cases, a consumer-reporting agency may not report negative information that is more than seven years old; 10 years for bankruptcies. 1998 amendments to the FCRA would permit the inclusion of criminal-conviction information, without time limitations.

- Covered credit information may only be distributed by consumer-reporting agencies for a recognized need, typically consideration of an application for credit, insurance, employment, housing, or other business. Reports to employers or containing medical information require the consent of the individual.

- Consumers must be permitted to opt out of lists sold by consumer-reporting agencies to firms for unsolicited credit and insurance offers.
- Consumers can sue for violations or seek assistance from the Federal Trade Commission and other federal agencies responsible for the enforcement of the FCRA.

d. Congressional and Executive Branch Activity

Congressional efforts. In a certain sense, the roster of enacted legislation represents only the tip of the congressional privacy iceberg. Over 75 privacy-related bills have already been introduced in the 106th Congress, which would, if enacted, address a broad spectrum of privacy issues ranging from online privacy to health-information privacy to financial-information privacy to public-record privacy. In addition, congressional committees have held numerous hearings on privacy issues to both examine the implications of privacy proposals before Congress as well as to oversee the privacy-related activities of federal departments and agencies.

The most prominent piece of privacy legislation to be enacted so far during the 106th Congress is Title V of the Gramm-Leach-Bliley Act (G-L-B Act). The principal focus of the G-L-B Act is modernization of the nation's banking laws and the elimination of many of the legal barriers that have separated banks, insurers, and securities firms since the Great Depression. The debate over the privacy provisions of the bill was heated and received significant media attention. At one point, representatives of the financial-services industry publicly suggested that the industry would oppose the bill, years in the making, if it contained unacceptable privacy provisions.

As enacted, Title V of the G-L-B Act requires that financial institutions take steps to protect the privacy of nonpublic financial information about consumers, including providing notice and an opportunity to opt out of most disclosures of nonpublic personal information to nonaffiliated third parties.

The enactment of the G-L-B Act, however, has not ended the debate. The Clinton administration, Senator Richard Shelby (R-AL), and others have already introduced measures to strengthen the privacy protections offered by Title V of the G-L-B Act.

A second privacy-related enactment came from an unlikely source, the Fiscal Year 2000 Transportation Appropriations Act.[45] Section 350 of the Act, sponsored by Senator Shelby, amended the Driver's Privacy Protection Act of 1994 to require that states obtain an opt-in from licensees before disclosing certain personal information from motor vehicle records, including opt-in requirements for purposes of look up, survey, and marketing. Senator Shelby has included a similar provision in the transportation appropriations bill for fiscal year 2001.

As if all of this congressional activity were not enough to underscore the increased importance and attention that privacy issues are receiving from Congress, on February 9, 2000, Senate Minority Leader Daschle (D-SD) announced the formation of the Senate Democratic Privacy Task Force, which will be headed by Senator Patrick Leahy (D-VT), to educate consumers and to work with industry, consumer groups, and the administration to address ways in which the privacy of Americans' medical records, financial records, records of Internet activity, as well as other personal information, can be protected.

The very next day, Senator Shelby, Senator Richard Bryan (D-NV), Rep. Ed Markey (D-MA), and Rep. Joe Barton (R-TX) held a news conference to announce the formation of the bipartisan, bicameral Congressional Privacy Caucus (CPC).[46] The purpose of the CPC is threefold: 1) educate members of Congress and staff about individual-privacy issues; 2) provide a forum for the discussion of individual-privacy issues; and 3) advocate for personal-privacy protections.

Clinton administration privacy efforts. The Clinton administration has been active in addressing privacy issues, supporting a variety a self-regulatory and legislative initiatives to provide increased privacy protections. In 1999, President Clinton named Ohio State University Professor Peter Swire to be the first Privacy Counselor to the President to coordinate the administration's position on privacy issues.

The president and the vice president have both spoken out on privacy issues. The president, for example, included remarks about consumers' financial privacy in his final State of the Union address. Specifically, the president stated that citizens' privacy must be safeguarded and, with respect to financial privacy, referred to the G-L-B Act: "[W]e've taken the first steps to protect the privacy of bank and credit-card records and other financial statements." The president also stated that he plans to send legislation to Congress adding to those protections. The president also mentioned medical-record privacy during the address, as he had the year before, stating that the administration would finalize health-information privacy regulations this year.

The vice president has also spoken on privacy issues, calling for Congress to enact comprehensive legislation to protect medical records. In addition, the vice president has called for an "electronic bill of rights" to protect personal information in the electronic age. One component of the administration's effort is a presidential memorandum ordering federal departments and agencies to review their information practices, ensuring "that new technologies do not erode Privacy Act protections while also examining how new technologies can be used to enhance personal privacy."[47] Other aspects of the plan include a web site, administered by the Federal Trade Commission (FTC), where individuals can opt out from various types of mailing lists.

The federal departments and agencies have also devoted considerable resources to the information-privacy issue, with the FTC taking an increasingly active role in a wide range of privacy issues. The FTC has entered into privacy-related consent decrees with numerous companies in the credit-reporting industry. In addition, the FTC is currently engaged in litigation with TransUnion, one of the major credit-reporting systems. In the TransUnion case, the United States Court of Appeals for the District of Columbia reversed a Federal Trade Commission ruling that TransUnion's practice of using identification and tradeline information from a credit report to create mailing lists for direct marketing violated the FCRA. The Court of Appeals remanded the case to the FTC for certain factual findings. On March 1, 2000, the FTC issued an opinion holding that TransUnion violated the FCRA by selling tradeline information for target-marketing purposes.[48]

The FCRA is only one of many weapons at the FTC's disposal for addressing privacy issues. The agency is charged with enforcing the Children's Online Privacy Protection Act and has taken a broad interest in privacy on the Internet, including online profiling issues. In addition, the FTC is one of over a half-dozen federal agencies with enforcement authority over the financial-privacy protections in Title V of the G-L-B Act.

The FTC also asserts authority under Section Five of the FTC Act, which prohibits unfair and deceptive trade practices, to prohibit companies from using personal information in ways that the agency believes to be unfair or deceptive. During the summer of 1998, the FTC successfully settled an action against web host GeoCities for allegedly violating Section Five by misleading customers as to GeoCities' handling of the personal information of its customers. The FTC has also launched an investigation of DoubleClick to determine if the online company's data practices constitute deceptive trade practices. Looking toward the future, the FTC's Section Five authority will be an essential enforcement mechanism for any safe harbor agreement between the EU and the United States (discussed below).

The Department of Commerce, which has been coordinating many of the Clinton administration's self-regulatory privacy initiatives, issued a draft "Elements" paper in January, 1998, setting forth the department's views on the necessary elements of a self-regulatory privacy-protection program.[49] Drawing upon long-standing fair-information-practice principles, the department believes, in order to be effective, self-regulatory programs must address the following areas: awareness, including privacy policies, notification provisions, and consumer education; consumer choice with respect to "whether and how their personal information is used"; data security; and consumer access to information that companies hold about that individual.[50]

In addition, the department emphasizes that in order for any self-regulatory regime to be effective, it must also include adequate enforcement provisions, including components such as readily available and cost-effective means for consumer recourse for the resolution of complaints; verification procedures to ensure that company practices comply with the company's stated privacy policies; and meaningful consequences for companies that fail to comply with the self-regulatory principles.[51]

The Department of Commerce has also spearheaded negotiations with the EU over the creation of a safe harbor mechanism to permit the continued flow of personal data from the European Union to the US in compliance with the data protection directive. The Safe Harbor Principles, which were formally approved by the European Commission in July, 2000, include seven principles: notice, choice, onward transfer, security, data integrity, access, and enforcement. In addition, the Principles are accompanied by fifteen sets of "Frequently Asked Questions" (FAQs) which provide additional detail with respect to: sensitive data; journalistic exceptions; secondary liability; investment banking and audits; the role of data-protection authorities; self-certification; verification; access; human-resources data; Article 17 contracts; dispute resolution and enforcement; choice (timing of opt-out); travel information; pharmaceutical and medical products; and public-record and publicly available information. Financial services are not covered by the safe harbor agreement, however the issue is to be revisited once the G-L-B Act has been implemented.

The Department of Health and Human Services (HHS) has also been active on privacy issues, supporting federal legislation to protect health-information privacy (no such legislation has yet been enacted, despite a self-imposed congressional deadline of August 21, 1999). In the absence of legislation, HHS has relied on statutory authority under the Health Insurance Portability and Accountability Act of 1996 to issue proposed health-information privacy regulations. The public comment period ended on February 17, 2000. Public response to the proposed regulations was overwhelming—over 50,000 comments, many of them critical of the proposed regulation. The Health Subcommittee of the

House Ways and Means Committee held a hearing on February 17 about medical-record confidentiality and, in particular, the impact of the proposed HHS medical-record privacy regulations on Medicare as well as on private-sector health care. At that hearing, Margaret Hamburg, HHS Assistant Secretary for Planning and Evaluation, said that finalizing the rule will take a while due to the high volume of comments. It is anticipated, however, that the rule will be finalized before the end of the year.

e. State Statutory Law

In addition to privacy protections found in federal law, law in each of the 50 states also provides a myriad of protections to individuals. The scope of these protections vary from state to state, as is often the case in our federal system. The wide variety of state legislation makes a detailed review impossible in a paper of this size, however, some broad observations are possible.

First, over one dozen state constitutions contain language protecting personal privacy rights.[52] These privacy protections take a variety of forms, but tend to mirror federal Fourth Amendment language protecting surveillance-privacy interests. Some states offer additional privacy protections. California's constitutional privacy-protection language, for example, found in Article I, Section 1, explicitly protects individual privacy as an "inalienable right." This language has been interpreted to apply not only to governmental agencies but also to private actors.[53]

Second, states frequently seek to provide additional protections in areas where there is already some level of federal protection, which is permissible provided that the federal law does not preempt state action and the state law is consistent with the federal statute. Over one-third of the states, for example, have enacted their own laws supplementing and further regulating the use of consumer-report information. In addition, many states are currently considering proposals to supplement the privacy provisions of the G-L-B Act.

Third, states often seek to regulate the use of personal information by state and local governments. Over one-third of the states have enacted their own "mini" privacy acts regulating the collection, maintenance, use, and disclosure of personal information by state and local government agencies. States also have adopted numerous more narrowly drawn statutes which extend confidentiality protections to particular information, such as information collected by the state for public-health reporting.

Fourth, while state privacy protections are frequently uneven, greater interstate uniformity exists in some areas where "model statutes" have been adopted. Almost 20 states, for example, have enacted the National Association of Insurance Commissioners (NAIC) uniform state law regulating the use of personal information by insurance companies and insurance support organizations. In September, 1998, the NAIC unveiled a model statute for regulating the use of health information by insurance companies and their support organizations. In addition, the National Conference of Commissioners on Uniform State Law is drafting a new health-information-privacy model law to replace the model it proposed in the 1980s, which was adopted in only three states. While states typically make some changes to these model statutes, the resulting statutes contain a high degree of uniformity.

Fifth, states stand ready to legislate in a wide array of areas to provide privacy protections. Several states have adopted statutes that regulate employers' use of personal information for employment purposes. Many states regulate the use of Social Security numbers; tax records; computer records; credit reporting and investigation; employment records; medical records; cable and video records; bank records; school records; electronic communications; polygraph testing; and arrest and conviction records. In recent years, the states have been very active in considering legislation to regulate genetic-record information and information obtained through, or generated over, the Internet or other online networks.[54]

State activity on privacy is not confined to the state legislatures. Governors and other state officials, particularly state attorneys general, have been increasingly active on privacy issues. The National Association of Attorneys General, for example, has devoted a considerable amount of time and attention to privacy issues in recent months. In addition, individual attorneys general, including those in Washington, Michigan, Minnesota, and New York, have filed a number of privacy-related legal actions and launched privacy initiatives in their states.

NONLEGAL SOURCES OF PRIVACY PROTECTIONS

In addition to federal and state legal protections, the privacy of individuals' information is also protected by nonlegal means including media scrutiny and public opinion, as well as self-regulatory efforts undertaken by the private sector. Privacy issues are frequently the subject of intense media and legislative scrutiny in the United States. The issue is marked by frequent crises and confrontations involving close broadcast and print media coverage, hostile and frequent Internet postings, legislative hearings, and, occasionally, court battles.

In February, 1998, for example, *The Washington Post* reported that two pharmacy chains, CVS and Giant, used, or planned to use, an outside contractor to send prescription refill notices and drug promotions, using prescription information supplied by the pharmacies.[55] Both companies took out full-page advertisements announcing the cancellation of the programs amid a flurry of editorial criticism and customer complaints.[56] CVS has since been sued,[57] with the plaintiff alleging that CVS breached its fiduciary duty as well as its duty of confidentiality to its pharmacy customers.[58]

Washington Post stories signaled the start of another privacy firestorm in January, 1999, when the *Post* reported that Image Data, a small New Hampshire company, had developed a product designed to combat check and credit-card fraud and identity theft using state DMV photographs. Under the Image Data plan, the company entered into contracts with several states, whereby Image Data was permitted to digitize DMV photographs of individuals and store the photographs in a database. Merchants could then access this database, using a small screen installed near the cash register, when a customer presented a check or credit card for payment, in order to assist the merchant in verifying the identity of the purchaser.

Image Data had entered into agreements with South Carolina, Colorado, and Florida to obtain driver's license photos and other information, and was testing its program in South Carolina when the project was featured in a *Washington Post* article on January 22. A public outcry ensued, with state officials receiving a torrent of angry calls protesting the plan (and a class-action lawsuit in Florida). Public ire appears to have been a product of several factors. As one South Carolina woman described it:

> We were livid [upon hearing about the Image Data program]. In my opinion, a South Carolina driver's license is a need, not a want. We have no choice but to give our information in order to have one. Then they turn around and sell it to a company, as personal as it is: my weight, my height, my address—my God, my image. There are endless possibilities as to what could be done with it.

As a result of the public outcry that has ensued, all three states have ended the transfer of photos to Image Data and sought to retrieve any photos already transferred.

A third example is the case of Internet advertising giant DoubleClick. During its four-year life, DoubleClick collected click-stream information from its participating web sites and then used that data to help those web sites customize the banner ads and pop-up ads that visitors see. DoubleClick could not identify the visitor, only the visitor's computer. The privacy firestorm began in November, 1999, when DoubleClick spent $1.7 billion to purchase Abacus Direct, the largest database of consumer catalogue activity. DoubleClick's plan, brilliant from a marketing perspective, was to marry its click-stream data with Abacus' offline data to identify specific consumers (not just their computers) and then create a profile of the consumers' interests and buying activity.

This plan produced a firestorm of criticism in the media, from privacy advocates and from consumers. Finally, on March 2, 2000, DoubleClick announced that it would not go forward with its plan to build personal profiles. Pressure to abandon the plan was intense; not only did DoubleClick receive a torrent of adverse media coverage, it also received over 100,000 consumer complaints in response to an online protest organized by the Center for Democracy and Technology. The FTC, as well as the Michigan, Connecticut, New York, and Vermont attorneys general, announced an investigation of DoubleClick's activities and several class-action lawsuits were filed. In addition, shortly before DoubleClick made its announcement, Internet-industry players such as search engine AltaVista Co. and Internet home-delivery service Kozmo.com Inc. took steps to distance themselves from DoubleClick. If that had not been enough, the company's stock price fell by more than 25 percent during the firestorm (it rebounded somewhat following the March 2 announcement).[59]

Public concerns about privacy are having an undeniable impact on corporate policy and practice as more and more industries and companies seek to self-regulate through industry standards and company privacy codes. Prominent examples of collective self-regulatory initiatives include efforts by the Individual Reference Services Group, the Direct Marketing Association, and the Online Privacy Alliance. In addition to cooperative efforts, many individual companies have also adopted their own privacy policies and codes. These policies reflect the growing importance the business community places on the privacy of personal information. [60]

Technology-based, nongovernmental solutions are another nonlegal source of protection for personal information. BBB*Online*, TRUSTe, and others have developed online privacy-seal programs, whereby companies who meet established privacy standards can affix the online seal to their Internet site to promote public confidence in the site's privacy practices. Other technology-based programs for the protection of privacy include: the Platform for Privacy Preferences (P3) advocated by the Center for Democracy and Technology and the Internet Privacy Working Group, which would permit users of Internet browsers to program the browsers to block sites that do not meet an individual's privacy needs; the Platform for Internet Content Selection (PICS), which is sponsored by the World Wide Web

Consortium at MIT, and serves as a content-rating system and may be expanded to function as a privacy-rating system as well; and the Open Profiling Standard (OPS) sponsored by companies including Netscape, IBM, American Express, and Hewlett Packard, among others, which would protect Internet-user privacy by permitting the user to block personal information that is typically sent to a web site by a user's computer.

TRENDS

While there is an incredible amount happening on privacy right now, a few trends that are likely to play out over the next few years can be identified:

- Public concern over privacy is likely to remain high. Technology is the moon that is pulling up the privacy tide. Until the public becomes accustomed to, and comfortable with, the new information technologies, and a consensus on privacy acceptable-practices develops, the public is likely to remain intensely concerned about risks to personal privacy.
- Privacy is a bipartisan issue. Nobody in the business community should have any illusion that the Republicans will be necessarily more sensitive to the importance of using personal information to drive down costs, deliver services, improve products, and improve public safety. The bipartisan nature of the issue was again highlighted in February, 2000, with the formation of a bipartisan Congressional Privacy Caucus. With public concern over privacy at such high levels, the bipartisan approach to this issue is likely to continue.
- Legislative activity is likely to continue almost unabated. With public-opinion surveys showing overwhelming public concern and the media fanning the flames by highlighting business practices, a continuing high level of legislative activity is almost a certainty.
- The traditional US approach of selective privacy regulation is eroding. There is increasingly widespread adoption of privacy programs like the Online Privacy Alliance principles, that are comprehensive "one-size-fits-all" measures. There is also an

increasing trend toward omnibus government solutions. While the draft safe harbor proposal is something of a hybrid between the traditional selective approach and the omnibus approach,[61] omnibus proposals or privacy packages are increasingly being introduced in state legislatures, including those of New York, California, Massachusetts, Hawaii, and Minnesota.

- Opt-out versus opt-in and affiliate sharing will be key issues. The debate over the G-L-B Act and Senator Shelby's amendments to the DPPA illustrate the contentious role that the opt-out/opt-in debate is likely to play in future congressional and state debates over privacy legislation. If business is to prevail on the issue, it will be necessary to demonstrate two things: opt-out really does work to protect privacy, and opt-in is an economic deflator. Title V also demonstrated the sensitivity surrounding affiliate sharing, an issue of growing concern to the public because of mergers of companies, such as the financial-services firms, that hold a wide range of personal data about them.

CONCLUSION

Information-privacy protections in the United States are strong and rapidly growing stronger. United States' protections for information privacy, however, cannot be measured simply by reference to a single omnibus law or by reference to the work of a single agency. To the contrary, the scope and substance of US information-privacy law are measured by reference to a wide array of sources of law and types of law, as well as self-regulatory measures.

Such law can be found in numerous state statutes which provide privacy and fair-information-practice-type protections for specific types of records or specific types of record-keeping relationships. Such law can also be found in dozens of federal statutes which provide notice, choice, access, data-quality, and confidentiality protections for specific types of records or specific types of record keepers. In addition, the measure of US law can be taken from an important body of constitutional and common-law jurisprudence. Finally, US information-privacy law is embodied in hundreds of state- and federal-agency regulations and administrative rulings.

Moreover, as a practical matter, much of the information-privacy protection in the United States does not even lie in law but, rather, is found in an array of self-regulatory mechanisms. These mechanisms include umbrella, cross-sectional privacy codes aimed mostly at e-commerce including, in particular, the Online Privacy Alliance standards. These mechanisms are found in emerging privacy-seal and verification programs such as TRUSTe and BBB*Online*. These mechanisms are also found in countless industry and company codes. Finally, but not to be overlooked, the robustness of the self-regulatory approach is sustained by an ever vigilant privacy-advocacy community and by the threat and reality of close media scrutiny.

Notes

[1] During the winter of 1999, the public deluged federal financial agencies with over 250,000 comments, mostly negative, regarding a proposed regulation that would have required banks to monitor customer transactions for suspicious activity; this year the Department of Health and Human Services reports receiving over 50,000 comments on its proposed health-information privacy rule.

[2] IBM Multi-National Consumer Privacy Survey (October 1999) available at http://www.ibm.com/services/e-business/priwkshop.html.

[3] In *Whalen v. Roe*, 429 U.S. 589, 599, 600 (1977), the Supreme Court discussed the various clusters of interests protected by the broad term "privacy."

[4] 5 U.S.C. § 552a.

[5] Atheneum (1967).

[6] *Records, Computers and the Rights of Citizens*, MIT Press (1973).

[7] Westin and Baker, Quadrangle (1972). See also Belair, "Information Privacy: A Legal and Policy Analysis" in *Science, Technology and Uses of Information*, National Science Foundation (1986).

[8] *Personal Privacy in an Information Society*, GPO (1977).

[9] See *e.g.*, *Katz v. United States*, 389 U.S. 347 (1967), holding that electronic eavesdropping by the government constituted a search and seizure and therefore must meet Fourth Amendment requirements.

[10] 426 U.S. 693 (1976).

[11] 425 U.S. 435 (1976).

[12] 429 U.S. 589, 605 (1977).

[13] In a subsequent information-privacy decision, *United States v. Westinghouse Electric Corp.*, 638 F.2d 570 (3rd Cir. 1980), the 3rd Circuit set out seven factors to consider when determining whether governmental information-collection practices infringe upon individual privacy. "The factors which should be considered in deciding whether an intrusion into an individual's privacy is justified are the type of record requested, the information it does or might contain, the potential harm in any subsequent nonconsensual disclosure, the injury from disclosure to the relationship in which the record was generated, the adequacy of safeguards to prevent unauthorized disclosure, the degree of need for access, and whether there is an express statutory mandate, articulated public policy, or other recognizable public interest militating toward access."

[14] 489 U.S. 749, 762 (1989).

[15] *U.S. Department of Defense v. Federal Labor Relations Authority*, No. 92-1223, February 23, 1994.

[16] 514 U.S. 1 (1995).

[17] Ibid., pp. 17-18 (O'Connor, J., concurring).

[18] Ibid., p. 26 (Ginsburg, J., dissenting).

[19] *Los Angeles Police Department v. United Reporting Publishing Corp.*, 528 U.S. 32, 120 S. Ct. 483 (1999).

[20] Cal. Gov. Code § 6254(f).

[21] *United Reporting*, 146 F.3d 1140 (9th Cir. 1998).

[22] *Los Angeles Police Department v. United Reporting Publishing Corp.*

[23] The Court's decision did not address the commercial-speech interests at issue in the regulation of the use of personal information in private records, an issue which also has drawn the attention of the Appellate Courts. The 10th Circuit Court of Appeals, for example, acted on First Amendment commercial-speech grounds to vacate a rule issued by the Federal Communications Commission which required consumers to opt in to most disclosures of their consumer proprietary network information (CPNI). *U.S. West, Inc. v. Federal Communications Commission*, 182 F.3d 1224 (10th Cir. 1999). cert. denied sub. nom. *Competition Policy Institute v. U.S. West*, ___ U.S. ___, 120 S. Ct. 2215 (2000). CPNI is information that relates to the quantity, technical configuration, type, destination, and amount of use of a telecommunications service subscribed to by any customer of a telecommunications carrier, including most information contained in telephone bills, which is made available to the carrier by the customer solely by virtue of the carrier-customer relationship. See 47 U.S.C. § 222(f)(1)(A)-(B).

[24] In a related development, on December 13, 1999, the Supreme Court issued an order in *McClure v. Amelkin*, 120 S. Ct. 630 (1999) (Order no. 99-200), setting aside a decision by the 6th Circuit Court of Appeals which struck down a Kentucky law limiting access to motor vehicle accident reports. The 6th Circuit struck down the law—which allows access to accident victims, victims' lawyers, victims' insurers, and the news media (but not for

commercial purposes)—after finding that the law violates commercial free-speech rights. The Supreme Court sent the case back to the 6th Circuit and ordered the lower court to restudy the case, taking into consideration the Supreme Court's decision in *United Reporting*.

[25] ___ U.S. ___, 120 S. Ct. 483 (2000). The 4th Circuit case was the first of four decisions issued by the Courts of Appeals on the constitutionality of the DPPA; two decisions upheld the constitutionality of the DPPA, two held it to be unconstitutional. See *Condon v. Reno*, 155 F.3d 453 (4th Cir. 1998) (holding DPPA is unconstitutional); *Pryor v. Reno*, 171 F.3d 1281 (11th Cir. 1999) (holding DPPA is unconstitutional); *Travis v. Reno*, 160 F.3d. 1000 (7th Cir. 1998) (upholding DPPA); *Oklahoma v. United States*, 161 F.3d 1266 (10th Cir. 1998) (upholding DPPA). The DPPA also has been challenged on First Amendment grounds; however, discussions of First Amendment challenges are omitted here. See *e.g.*, *Travis v. Reno*; *Oklahoma v. United States*.

[26] "The powers not delegated to the United States by the Constitution, nor prohibited by it to the States, are reserved to the States respectively, or to the people." US Constitution, Amendment X.

[27] 18 U.S.C. § 2721 et. seq.

[28] 18 U.S.C. § 2721(a).

[29] 18 U.S.C. § 2721(b).

[30] 18 U.S.C. §§ 2723(a) & 2724(a).

[31] The Court concluded that "the DPPA does not require States in their sovereign capacity to regulate their own citizens. The DPPA regulates the States as the owners of databases. It does not require the South Carolina Legislature to enact any laws or regulations, and it does not require state officials to assist in the enforcement of federal statutes regulating private individuals. We accordingly conclude that the DPPA is consistent with the constitutional principles enunciated in [*New York v. United States* and *United States v. Printz*.]" *Reno v. Condon*, 120 S. Ct 666, 672. In addition, the Court disagreed with the 4th Circuit's holding that the DPPA exclusively regulated the states, finding instead that the "DPPA regulates the universe of entities that participate as suppliers to the market for motor vehicle information— the States as initial suppliers of the information in interstate commerce and private resellers or redisclosers of that information in commerce." Ibid. As a result, the Court did not address the "question whether general applicability is a constitutional requirement for federal regulation of the States."

[32] For the most part, this "common law" privacy tort has a statutory grounding. See Trubow, *Privacy Law & Practice* (Matthew Bender, 1991) at Section 1.05 and the cases cited therein.

[33] *Restatement (Second) of Torts* § 652D (1977).

[34] *Privacy Law & Practice*, p. 692 (quoting *Restatement (Second) of Torts* § 652D cmt. A; internal quotation omitted).

[35] *Doe v. Methodist Hospital*, 690 N.E.2d 681,692 (Ind. 1997).

[36] See *Hammonds v. Aetna Casualty and Surety Co.*, 243 F.Supp. 793 (N.D.

Ohio 1965); *Milohnick v. First National Bank of Miami Springs*, 224 So.2d 759 (Fla. Ct. of Apps. 1969).

[37] *Doe v. Roe*, 400 N.Y.S.2d 668, 674 (N.Y. Sup. Ct. 1977) ("implied covenant of secrecy").

[38] 237 F.Supp. 96 (N.D. Ohio 1965).

[39] See *Office of Technology Assessment, Protecting Privacy in Computerized Medical Information*, 43 (1993).

[40] 5 U.S.C. § 552a(b) (1996).

[41] 5 U.S.C. § 552a (1996).

[42] See 64 Fed. Reg. 59917 et. seq., November 3, 1999, as amended by 65 Fed. Reg. 427, January 5, 2000.

[43] 15 U.S.C.A. § 1681 et. seq.

[44] See a summary of a consumer's rights under the FCRA in the FTC's model notice for distribution to consumers. 16 C.F.R. Part 601, Appendix A (1998).

[45] Pub. L. No. 106-69.

[46] The CPC supports the following four privacy principles:

1. Notice. Whenever private companies or government agencies plan to collect, use, and/or disclose personally identifiable information, they must notify individuals in a clear and conspicuous manner. Individuals must also be notified about the intended recipient of personally identifiable information and the purpose for which the information will be used.

2. Access and Correction. Individuals must have access to personally identifiable information about themselves maintained by private companies and governmental agencies in order to review the information for accuracy, timeliness, and completeness. Individuals must also have the opportunity to correct inaccurate information.

3. Consent. Private companies and government agencies must obtain individuals' affirmative consent before using and/or disclosing individuals' information for a purpose other than that for which the information was originally provided.

4. Preemption. In order to provide individuals with the strongest possible privacy protections, federal law must not preempt stronger state privacy protections.

[47] Press Release, "Vice President Gore Announces New Comprehensive Privacy Action Plan for the 21st Century," Office of the Vice President, May 14, 1998.

[48] *In re Trans Union*, available at www.ftc.gov/os/2000/03/index.htm. The FTC also held, for the first time, that age data is a consumer report when used or expected to be used for an FCRA-permissible purpose.

[49] Department of Commerce, "Elements of Effective Self-Regulation for Protection of Privacy," discussion draft (January 1998).

[50] Ibid., pp. 1-2.

[51] Ibid., p. 2.

[52] Fred H. Cate, *Privacy in the Information Age* (1997), pp. 66-68.

[53] Ibid., p. 67. See *Urbaniak v. Newton*, 156 Cal. Rptr. 55 (Cal. Ct. App. 1979); *Division of Medical Quality v. Gherardini*, 277 Cal. Rptr. 354 (Cal. Ct. App. 1991). See also Paul M. Schwartz, "The Protection of Privacy in Health Care Reform," 48 *Vanderbilt Law Review* 295, 320-321.

[54] See "Privacy Legislation in the States 1999 Trends," *Privacy and American Business*, Alan Westin & Robert Belair, eds. (September/October 1999).

[55] Robert O'Harrow, Jr., "Prescription Sales, Privacy Fears: CVS, Giant Share Customer Records With Drug Marketing Firm," *The Washington Post*, February 15, 1998.

[56] Robert O'Harrow, Jr., "Giant Stops Sharing Customer Data: Prescription-Marketing Plan Drew Complaints," *The Washington Post*, February 18, 1998; Robert O'Harrow, Jr., "CVS Also Cuts Ties to Marketing Service," *The Washington Post*, February 19, 1998.

[57] *Weld v. CVS*, (Mass. Superior Ct. Suffolk) No. 98-0897 (1998).

[58] "Class-Action Suit Targets CVS Over Use of Prescription Data," *Privacy Times*, Evan Hendricks, ed., April 3, 1998, pp. 1-2.

[59] "DoubleClick Cries 'Uncle'...Sam (Sort of)," *Privacy Times*, March 3, 2000, pp. 5-6. See also *Bloomberg News*, "DoubleClick in Settlement Discussions," CNET News, March 23, 2000, at http://aolcom.cnet.com/news/0-1005-200-1582990.html.

[60] See generally *Privacy & American Business, Handbook of Business Privacy Policies and Codes Volume 4* (1997).

[61] The draft Safe Harbor Principles are omnibus, while the accompanying Frequently Asked Questions are often selective in their approach.

Myths in the Privacy Debate

Duncan A. MacDonald

INTRODUCTION

I want to dispel some of the myths in the privacy debate, but I am not sure where to begin, because privacy is so hard to pin down. Like a myth itself, privacy can have a myriad of different meanings to different people at different times, and it has always been that way, even from antiquity.[1]

The desire for privacy probably originated as a survival instinct, the kind that drives animals to mark off and make claim to a special territory in which to hunt, live, procreate, and protect family from the reach of predators and competitors. As such, it is possessive and in a sense anti-others. In organized societies, it has a political texture that essentially is anti-authority. In its modern flowering, privacy is closely tied to property rights—private property as envisioned in Lockean political philosophy.[2] Not surprisingly, it thrives most abundantly in capitalist economies, especially those with strong traditions of upholding individual freedoms, like free speech and expression.

By and large, it is a dead letter in command economies, theocracies, and to some extent in homogeneous cultures.[3] People assert it in some places to undermine religious domination and in others to uphold religious and philosophical freedoms. As a rule of thumb, the bigger the governmental bureaucracy in any country, the greater likelihood that it will invade the privacy of its citizens and influence its social culture to cause citizens to do the same against each other.

Throughout history, privacy as a concept is seen always in transition, always being redefined by new information.[4] Contrary to current popular belief, technology more often than not has expanded its possibilities, mostly because of improvements in printing, housing, and transportation and distribution systems. The same holds true for economies with a growing middle class. As individuals accumulate wealth, their ability to weave private spaces into their lives increases.[5]

The intensity of the privacy debate today versus the debate in the past results from numerous factors. Certainly, the horrors of Nazism, fascism, and communism jolted Western nations into realizing how important privacy is and how easily it is lost. Most recently, the European Directive on Data Protection has challenged us to consider whether Congress should pass a similar data-protection law. The directive itself reflects the fear of the democracies of the European Union that information technology might be used in the future to subjugate people to private-sector dictators.[6]

Put another way, their fear is that technology will enable businesses to know enough personal information about people to manipulate their economic decisions. It is a fear that mysteriously disregards the possibility that people will learn to use technology to the opposite effect—for protection against economic control.

There is no question that businesses are using new technologies more than ever to collect information about consumers, but to a large extent the debate is about why they are collecting so much. Privacy advocates say it is to exploit consumers. But businesses say it is only to better understand what consumers want, so that they can supply it efficiently. They add that because today's consumers are more financially complex than they were a generation ago, they have no choice but to pursue whatever useful information they can find.

Without question, consumers own more, move around more, and buy more products from significantly more entrepreneurs than their forebears. And they pay with an ever-expanding variety of payment vehicles. A generation ago, they made most of their purchases as captives of local stores who knew them more intimately than any modern company could ever hope for. In contrast, today's consumers can transact anonymously on and offline with a seeming infinity of institutions across the planet, and thereby scatter their commercial information in ways that frustrate anyone bent on trying to figure them out.

But that is exactly what businesses must do to succeed. The laws of supply-and-demand require businesses constantly to learn as much as they can about what consumers want. And the more particular and shifting consumers' wants, the deeper businesses must probe. This information-seeking process, of course, works both ways, with consumers having constantly to keep up with businesses and the vast array of their products and services.

THE MYTH THAT WE NEED MORE PRIVACY LAWS

Although businesses and consumers need free access to information about each other to serve their respective needs, our public debate is only about how the former collects and uses information. This paper will focus on myths in that debate, starting with two that attract the most attention, each a flip-side of the same coin. One is that US law is deficient on privacy; the other is that we need more laws to protect it.

On the contrary, there is an abundance of state and federal law in the US governing privacy in the public and private sectors—statutes, regulations, common law, and contractual rights—and it is growing rapidly.[7] At the top is the US Constitution, arguably the oldest and most successful privacy law in the world. The Constitution says a lot about privacy without ever mentioning the word. It doesn't have to, of course, because of its broad guarantees of fundamental freedoms and its strict limits on government actions that interfere in people's lives. The Constitution says, in so many words, that what people do with their freedom is their private business, not government's.

Thirty-five years ago the Supreme Court reiterated this principle in the much-disputed landmark decision of Justice William O. Douglas in *Griswold v. Connecticut*.[8] Perhaps more than any other Supreme Court decision in our history, *Griswold* opened a searing debate in America about privacy.[9] I want to argue that *Griswold* means government must stay out of private-sector privacy matters—and that means no regulation of business information practices, except in response to extreme situations, for example, to prevent crime[10] and abuse of sensitive personal information, like medical records. Whether it allows room to require disclosure of business information practices is open to question.

Griswold involved the punishment of an organization and its "Medical Director," who were in the birth-control business and whose crime was to prescribe contraceptives in violation of Connecticut state law. In upholding the decision of the Connecticut Supreme Court that the law in question violated "the right of marital privacy," Justice Douglas wrote, "[T]he First Amendment has a penumbra where privacy is protected from governmental intrusion." He called it a "peripheral right," and noted that "guarantees in the Bill of Rights have penumbras, formed by emanations from those guarantees that help give them life and substance." His closing words were that our "right of privacy [is] older than the Bill of Rights."

We should take *Griswold* on its face[11] and recognize that the First Amendment is the cornerstone of privacy in America; moreover, that its language protecting free speech, press, expression, religion, and assembly allows people to create sanctuaries—spheres of privacy—that enable a truly private life, without which, as *Griswold* says, the "express guarantees [could not be] fully meaningful." The First Amendment liberates people to think, write, and speak freely, hold alien philosophies, go where they want, be alone or in organized groups, practice traditional or new religions, reject religion altogether, withdraw from public life, transact regularly in commercial markets, and on and on. These rights are private, and that means government has no role to play in whether and how people choose to use them. It means government cannot occasionally deny or censor them, or interfere with peoples' beliefs or choice of friends, neighbors, or social/political organizations. It can intervene only in extreme cases.[12]

Griswold in effect tells us that privacy must be held to the same First Amendment standard as for free speech, press, religion, and assembly: When it comes to protecting those rights, citizens must fend for themselves. As with free speech, they must determine on their own what privacy means, and how and when to use it. And as with other First Amendment rights, they must learn how to pursue, protect, and exercise it through self-reliance.[13] As the opening words of the First Amendment state, government has no role here: "*Congress shall make no law.*"[14]

THE EXTINCTION OF PRIVACY?

To get around this injunction, privacy advocates rely on another myth—that privacy is at risk of extinction in America, due in good part to the Internet.[15] We are told, for example, that people use the Internet less than they would because of fear of losing their privacy. This is an exaggeration. Peoples' use of the Internet is increasing exponentially, perhaps more rapidly than for any other product or medium in history.[16] In 1999, Americans sent well-over one trillion e-mails, most of them unprotected by encryption. They accommodate the slight risk that others might spy on their e-mails because of their long usage of phones, which they know from experience are less protective, not to mention less versatile and more expensive.

Further belying a fear of the Internet, consumers' e-commerce transactions are growing at an explosive rate of 300 to 400 percent annually, notwithstanding the well-known fact that many Internet entrepreneurs capture and use consumers' browsing and transaction information for marketing purposes. Most consumers put up with this because they know they can: 1) get a better deal online; 2) block the information capture in most cases; and 3) resist any subsequent marketing solicitations that ensue. Under the *Griswold* view of privacy, they have little choice but to fend for themselves.

The First Amendment often puts consumers in this position. For example, when they shop on or offline for a movie, book, music CD, live entertainment, or just a TV or radio program, they will often encounter things that deeply offend their moral, political, religious, or civic beliefs. It might be sexually explicit advertising or songs that glorify sexism or violence. But whatever the case, the First Amendment will not allow them to turn to government for a remedy. It tells them, in effect, that their only recourse is to turn away. Or, if they are sufficiently motivated, to use their right of free speech to try to persuade the offenders to change their ways or to persuade others not to give them business. In either case, change can only occur through *private action.*

Private action has stood us well in the marketplace. The alleged risks that the Internet and information-technology industries provoke are not unlike what other industries have faced and resolved without government intervention. Take any industry and look at its products ten, twenty, fifty, one hundred years ago. To pick an example, automobiles at the turn of the century didn't have a roof, doors, heating, front windows, a radio, air conditioning, or reliable tires—most of the conveniences we consider essential today. They broke down constantly and were very dangerous. But as the century rolled on, the auto industry, listening to consumers, effectively addressed these problems and got us to where we are today: reliable products that Americans love. But imagine if Teddy Roosevelt's Congress, at the dawn of automobiles, had the hubris to require the industry to fix the flaws in its cars immediately. Would we have better cars today?

Will we have a better information industry and wiser use of information technology in the future if government attempts to fix the perceived and anticipated privacy flaws of both, instead of leaving the quest for solutions to free markets? Will regulation lead to efficient, cost-effective privacy protection? Since free markets have given us so many of the privacy opportunities we have today, and since government historically has been the greatest threat to privacy, why would anyone prefer the latter?

The point is simple: Economic markets create competitors and put them through an unending, rigorous process to win consumer favor through invention, product improvement, attractive packaging, efficient distribution, customer service, price, trust, and scores of other attributes. Markets respond to flaws in every industry, figure things out, and provide value without government involvement. There is no reason, therefore, to believe that the burgeoning information industry, which has so richly enhanced our lives, will nonetheless uniquely fail us on privacy protection.

In many respects, the information industry represents a triumph of the First Amendment—the maximum, historically unparalleled democratic flow of information to ensure individual autonomy. It is only natural that there is some confusion about how best to deal with the mass of information it makes available to everyone. But it is foolish to suggest at this early stage of the industry that government should intervene to set things right. Trial-and-error in the market and consumer self-reliance will do that, as they always have.

Privacy advocates, therefore, should pay close heed to *Griswold* and the First Amendment's admonition that *"Congress shall make no law"* governing privacy—no government intervention, except in response to extreme situations. Short of an extreme, the Constitution trusts private forces will work things out.[17] Accordingly, there should be no privacy legislation if: 1) the privacy harm is not definable, serious, and provable (*i.e.* is based only on a guess about what might happen); 2) the harm is of a kind that the marketplace has effectively resolved in the past without government intervention; 3) consumers can deal with the harm on their own without significant cost and effort; 4) the harm shows signs that it will abate through industry self-regulation, new protection technologies, or consumer education, self-reliance, or acceptance of *quid pro quo* (*i.e.* value for what is given up); 5) it discriminates by applying only to business practices and not to all other organizations that engage in similar practices, such as government agencies, schools, charities, political parties, *etc.*; 6) the legislation will cost consumers more than the harm it seeks to eliminate; and 7) there is another constitutionally less-harmful alternative. To be safe, the new legislation should have a quick sunset, because privacy considerations change rapidly and privacy risks are constantly reduced by new inventions and business practices.

Based on what we know about the status of privacy in America today, it would seem that few, if any, new laws are justified. Privacy is not seriously being harmed by industry, and, in any event, consumers have the means to manage what they don't like. They can utilize a number of tools to protect themselves in the face of a perceived privacy risk—or they can accept the risk in return for an economic benefit.

THE MYTH OF MANIPULATION

The privacy cognoscenti won't buy this. They are riled not only that businesses compile and mine information they get on and offline; they are also convinced that businesses use the information to manipulate consumers. Most importantly, they believe the manipulation will be successful. They have to believe this, for without the certainty of manipulation their case that privacy harm is serious falls apart. What is left for them to hang their hats on? Junk mail, occasional telemarketing calls, information that slumbers in a database until it goes stale, customized web-site pop-ups?

Of course, there is no reliable evidence that manipulation occurs; nor that marketers believe manipulation is possible[18] or that consumers believe they are being manipulated. But there is a recent article in the *Harvard Law Review* that strongly asserts the opposite: It finds significant consumer manipulation.[19]

The article insists that "because individuals exhibit systematic and cognitive processes that depart from axioms of rationality, they are susceptible to manipulation by those in a position to influence the decision making context." Adding to their bleak picture of consumers' intelligence and lack of willpower, the authors argue that "because a multitude of non rational factors influence individual decision making, consumers cannot be expected to engage in efficient product purchasing analyses." Reduced to its bare essentials, the authors speculate that Americans have become puppets to sellers who cause them to buy products they don't, or shouldn't, want. Not surprisingly, the authors' solution is aggressive government intervention.

The article is worth reading, as it is in the *Harvard Law Review* and thus will be taken more seriously than it should. Undoubtedly, it will soon show up in privacy position papers and memoranda in governmental departments. As proof of the pudding, it may already have played a role in motivating US Attorney General Janet Reno to get further involved in the tobacco wars. The recent civil action by the Justice Department against tobacco companies strongly reflects the theory of the article.

The article, in any event, is wrong. Regardless of the volume of personal information that marketers use to fashion solicitations, manipulation of consumer purchasing decisions is extremely difficult in a competitive economy. For every product offering that might entice a thoughtless, perhaps manipulated, decision, there are scores of others in different colors, sizes, shapes, packaging, and prices, each one luring the consumer away from the would-be manipulator. Competition, in short, creates a system of checks and balances where no one can have the upper hand with consumers for long, if at all.

It is a certainty that whenever a company, via data mining, discovers a predilection of a consumer, scores of others will soon make the same discovery, and still others will make their own discoveries about different predilections. For example, if I buy a pair of hiking boots from a department store with a credit card, both the store and card company may use the information to try to get me to make another, related purchase, say, of outdoor products. If I go on the Internet to search for hiking equipment and places to hike, still more solicitations might ensue. But because I am a complex, diversified buyer, hiking is only a modest fraction of my commercial decisions. I'll buy scores of other products and services that information magnets will capture and perhaps turn into still more solicitations. The evidence of these possibilities is in my mailbox every day: businesses checkmating each other and manipulating nothing. For all their efforts, I simply ignore their solicitations. I am in control.

In the near future, consumers will have even more control, thanks to smart cards and software that will make them all but anonymous at points of sale on and offline. Other software soon will make it easy for consumers to identify organizations that maintain information about them—retailers, employers, schools, health-care providers, and politicians—and get access to that information with an opportunity to correct what is erroneous. Powerful new tools, indeed, that the marketplace, not government, is providing. These tools will shift the balance of power in consumers' favor, so that by the middle of this decade, it is likely that the paranoia about being watched will mostly be on the institutional side: government and business.

Let's pause on this point: consumers snooping on businesses. If a consumer wants to find out about shoes at a department store, credit cards at a bank, hotels in Alberta, and so on, all she has to do is go onto the Internet and ask the world. In a flash, she will get a massive amount of valuable information from other consumers, consumer advocates, government agencies, infomediaries, the media, competitors, and others, each cautioning her how to protect herself, how much to pay, what outlets to avoid, and the like. The Internet gives her unprecedented tools to eliminate guessing about brands and product quality.

In comparison, the information businesses gather about consumers' transactions, on and offline, is sketchy and at best enables little more than a solicitation crapshoot—a game against odds that they will contact the right person on the right day with the right offer and make a sale. And, of course, not make a contact in the wrong way and lose the consumer forever. In short, what the business community gets about consumers is crumbs. To suggest that consumers nevertheless need government protection seems excessive, except perhaps when the government is the culprit.

INTERNET SALES TAXES & PRIVACY

We know from the encryption debates that politicians often are of a mixed mind about marketplace tools that protect privacy. They like them up to a point, but they are starting to wonder whether too much privacy will diminish their ability to govern. This is especially so on the issue of taxation of e-commerce transactions. Tax-enforcement agents across the United States are fearful that consumers are going to use the Internet to try to avoid paying sales taxes.[20]

The majority of them—states, cities, counties, villages, et al., maybe 30,000 to 50,000 taxing jurisdictions in all—don't want to give up a penny. What many of them want is the creation of a national data bank to track e-commerce transactions of every kind: by price, item, place of purchase, place of delivery, etc. Their data bank will resemble the Federal Reserve or the bank-card associations' settlement systems, except for all the personal information it will collect and distribute to taxing authorities. Nothing of its kind has ever been created in the US. Whether their data bank can pass First Amendment muster remains to be seen. Moreover, because of the Compact Clause in the US Constitution (Article 1, Section 10), the states probably cannot create the bank without the approval of Congress, which seems unlikely. The combination of a data bank and taxes makes it too hot to handle.

It gets worse. Several states want the credit-card industry to play a major role in the Internet-tax-collection effort. The reason is simple: credit cards pay for virtually all e-commerce transactions and card issuers capture relevant details of each transaction for billing purposes. Because the issuers have information the states need, the states want to involve them in the collection effort. The attraction for the issuers is the additional discount revenue they will make from settling billions of dollars of sales taxes, as well as the political allies they will make in legislatures on other matters of importance, like protection of their information-sharing practices.[21] This is another reason to treat privacy within the "penumbras" of the First Amendment. By rigorously keeping government out of the privacy picture, neither side will be able to make deals to subvert marketplace solutions.

Credit-card issuers would be fools to hop in bed with the tax collectors. In doing so, they will commit two serious errors. They will exacerbate the growing distrust that customers already feel about their information practices, and provoke a new distrust that they have sold out to the worst snoopers of all. Just as bad is the risk that politicians will abuse the relationship by using it to raise new taxes, knowing that the message will come from the card issuers and not themselves.[22]

Let's face it, governments constantly try to find ways to snoop on citizens to achieve objectives like collecting taxes, dealing with crime, imposing moral standards, distributing benefits, and the like. But when government does it, there is a difference in contrast to business information practices: there are no markets to balance or erase its egregious effects—no opt-in, no opt-out.

OPT-INS, OPT-OUTS

The opt-in/opt-out issue, of course, is at the center of the political debate about business information practices. One side of the debate says the law should not allow businesses to share consumer information with third-party marketers without the consumer's written consent at the inception of their relationship. The other side says businesses should have the discretion to share the information, subject to the consumer's right at any time to opt out. In each case, disclosure is a presumed feature of the opt-in/opt-out right.

There are myths of sorts on both sides of the debate. All businesses seem to read from the same hymnal when the opt-in issue is on the table. They claim that mandating an opt-in will kill their marketing efforts, thereby increasing their costs and the price of their products. They add that without the freedom to use information, customer service will suffer dearly. Interestingly, few, if any, of them know for sure that an opt-in exercise will lead to those results, because they have never tested it. They just seem to assume that consumers will abandon them *en masse*. If this is so, it is odd that any business would want to be in that position, much less insist on the right to continue it.[23]

It is also odd that businesses believe they cannot find the words, and perhaps the incentives, to persuade their customers to collaborate with what in most cases is a good thing: information use that leads to bargains. If the business community is to carry the debate against restrictions on information practices, it must conduct opt-in experiments. Until it has empirical proof showing otherwise, it should stop arguing that the roof will collapse because of opt-ins. Who knows, businesses might even discover from the exercise that their information practices cost more than they are worth.

In any case, since it is highly unlikely that legislatures, including Congress, have the constitutional power to outlaw secondary use of transaction information by the private sector, the practice will continue to be legal. And because it is legal, the only question is how consumers with a concern can stop it. Keep in mind that most consumers do not show concern, or at least do not act on their concerns when given the opportunity. They ignore even the simplest opt-out procedures. Moreover, they almost never inquire about the information practices of the companies or banks they do business with. In the face of this apathy and as if to manufacture concern, privacy advocates insist that affirmative action in the form of an opt-in is the only way to protect consumers.

The opt-in approach, of course, is not a norm in business practice or the law. And that begs the question: Should the law require it to resolve a dubious privacy issue? Why impose a signature requirement[24] when so much else of consumers' transactions happens without a signature?[25] If the use of information to market products deserves such treatment, then many other, more important, aspects of consumers' transactions should also be carved out to include a signature. As it is, something like this happens when a consumer transacts for a mortgage. Between the application date and closing, the hapless consumer can end up providing a score of signatures or initials on more than a hundred pages of documents that nobody in their right mind would ever read, much less be able to understand or justify. Twenty years ago the process was relatively simple and it worked, but today a kind of madness has taken over that only lawyers can like. The opt-in approach for privacy risks is taking us down the same path.

Maybe the business community should offer to accept an opt-in requirement if Congress in turn will reimpose an opt-in for class-action lawsuits. Rule 23 of the Federal Rules of Civil Procedure used to operate on an opt-in basis. Until 1966, each member of a class seeking money damages had to sign up to be included in the case. According to a recent Rand Institute study, the change in Rule 23 to what now is an opt-out standard caused the number of class actions to "multiply many times over."[26] One must suspect that some of the reason for the exaggerated demand for privacy legislation is because of all the business it will give to class-action lawyers. But if an opt-in requirement is to become part of the equation, Congress should be consistent and require it for class actions also.

OPT-OUT FLAWS

The opt-out argument likewise is flawed. It holds that businesses should have a presumptive right to use much of the information they collect from a consumer until the consumer tells them to stop. Businesses prefer this approach because they believe, probably correctly, that the more information they have about large numbers of consumers, the better they will get at providing them with what they want.

Keep in mind that if a business provides an opt-out right at the inception of a relationship, that right arguably is simultaneously an opt-in right, because it gives the consumer exactly what an opt-in does: the ability to prevent the use of information from the start. Of course, this presumes: 1) a disclosure of the right, which many, perhaps most, businesses do not provide or provide only in gobbledygook; and 2) the consumer will read the disclosure, an unlikely event close to 100 percent of the time.

Privacy advocates argue that disclosures are an imperative of consumer protection. But are they really? Hasn't the daily drum beat of critical media, political, and academic coverage of business information practices inoculated almost everybody about what is going on? Don't most consumers know what to do, but simply not do it? How many of them ask a business up front, before a relationship or transaction ensues, if it will use their information for secondary purposes?

Of course, if the business admits it will use her information, a concerned consumer has many options. She can demand an opt-out before going forward, request a *quid pro quo* (*e.g.* a discount), walk away, pay with cash (or anonymously, if online), or accept that the information use will be harmless and perhaps even beneficial. But if she does nothing, in the case of most established businesses, the worst harm will be a few pieces of junk mail or telemarketing calls, each of which is easily resistible. The benefits, on the other hand, could be cheaper, customized products and better services.

Putting the burden on consumers to fend for themselves on information matters, without government intervention or lengthy disclosures, might seem harsh, but it is no more harsh a responsibility than what they already face when they shop. They know they must regularly ask about price, durability, perishability, safety, warranties, service, maintenance, size, weight, aesthetics, returns, dispute mechanisms, and on and on. They know they pretty much live in a *caveat emptor* world that by and large serves them well. And they know they are not helpless. So what is it about information use that provokes so many demands for special, elevated protection by government? If consumers can fend for themselves on so much else—matters far more complex, risky, and important to them than the use of transactional information for marketing purposes—why not the same for information practices?

Why not let them freely determine how much privacy they want? That's what they do most of the time anyway. For most people, for example, their residence is their most cherished privacy retreat. Yet it goes without saying that some residences are more protective of privacy than others. Tenement apartments are less private than suburban homes, and the latter are less private than the modern castles of the rich. While the privacy ideal might be the castle, it should not be government's task to get people there. It is up to individuals to figure on their own how much privacy they want and how to get it. Most people, of course, don't give the ideal a second thought. They pragmatically tolerate that a nearby neighbor may occasionally overhear their spats or goofiness, because they know the invasion isn't worth a fuss. By the same token, when left to deal with most business information practices, most of them sensibly shrug their shoulders and move on to more important matters.

Pragmatism probably explains why most consumers do not opt out when a business gives them the chance. Consumers know that the risks concerning secondary use of their information are modest at best and that, in any event, trying to prevent all of them is probably impossible.[27] Consumers interact with too many organizations that capture, buy, and share their information.

On any given day, most consumers probably deal with a score of businesses on and offline that record various information about them: utilities, phone companies, retailers, manufacturers, banks, investment advisors, insurers, credit-card companies, magazines, plumbers, carpenters, restaurants, grocers, and on and on. Depending on how the consumer pays, others also might capture the information, like merchant banks for card transactions, credit-reporting agencies, network providers, and the like. Noncommercial organizations on a daily basis often do the same thing—charities, schools, government, the dreaded Motor Vehicle Bureau, politicians,[28] *et al.* Still other organizations capture information without any interaction with the consumer.

It is no secret that some of them repeatedly trade the information with others, subjecting it to a kind of multiplier effect, where the information in theory might pass on and on many times before it loses its relevance. Recapturing it, much less trying to find out where it went, would be impossibly expensive and time consuming for even the wealthiest consumer—and quite frankly not worth the fuss, because, in the end, what happens to the information in most cases is rarely harmful to anybody.[29] Most of it in fact is never used, in good part because it is unusable. If every trade of information led to a solicitation, consumers would receive scores of junk mail and telemarketing calls every day.

Trying to stop information sharing before it commences likewise seems out of reach for most consumers. There is simply too much to stop, too many privacy practices to investigate: organization-by-organization, product-by-product, account-by-account, and disclosure-by-disclosure, each one written differently, but mostly all in gobbledygook. And then there is the enormous effort afterwards to monitor for results. Who has the time, and why expend it on what is mostly harmless in any event?[30]

The privacy police would have us believe that someone "live" in each of the established organizations we regularly deal with is snooping into everything we do in search of information to manipulate or harm us.[31] It is amazing that people fall for this. Today the snoopers mostly are algorithms that have been fashioned to slightly increase the existing slim chance that the organization using it might get a person to buy something, complain a little less often, make a donation, offer services, fill out a form, etc.

Sophisticated information algorithms have been used by the credit-card industry for a long time. Ten years ago the industry was happy with a 2 percent response rate to the solicitations it shaped with the help of algorithms—about a billion such solicitations per year. In 1999, the solicitations exceeded three billion, but the response rate dropped to only 1 percent. It tells you something: Despite all the new information that is available and being used, it is mostly useless in increasing acceptance rates.

That most data gathering by most organizations is harmless doesn't mean that consumers shouldn't be told in disclosures about what is going on. But the trouble with disclosures is that consumers do not read them. There are too many disclosures to read covering too many aspects of their lives—about companies, products, services, labor practices, safety warnings, discrimination, costs, duties, fines, and the like, virtually all written in gobbledygook and lost amidst a plethora of other information. The problem is information overload: so many public and private notices that people have learned to disregard them. It is a stretch for anyone to say that for once, in the case of privacy, a new disclosure law will work. About the only thing it will accomplish is temporary removal of the issue from the politicians' backs.

SECURITY IS THE ISSUE

For most consumers the issue in the end is not opt in or out, junk mail, telemarketing calls, those mysterious web-site pop-ups that know who they are, or another disclosure law to ignore; it is whether somebody will get access to their information and steal from them. More than anything else, consumers want security against crime. And that means they do not want key information like their Social Security or bank account numbers, income, and the like to get into the hands of crooks, who might use it to borrow in their names or break into their accounts.

For the most part, this has not been a problem. Most established businesses have excellent security systems and rarely experience a breakdown. But when they do, they fix it quickly and provide a fair remedy for victims. Anything less and the market, especially the media, will punish them severely.

CONCLUSION

Let me conclude my observations about myths in the privacy debate by repeating my belief that we should trust the market to resolve the privacy issues that disturb us so much today. They are not unlike the problems that any new industry faces. To assume, as so many do, that information technology will bring us in only one direction—a world where businesses use information to manipulate consumers' economic decisions—is itself manipulative. By promoting fear it lays the groundwork to usurp important constitutional principles. Like it or not, if privacy is a First Amendment right, as *Griswold* insists, we have little choice but to defend it on our own, just like free speech. The First Amendment tells us we must be patient in areas where use of the freedoms it covers might take a long time to bear fruit. Accordingly, it denies us recourse to legislation to speed things up.

But that should not be cause for despair. Competition forces entrepreneurs to listen to consumer demands and supply what they want. Privacy demands cannot be an exception to that rule, regardless of the dire predictions of some privacy-legislation advocates. As it is, new inventions and processes are being tested and implemented every day by industry. There are only two things that can hold them back: 1) premature legislation that will shift the debate and initiative from the marketplace to the courts (where lawyers will work their alchemy); or 2) consumer disinterest. Polls, of course, show that consumers are very interested in protecting their privacy from information-technology intrusions. But when given the opportunity to mitigate the intrusions, only a small percentage of consumers takes action.

But that, too, should not be a cause for despair. It can mean a thousand things. For example, it can mean consumers lack motivation because they are confused about the risks, harms, and solutions; or because they trust that the marketplace or government will eventually set things straight. It is likewise possible that there is inaction because privacy is an enigma to so many people. It is in the eye of the beholder and can be defined, measured, shaped, priced, protected, traded, and discarded in any number of different ways. It comes in degrees. It is like free speech; it has pluses and minuses, and succeeds best when left alone. If we leave it alone, privacy will be safe in America.

Notes

[1] For a comprehensive history, see Philippe Aries and Georges Duby, eds., *A History of Private Life*, 5 vols. (Cambridge, Massachusetts: The Belknap Press of Harvard, 1987).

[2] In *Two Treatises of Government* John Locke wrote that the "preservation" of private property is "the great and chief end...of men...putting themselves under government." (New American Library, 1963), p. 395.

[3] I would loosely define a homogeneous culture as one with a dominant religious, racial, or ethnic group that demands conformity with norms, customs, rituals, language, prejudices, castes, and the like. A majority of the countries of the world fit the definition, including many in Europe. Conformity, I would add, is an enemy of privacy, because it constantly requires submission to group standards via observation and sanction. The flip-side might be that multi-diversity protects privacy by fostering pockets of resistance—nonconformity via private, individual actions. If so, the US arguably is a much more privacy-oriented culture than it is given credit for.

[4] For example, the right to arrange the marriage of children in many cultures has been a private right of parents for centuries. The spread of liberal democracy because of trade, migration, and telecommunications technology has replaced it with the private right of offspring to make their own decisions. In short, new information undermined old information.

[5] For example, via separate rooms and beds for each member of a household in a privately owned home as opposed to a single room in a rented apartment. Wealth also enables greater leisure time to enjoy private possessions. Without space and time, privacy is an ephemeral right. What is often forgotten is that businesses constantly increase the opportunity for consumers to enjoy privacy by reducing the time it takes to conduct transactions. ATMs and PC banking, for example, have reduced to minutes what took hours not more than 15 years ago. The Internet has done the same thing by making shopping faster—and more private—than ever. The less time consumers have to spend transacting, the more time they will have for private actions, like reading a book, courting a friend, participating in the political process, hiding in the hills, etc.

[6] It is ironic that Europeans, who have been victimized so much in this century by pernicious governments, nonetheless trust the public sector more on matters of privacy than the business sector. This is in strong contrast to the US, where law reflects greater distrust of government.

[7] Privacy advocates most often point to the Fair Credit Reporting Act as a successful privacy-protection statute. Their affection for FCRA is strange,

for it allows massive trading of intimate, and often sensitive, consumer information for credit, insurance, marketing, and employment purposes. To listen to their current arguments against information sharing, one would think they would want to repeal FCRA or at least amend it to allow consumers to opt in. But they wouldn't dare, because FCRA has proven so successful. It is crucial to our economy. Among other things, it benefits consumers with the most efficient, egalitarian, lowest-priced credit system in the world. And it does this by what privacy advocates in other contexts would condemn as an invasion of privacy. Our credit-reporting system tells us we have less to fear about information sharing than the advocates would have us believe.

[8] 381 U.S. 479, 85 S. Ct. 1678, 14 L.Ed. 2nd 510 (1965).

[9] I am not unmindful that *Griswold* and its author are anathema to many scholars and political groups, who view the decision as reflecting more the personal politics of Douglas than sound constitutional jurisprudence. I would argue, however, that *Griswold* is a reality and that we should consult it to help us deal with our generation's privacy issues.

[10] For example, against identity theft and exploitation of children.

[11] *Griswold* upheld more than just the right of a doctor and Planned Parenthood to enable a married couple in Connecticut to receive contraceptives; it sanctioned the *business right* to sell the contraceptives and information about them. As such, *Griswold* not only told the state to stay out of the couple's bedroom but to stay out of the business transaction, treating both as private places protected by the Constitution. The Court did this despite significant public opposition at the time to liberalized distribution of birth-control products and services. There are parallels here to current privacy issues that reason, once again, for government not to interfere.

[12] One extreme of course is crime, and yet the Constitution is so distrustful of government that it allows the search and seizure of information about a crime only under strictly defined circumstances. The Fourth Amendment prohibits "unreasonable searches" and requires a determination of "probable cause" before a search can begin. The Fifth Amendment adds a layer of protection, prohibiting forced self-incrimination or "deprivation of life, liberty or property without due process of law." Coming after the First Amendment, it is only natural that the Fourth and Fifth are so deferential to privacy protection, even for criminals.

[13] The argument that people need privacy-disclosure laws to enable informed self-reliance is attractive, but constitutionally suspect. The First Amendment doesn't allow government to force religions to tell us about their intimate standards and rituals or require newspapers to disclose their sources so that we can make more informed judgements about articles. So by what justification can privacy merit different treatment? If privacy is a First Amendment right as *Griswold* has held, government must butt out.

[14] Based on a long line of Supreme Court decisions, the First Amendment applies equally to the states through the Fifth and 14th Amendments.

[15] "Our fundamental right of privacy has been almost completely eroded by rapid advances in computers." Richard Wolf, "States Move To Protect Online Privacy," *USA Today*, January 20, 2000.

[16] But see Robert Samuelson, "The Internet and Gutenberg," *Newsweek*, January 24, 2000. Samuelson says railroads, air flight, automobiles, and TV grew just as fast and had as great an impact as computers and the Internet.

[17] The risks that business practices impose on people's privacy are no greater than risks they face from the assertion of other First Amendment rights. For example, free speech and free press often lead to abuses the law cannot resolve. Media bias or apathy can make or break the reputation of people, organizations, political movements, businesses, and the like. Their actions can have a costly influence on government action (regulatory & judicial), market determinations, cultural acceptances, etc. The Supreme Court's decisions on obscenity and abortion have been convulsive by any measurement, but defended in any event as the raw price we often have to pay to be free. What we don't like about any of these decisions we must deal with on our own and not through governmental protections.

[18] If marketers believed manipulation were possible, they wouldn't keep it a secret for long—it would show up in speeches at their trade conferences, in trade- and B-school literature, in discovery and testimony at lawsuits, etc. I have dealt with among the best marketers in American industry for almost three decades and never once heard the word. They would laugh at the charge.

[19] Jon D. Hanson & Douglas A. Kysar, "Taking Behavioralism Seriously: Some Evidence of Market Manipulation," 112 *Harvard Law Review* 1420 (May 1999).

[20] Only a small number of states welcome elimination of sales tax on Internet transactions—often to help promote a local high-tech industry.

[21] The morass here might turn out like the mess we have with political action committees.

[22] See *Review and Outlook*, "George's Web," editorial, *The Wall Street Journal*, January 28, 2000.

[23] Businesses are well-aware of public and private polling that shows strong consumer views in favor of the right to opt in. But there is insufficient polling to indicate how many consumers would exercise the right not to opt in or what would motivate them to opt in. Moreover, since we have no idea how much, if any, an opt-in requirement will add to the cost of transactions, we have to be suspicious about the accuracy of the polling.

[24] Many of the opt-in proposals would require a signature, initial, or check mark in a box to make them effective.

[25] For example, few, if any, credit-card companies require a consumer's signature to open a card account, even when credit lines can run in the tens of thousands of dollars. Consumers in turn can use their cards for mail order, e-commerce, and many in-store transactions for big-ticket purchases without ever signing anything.

[26] "Class Action Dilemmas," Executive Summary, Rand Institute for Civil Justice (1999), p. 1.

[27] In the near future, software and perhaps infomediaries will enable a measure of success here, perhaps against big companies, but it is questionable whether the effort will make a big difference in stopping information mining by small and unseen players. Short of legislative prohibitions against the information practices that exasperate privacy advocates—a seemingly impossible task for any legislature—the best thing for everybody to do is to continue to debate the issue and look for private solutions.

[28] An Internet site recently reported that "the two leading Republican presidential candidates, Sen. John McCain and Texas Gov. George W. Bush, have contracted with Aristotle Publishing (http://www.aristotle.org) to target web users by matching web browsing habits and web site sign-up data with actual voter registration records." There's a message here.

[29] If the sorting of benign information by machines is so harmful that government must erect a barrier around it, then why shouldn't government carry the protection a step further and apply it in other spheres? For example, should it require restaurants to have more space between tables to prevent diners from eavesdropping on each other? The point here is that privacy exaggeration can lead to a slippery slope, to paranoia that corrupts the smart use of law and citizen self-reliance.

[30] This is not to say that consumers should give up on the various tools that are available to them. It is just to recognize that they should be selective. Perfect privacy comes only in the grave. Privacy protection has always come at a price and can be very expensive for those obsessed about it. Those who desire impregnable fortresses to keep away the world will find it is impossible and ultimately lonely.

[31] Much of the privacy debate results from fear mongering—privacy advocates instilling images of voyeurism by live people, as though data workers were peering one-on-one into individuals' windows, looking for information to embarrass them.

Privacy Concerns: Perception Versus Reality

Peter Gray

SYNOPSIS

The privacy and security of consumer information have become significant public-policy concerns in the US and abroad. These concerns are receiving increased attention from Congress, state legislatures, the administration, domestic and foreign regulators, privacy advocates, and the media. With such exposure, the political temptation to enact legislation to protect consumer privacy and security becomes hard to resist. Under the assumptions that consumers are powerless to protect their privacy and businesses do not have the will to do so, some may view legislation and regulation as the ideal solution, rather than a last resort. But enactment of legislation to protect consumer privacy and security can profoundly affect both online and off-line information businesses, including the financial-services industry, and may have unintended consequences. This chapter focuses on key privacy and security concerns, the role of self-regulation, the rationale offered for public-policy changes, the role of consumers, the European influence on US privacy policy, and the current trend towards more regulation.

INTRODUCTION

Privacy protection has been a public-policy concern for decades. However, rapid changes in technology, accelerated public acceptance of the Internet and electronic commerce, and the development of more sophisticated methods of collecting, analyzing, and using personal information have made privacy a major socio-political issue in the US, Europe, and other areas. Privacy issues increasingly have attracted the attention of the media, politicians, government agencies, businesses, and privacy advocates. In addition, the public has become increasingly sensitized to the protection of their personal information.

Nonetheless, many consumers balance their privacy preferences against other values and interests. Their actual behavior in the marketplace continues to demonstrate their willingness to trade off various degrees of personal privacy for discounts on merchandise, free products and services, points, and other benefits.

Critics of current information and data-protection practices frequently point to opinion polls, consumer surveys, and privacy violations by businesses and governments to demonstrate the erosion of personal privacy. For example, a 1998 survey by Privacy and American Business showed that 81 percent of Internet users expressed concerns about potential threats to their personal privacy while online. Over 70 percent were worried about unauthorized access and use of their e-mails, web-site tracking, and personal profiling.[1] Based on such findings, it has generally been assumed that many people are reluctant to use the Internet for online shopping.

National privacy surveys by Lou Harris and Associates and Opinion Research Corporation over the last 20 years also show a rising trend of public concerns about personal privacy.[2] Politicians and privacy advocates cite the results of such public-opinion polls and anecdotal examples of privacy violations to promote stronger consumer-protection legislation and regulations.

Growing media coverage of privacy abuses further attracts the attention of legislators, regulators, and the public. Indeed, many recent news stories give the impression that personal privacy no longer exists. For example, recent articles highlighted accusations that the IRS sent personal tax data to lenders via e-mail; states sold driver's license photos; banks sold customer information to marketers; and companies compiled massive databases of personal shopping habits without the knowledge and consent of consumers.

When stories like these give the impression that consumers are powerless to protect their own privacy, they provide momentum behind legislative proposals to try to restrict the collection and use of personal information. But such legislation may curtail cross marketing, data mining, customer profiling, and other activities that could benefit consumers and businesses.

Businesses have adopted a number of strategies to reassure their customers and forestall the most onerous versions of "privacy protection" legislation. They are adopting privacy policies and displaying privacy seals on their web pages. Software vendors are promoting new privacy-protection systems. US businesses and the federal government continue to pursue international negotiations to prevent disruptions of cross-border data flows. Yet class-action lawsuits also are being filed against companies for alleged privacy violations.

Is all this effort and expense merited, or are we suffering from P4 (Preoccupation with Protecting Personal Privacy) syndrome?

Unfortunately, with all the emphasis on privacy protection, much less is known about consumers' attitudes and behavior toward information security. How concerned are consumers about hackers who might gain unauthorized access to their financial accounts or personal files? Do consumers approve or disapprove of security measures, such as unique identifiers in computer chips and software that help authenticate computer users? Do consumers agree that personal security identifiers can help to prevent fraud and systems intrusions, and that increased security measures can enhance their privacy by better protecting personal information?

Some people may consider security and privacy as separate matters; others may view them as related elements of personal-data protection. We do not have enough evidence to indicate if consumers are willing to trade off aspects of personal privacy for greater security, or whether such trade-offs are necessary. Even if we did, there never will be a single, easy solution to privacy and security protection. Instead, privacy and security preferences can best be achieved through a combination of company and industry initiatives, consumers' actions to protect themselves, enforcement of existing laws and regulations, and, if truly necessary in some cases, enactment of new laws and regulations.

In the US, the scope of data-protection laws and regulations varies by industry and geography. For example, the financial-services industry is already covered by a variety of privacy-protection laws and regulations that apply domestically and overseas. However, the growing convergence of diverse financial institutions has raised new concerns about sharing of personal information internally and with third parties. The recent political push for more sweeping regulatory solutions to privacy concerns also has focused on several other relatively unregulated sectors of the information economy: medical and health records, information gathered on the Internet, and data files collected and administered by many state and local governments.

THE ROLE OF PRIVACY SELF-REGULATION

The private sector, quite naturally, prefers a self-regulatory approach to privacy protection. But the US government increasingly has urged industry to develop meaningful ways to provide consumers with better privacy-disclosure policies and greater consumer control over personal information. Companies are being prodded to develop mechanisms that protect information security and data integrity, and to strengthen and enforce their existing privacy policies.

The private sector has responded with a variety of self-regulatory initiatives in an attempt to forestall potentially onerous legislation or regulations that could impede both offline and on-line business opportunities. For example, the Direct Marketing Association, which offers consumers the opportunity to opt out of mail and telephone solicitations, expanded that program to include Internet solicitations. Many trade associations have developed privacy guidelines or best-practices for their members. A growing number of companies that collect information about consumers in their databases have adopted their own privacy audits and standards, and they disclose their privacy policies and practices in print and on their web pages.

The Better Business Bureau developed the BBB*Online* Privacy Program to verify, monitor, and review company privacy policies and practices; provide a consumer dispute-resolution mechanism; award web-page seals to companies that comply with good privacy practices; and provide educational programs.

TRUSTe and the American Institute of Certified Public Accountants also offer privacy-assurance programs to companies that meet their privacy standards. In addition, new technological solutions are being applied to better protect consumer information.

THE RATIONALE FOR PUBLIC POLICY

In the privacy arena, the rationale for US public policy appears to be based on a series of assumptions that rely heavily on public-attitude polls, media exposure of abuses, potential threats to personal privacy, laws and regulations of other countries, and the misinterpretation of statistical data and anecdotal information. The best illustration of this phenomenon can be found with respect to the Internet and online-privacy protection. Consider the following assumptions and compare them to the reality of the marketplace:

Assumption: Consumers are universally concerned about the privacy of their personal information, both offline and online.
Reality: Some people are more privacy-sensitive than others. Some care most about protecting sensitive information, like their medical records. Others don't seem to care, and they are willing to trade personal information for free or low-cost products and services, greater convenience, and other benefits.

Assumption: Consumers consider privacy as more important to them than convenience, security, reliability, value, choice, customer service, speed of access, and other benefits.
Reality: Individuals have a hierarchy of needs and preferences, which may change over time. For example, a consumer seeking the lowest-cost airfare available may be willing to divulge a degree of personal information in order to get the ticket. Someone who pays bills online may value the security and reliability of that service more highly than privacy. While the opportunity for lower costs remains a primary reason why millions of investors have opened online brokerage accounts, security and service availability are important, too. In the case of researchers surfing

the Web, they may be primarily interested in obtaining greater bandwidth to speed access to, and retrieval of, information, with little or no concern about privacy.

Assumption: Consumers who say they are concerned about their privacy won't surf the Internet or shop and buy online.

Reality: People often behave and act differently from what they say or believe. This particular example of cognitive dissonance may help to explain the discrepancy between public-opinion polls, which point to privacy concerns as a major deterrent to Internet use, and explosive growth in consumer online shopping and purchasing. According to Forrester Research Inc., the number of US households on the Internet grew from 5.8 million in 1994, to 38.8 million in 1999, and the company forecasts 59.8 million online households in 2003.[3] Jupiter Communications reported that the number of US online buyers grew from 18.8 million in 1998, to 28.8 million in 1999, and it predicts 85 million buyers by 2003.[4]

Assumption: Most consumers are worried about unauthorized access to their e-mail messages.

Reality: Despite the availability of various methods to ensure the privacy of their electronic communications, most people don't attempt to encrypt their messages or use anonymous identities. Their actual behavior demonstrates a clear lack of public concern over the privacy of e-mail messages.

Assumption: People have no control over their personal privacy in cyberspace, and they are powerless to protect themselves from privacy intrusions.

Reality: Consumers have a variety of ways to control their online privacy by using technological and other means to protect their personal information. They can disable cookies, encrypt messages, do business with companies that they trust, and use commercially available privacy-enhancing software. They can also refuse to provide personal information, use anonymous identities, employ filters to block unsolicited commercial e-mail

(SPAM), and configure their browser setup and preference specifications with a pseudonym.

Assumption: Consumers will not do business with companies that don't have privacy policies or privacy seals posted on their web sites.

Reality: Most people want to deal with companies that they trust and in which they have confidence. Good privacy policies and practices are an important element of trust. But good value and product quality, company reputation, excellent customer service, fair and prompt dispute resolution, and other factors besides privacy are also important. Annual consumer-complaint surveys by the Federal Trade Commission and state consumer-protection agencies show that fraud, misleading claims, refund and billing disputes, service availability, and failure to deliver promised merchandise predominate. Consumer complaints about online or offline privacy violations are rare.

In conclusion, there is a critical need to examine the assumptions that tend to drive and shape privacy policy. Legislation and regulations are not the panacea for comprehensive online or offline privacy protection, and they should be used as a last resort. Instead, existing laws and regulations should be enforced, consumers should become better informed and empowered to protect their own privacy, and businesses should compete for the public's trust.

CONSUMER INFLUENCE AND CONTROL OVER PRIVACY

Consumers are increasingly aware that ubiquitous and more-powerful computers, sophisticated data-analysis software, and widespread access to the Internet make it easier for both legitimate and shady businesses, as well as government agencies, to collect, access, and use personal information. Consequently, consumers have become more assertive in demanding that their personal information be protected, and that they be given greater control over the collection and use of such information. The following examples illustrate the influence of the public and the media on changing the privacy policies or practices of businesses and government agencies:

(1) South Carolina, Florida, and Colorado decided to sell 22 million drivers' photo images and personal data from their motor vehicle license files to Image Data, a private company in New Hampshire that is building a national database to help reduce identity theft, fraud, and other crimes. Media exposure and negative public reaction forced Florida to cancel its contract with Image Data; the Colorado legislature to consider a ban on the transfer of state motor vehicle records; and South Carolina to appeal its contract. Other states are considering imposing restrictions on sales of public information.

(2) Last year, federal banking regulators issued proposed anti-money-laundering regulations that would require banks to monitor customer accounts and report suspicious financial transactions to law-enforcement authorities. Privacy advocates warned the public that this was a government attempt to invade the privacy of consumers' confidential financial information. Consumers responded by sending thousands of e-mails to legislators and other policymakers. As a result, federal banking regulators decided to scrap the proposed rule.

(3) Intel's Pentium III computer microchip contained a processor serial number that was designed to combat online fraud, improve the security of e-mail messages, and limit computer theft by enabling web-site operators to track or trace consumers' online activities. Under the threat of a consumer boycott and negative publicity, Intel changed its software to permit users to deactivate the identification feature.

(4) Microsoft imbedded a unique serial number into its software that identified an individual computer user, the computer being used, and documents created on the computer in order to help the company diagnose and solve users' problems. Under pressure from privacy advocates, Microsoft agreed to modify its software to prevent the automatic transmission of personal information without proper customer authorization.

(5) RealNetworks used its software to collect users' personal information and music preferences online, without their knowl-

edge or consent. Extensive media coverage and public criticism caused the company to change its procedures and software to avoid tracking customers without their consent. The company faces a series of class-action lawsuits alleging violations of various state and federal laws by not complying with its own stated privacy policy.

(6) DoubleClick has been criticized by privacy advocates for tracking advertising click-throughs and profiling consumers who surf the Web. Negative publicity and the threat of legal action caused the company to change its privacy policy to allow consumers to opt out of profiling.

The above examples illustrate how the public, media, and privacy advocates effectively expose and oppose perceived threats to personal privacy. The Internet and modern communications systems are shifting market power toward consumers, who can decide just how much privacy they want. This market power may be expressed through competitive pressure against private companies to preserve market share, retain customers, maintain their reputation, and enforce their own promises. However, to the extent that consumers have insufficient market alternatives to government activities that threaten their personal privacy, they must rely on political power to protect those interests.

BALANCING PRIVACY CONCERNS WITH THE BENEFITS OF INFORMATION SHARING

Companies increasingly have the ability to customize their products and services to suit the individual consumer. In meeting the specific needs of individuals, however, companies often must tailor their marketing efforts based on consumers' personal information about their shopping habits, likes and dislikes, as well as demographic and other characteristics. Yet at the same time, consumers can and should decide the degree of personalization or anonymity they want from marketers.

For example, online behavioral tracking allows companies to know about consumers' interests and preferences, so they can target products and services that meet specific needs. Collaborative filtering software can be used to compile customer tastes and purchasing behavior, segment consumers into like-minded groups, and use the preferences of some to predict the buying inclinations of others in the group.

The benefits of such methods of market analysis to both consumers and companies are clear. Consumers do not get deluged with unwanted ads and solicitations, and companies save money by targeting their messages to a receptive audience rather than to people who are unlikely to want or need their products or services. Furthermore, use of such software actually *reduces unwanted intrusions* on consumers' privacy.

To help assuage consumer concerns about online security, various electronic authentication methods have been developed to allow buyers, sellers, and other parties to verify each other's identities and to ensure that electronic messages, documents, or communications have not been altered or tampered with during transmission. Electronic authentication techniques can provide a greater level of user confidence in transacting over the Internet. Such techniques also have the potential to reduce online fraud, unauthorized access to personal information, and network security breaches. This technology enables consumers and businesses to conduct many different types of electronic transactions—including the purchase and sale of goods and services, as well as the payment, receipt, and settlement of funds—more quickly, easily, and securely than paper-based transactions.

In conclusion, the common assumption that consumers are powerless to protect their own privacy and security should be challenged. Consumers who are concerned about their privacy or security can and do take action. Businesses tend to respond quickly to both consumer sentiment and market competition. Government responses may not be as immediate, but they are tuned more to the buildup of sufficient political pressures.

EUROPEAN INFLUENCE ON US POLICY

The European Union (EU) adopted a comprehensive data-protection directive in 1995, effective in 1998. The directive includes a prohibition on the transfer of personal information from EU-member countries to other countries that do not provide European consumers with an "adequate" level of privacy and security. The European standard for adequacy is generally stricter and more comprehensive than that of the US and most other countries. Therefore, if certain industry sectors are considered to have inadequate data-protection safeguards in place, multinational companies with offices in Europe could be blocked from transferring information on European citizens to the US and other countries. Such blockages could affect Internet, intranet, and extranet transactions, as well as computer records and paper-based information on consumers. If enforced, the directive could seriously impede both electronic and traditional commerce activities. Meanwhile, authorities in the US, Latin America, and Asia are considering data-protection legislation modeled on the EU directive.

Government officials from the US and EU have been negotiating in an attempt to avoid blockages of data flows and disruptions to trade and e-commerce, so enforcement of the directive has been delayed to give the parties time to consider alternative solutions. The US Department of Commerce has developed a safe harbor concept that would protect US companies from data-flow blockages if they agree to adhere to prescribed privacy principles. But an agreement with the European Commission, representing the EU, and the US has been elusive, and some European countries may decide to enforce their privacy laws and penalize companies that violate them. In any event, the directive has raised the sensitivity of US policy-makers to protecting the privacy and security of US consumers, and legislative and regulatory initiatives to do so can be anticipated. Meanwhile, to avoid disruption of their operations in Europe, US multinational companies are developing contractual approaches to data protection that comply with European laws.

THE TREND TOWARD GREATER PRIVACY REGULATION

Two key public-policy issues face lawmakers and regulators: Can the private sector be trusted to adequately protect consumer privacy and security? Or should government be trusted to impose stricter regulations to guarantee such consumer protection?

Those who advocate stricter regulation rationalize that it will cause more people to use the services of legitimate businesses and be protected from disreputable ones. They argue that more people will participate in electronic commerce if they have confidence that those who violate their privacy or security will be punished. Opponents of greater regulation say that heavy-handed privacy laws and regulations will stifle market opportunities and burden existing operations. Legislation designed to further protect consumer data may make some segments of the public, particularly those who are privacy sensitive, feel more secure. However, it may also disrupt the flow of information, and add to the cost of products and services for all consumers.

Congressional concerns over the privacy and security of personal information have led to passage and recent enactment of legislation that sets various privacy-protection goals, such as: protecting children who use the Internet; criminalizing identification theft and fraud; prohibiting the federal government from requiring Social Security numbers to be placed on driver's licenses; requiring consumer opt-in before personal information from driver's licenses and registration files can be used for marketing purposes; prohibiting the assignment of unique identifiers to health records; and protecting financial information. In addition, many states have enacted privacy laws affecting health care, direct marketing, telecommunications, financial services, and other areas.

Last year, Congress enacted the Financial Services Modernization Act, which applies broadly to banks, thrifts, credit unions, insurance and finance companies, securities firms, retailers, and others that offer consumer financial services. The legislation includes the following new consumer-privacy provisions:

- All covered institutions are required to clearly and conspicuously disclose to consumers their privacy policies on the sharing of nonpublic information.
- Disclosures on sharing of such information must take place when a customer relationship is first established, and annually as long as the relationship continues.

- Unlimited intracompany sharing of customer information is permitted, but customers must be given the opportunity to opt out of sharing personal information with third parties, with limited exceptions.
- The transfer of customer account numbers to third parties for marketing purposes is prohibited.
- States are permitted to enact stricter privacy-protection laws, so long as they do not preempt relevant provisions in the Fair Credit Reporting Act.
- Both federal and state regulatory authorities may enforce the privacy provisions of the act.
- The federal regulators are required to establish standards to ensure the confidentiality and security of customer information.
- The federal regulators are directed to study the appropriateness of information sharing between company affiliates, including the benefits and risks to consumers.
- Pretext-calling by information brokers who phone financial institutions to obtain customer information with the intent to defraud is prohibited.
- Remedies for violations of the act's privacy provisions are established.

Despite concerns over the privacy of their personal information, most customers who have an existing account relationship with a financial institution do not object to information sharing between different business units within a corporate family. In fact, customers often expect their financial institutions to know that they already have an account relationship when they apply for another financial product or service, or when they have an account inquiry or complaint. Furthermore, intracompany sharing of personal information provides a greater level of privacy protection for consumers, since third parties do not get access to customer data if the consumer chooses to opt out. By allowing financial institutions to directly offer their customers a wider array of products, less customer information is shared with third parties and personal privacy is enhanced.

As more consumers use the Internet to bank, pay bills, purchase insurance, shop online, save money, buy and sell securities, and engage in other financial transactions, financial-services companies are designing their web pages to offer a convenient, lower-cost way to access a wider range of financial products and services. For example, a customer seeking an online auto loan can also choose to buy auto insurance from the same source. An individual who wants to invest a sum of money can access a variety of choices among securities and get investment advice based on his or her risk profile. A credit-card holder who wants a mortgage may be able to get preferential terms or rates from the same company. Without the ability to share information between the bank, insurance, credit-card, mortgage, securities, and insurance affiliates of the financial-services company, consumers would not have the opportunity to take advantage of such benefits.

Notwithstanding such benefits, both federal and state legislatures are considering further restrictions on information sharing. For example, New York state is considering legislation that would require companies to get the consumer's prior consent (opt-in) before information may be shared with third parties. In addition, proposed federal and state legislation would require prior consent of the customer of a financial institution before information may be shared between company affiliates. Legislation has also been proposed to restrict data mining and consumer profiling, the collection and use of medical and health information, access to and use of public-record information, unsolicited commercial e-mail, and Internet privacy.

There is a clear trend toward more stringent regulation of consumer privacy and security, despite industry self-regulation efforts, the availability of new technology to protect consumers, and the public's ability to protect itself. While the generally accepted practice of most businesses is to permit consumers to opt out of the collection and use of personal information, companies are moving toward obtaining consumers' informed consent, getting permission to market products and services, and providing the opportunity to opt in under certain circumstances.

Meanwhile, legislative precedents have been established for mandatory consumer opt-in requirements. The Communications Act of 1934, as amended by the Telecommunications Act of 1996, established an important opt-in precedent. Section 221 (47 USC 221) of the act permits a telecommunications carrier to disclose customer proprietary network information (CPNI) for marketing purposes only when the customer provides an affirmative, written request. The Federal Communications Commission (FCC) regulations to implement the CPNI provisions were subsequently vacated by the 10th Circuit Court of Appeals on First Amendment grounds, but the FCC plans to appeal the decision. Section 631 of the act (47 USC 551) protects cable-TV subscribers' privacy by restricting cable operators from collecting or disclosing personally identifiable information without receiving prior written or electronic consent. To protect children from online predators, the Children's Online Privacy Protection Act of 1998 (PL 105-277) makes it unlawful for online services to collect or use personal information about a child for marketing or other purposes without obtaining parental consent. In 1999, the Driver's Privacy Protection Act of 1994 (DPPA), which permitted consumers to opt out before motor-vehicle-record information could be disclosed for marketing purposes, was amended to require consumer opt-in permission. And in January, 2000, the Supreme Court unanimously upheld the constitutionality of the DPPA. Thus, states may not disclose personal information from drivers' files without obtaining their affirmative consent.

What are the implications of this trend toward requiring companies to obtain consumer consent before they may use personal information? Most industry officials believe that both traditional and electronic commerce activities will be constrained, because experience demonstrates that most people will not provide advance consent to disclose personal information to marketers and other third parties. Consequently, consumers' opportunities to obtain new, improved, or lower-cost products and services may be lost. Personalized marketing will become more difficult and expensive, the volume of unwanted junk mail will increase, and market efficiencies will be reduced.

To cope with such threats, businesses must become more sensitive to both the privacy concerns of consumers and the political popularity of protecting the confidentiality of consumers' information. To avoid onerous restrictions on the collection and use of consumer information, businesses must demonstrate responsible behavior and convince policymakers of the costs of over-regulation.

CONCLUSION

Both privacy and security are politically popular areas of concern, with growing public awareness and activism in the US, Europe, and many other countries. Opinion polls indicating high levels of consumer privacy concerns and media coverage of privacy and security breaches make data protection an irresistible area for attention by regulators and politicians. Therefore, the temptation to legislate and regulate to protect the public often outweighs the consequences of restricting both offline and online commerce. Furthermore, legislation that is designed to apply to offline business operations may have a significant effect on online activities, and vice-versa. To deter enactment of restrictive legislation, the private sector must demonstrate that it is acting fairly and responsibly to protect consumer privacy and security.

The political bottom line is that the burden remains on business to show that additional data-protection laws or regulations should only be necessary to deal with specific abuses that cannot be cured by other means, or (perhaps) when private-sector actions truly fail to enhance consumer confidence adequately. Legislators should not rush to enact new proposals to protect consumer privacy and security unless the public benefits clearly outweigh the risks of not acting.

Finally, consumers have a crucial role to play. They should exercise greater control over their own privacy and security by only doing business with companies they trust, and they should employ technological and other means to protect the confidentiality of their personal information.

Notes

[1] Louis Harris & Associates and Dr. Alan Westin, "E-Commerce and Privacy: What Net Users Want" (1998).
[2] Ibid.
[3] "The Digital Economy Factbook" (1999).
[4] Jupiter Communications Survey (1999).

Public Policy and the Privacy Avalanche

Fred H. Cate

The open flow of information is under attack in the United States as never before in an effort to protect privacy. This issue has united the far right and far left, Republicans and Democrats, federal and state governments, the Eagle Forum and the ACLU, even Phyllis Schlafly and Ralph Nader. It is an issue that in the last two years has generated an avalanche of litigation, legislation, administrative regulations, hearings, press reports, and proposals for more to come in the future. In the past year alone, we have seen comprehensive financial-privacy legislation enacted by Congress,[1] the first federal law prohibiting access to historically open public records without individual "opt-in" consent,[2] sweeping health-privacy rules proposed by the Clinton administration,[3] children's online-privacy rules promulgated by the Federal Trade Commission,[4] multimillion-dollar settlements of privacy lawsuits,[5] a multistate attorneys general privacy investigation of major banks,[6] the negotiation of a privacy "safe harbor" with European regulators,[7] the appointment of the first-ever privacy official,[8] 356 privacy laws enacted by states,[9] and, most recently, two proposals from the Federal Trade Commission that Congress enact legislation protecting online privacy and guaranteeing individual access to, and an opportunity to correct, personal information.[10]

This unprecedented attention to privacy both reflects and has contributed to widespread popular concern. People are worried about their privacy; poll after poll tells us this. In one 1999 poll published in *The Wall Street Journal*, 29 percent listed loss of privacy as the issue that most concerns them about the next century—ahead of terrorism on US soil (23 percent), world war (16 percent), global warming (16 percent), or economic depression (13 percent).[11] This concern is prompted largely by extraordinary technological innovations that are dramatically expanding

94

both the practical ability to collect and use personal data, and the economic incentive to do so. Computers and the networks that connect them have become a dominant force in virtually all aspects of society in the United States and throughout the industrialized world. Today, information services and products constitute the world's largest economic sector. Institutions and individuals alike are flocking to the Internet—particularly to the World Wide Web—in record numbers, making it the fastest-growing medium in human history.[12] As a result, information, long the "lifeblood that sustains political, social, and business decisions,"[13] has taken on new and dramatically greater importance.

THE PRIVACY AVALANCHE AND CORE INFORMATION VALUES

The problem is that this new legislative and regulatory approach towards dealing with privacy ignores or repudiates a number of core values, especially those reflected in the US Constitution. I want to address briefly six of these.

OPEN INFORMATION FLOWS

The first is the concept of a free flow of information. The free-flow concept is not only enshrined in the First Amendment, but frankly in any form of democratic or market economy. In the United States, we have placed extraordinary importance on the open flow of information. As the Federal Reserve Board noted in its report to Congress on data protection in financial institutions, "it is the freedom to speak, supported by the availability of information and the free-flow of data, that is the cornerstone of a democratic society and market economy."[14]

The significance of open data flows is reflected in the constitutional provisions not only for freedom of expression, but for copyrights (to promote the creation and dissemination of expression) and for a post office (to deliver the mail and the news). Federal regulations demonstrate a sweeping preference for openness, reflected in the Freedom of Information Act,[15] Government in the Sunshine Act,[16] and dozens of other laws applicable to the government. There are even more laws requiring disclosure by private industry, such as the regulatory disclosures required by securities and commodities laws, banking and insurance laws, and many others. This is a very basic tenet of the society in which we live.

The importance of an open flow of personal information reflects the very practical benefits that such accessibility brings. Personal information helps businesses "deliver the right products and services to the right customers, at the right time, more effectively and at lower cost," Fred Smith, founder and president of the Competitive Enterprise Institute, has written.[17] Federal Reserve Board Governor Edward Gramlich testified before Congress in July, 1999, that "[i]nformation about individuals' needs and preferences is the cornerstone of any system that allocates goods and services within an economy." The more such information is available, he continued, "the more accurately and efficiently will the economy meet those needs and preferences."[18]

Federal Reserve Board Chairman Alan Greenspan has been perhaps the most articulate spokesperson for the extraordinary value of accessible personal information. In 1998, he wrote to Congressman Edward Markey (D-Mass.):

> A critical component of our ever more finely hewn competitive market system has been the plethora of information on the characteristics of customers both businesses and individuals [sic]. Such information has enabled producers and marketers to fine tune production schedules to the ever greater demands of our consuming public for diversity and individuality of products and services. Newly devised derivative products, for example, have enabled financial institutions to unbundle risk in a manner that enables those desirous of taking on that risk (and potential reward) to do so, and those that chose otherwise, to be risk averse. It has enabled financial institutions to offer a wide variety of customized insurance and other products.

Detailed data obtained from consumers as they seek credit or make product choices help engender the whole set of sensitive price signals that are so essential to the functioning of an advanced information based economy such as ours.[19]

Unfettered use of personal information benefits consumers not only by allowing businesses to ascertain and meet their needs accurately, rapidly, and efficiently, but also because it:

- enhances customer convenience and service;
- permits consumers to be informed rapidly and at low cost of those opportunities in which they are most likely to be interested;
- improves efficiency and significantly reduces the cost of many products and services;
- facilitates a wide range of payment options, including instant credit;
- allows for real consumer mobility, so that consumers can obtain credit, write checks, enjoy frequent-shopper recognition, return goods or have them serviced, and enjoy a wide range of other benefits when they travel or move;
- promotes competition by facilitating the entry of new competitors into established markets, reduces the advantage that large, incumbent firms have over smaller start-ups, and encourages the creation of businesses specialized in satisfying specific consumer needs; and
- facilitates the detection and prevention of fraud and other crimes.

These are real, tangible benefits that consumers enjoy every day and that are not possible without reliable access to personal information. As just one example of these practical benefits, Walter Kitchenman has calculated that mortgage rates in the United States are as much as two full percentage points lower because of the rapid availability of standardized, reliable consumer credit information.[20] With outstanding mortgage rates approaching $4 trillion, American consumers save as much as $80 billion a year because of the efficiency and liquidity that information makes possible. Such information further reduces the cost of credit by facilitating the prevention and early detection of fraud, debt collection efforts, nationwide competition, and consumer mobility, thereby increasing both the availability of, and the range of people who qualify for, credit.[21]

In a recent report on public-record information, Richard Varn, Chief Information Officer of the State of Iowa, and I examined the critical roles played by public-record information in our economy and society. We concluded that such information constitutes part of this nation's "essential infrastructure," the benefits of which are "so numerous and diverse that they impact virtually every facet of American life...." The ready availability of public-record data "facilitates a vibrant economy, improves efficiency, reduces costs, creates jobs, and provides valuable products and services that people want."[22]

Perhaps most importantly, widely accessible personal information has helped democratize opportunity in the United States. Anyone can go almost anywhere, make purchases from vendors they will never see, maintain accounts with banks they will never visit, obtain credit far from home, all because of open information flows. Americans can take advantage of opportunities based on their records, on what they have done rather than who they know, because access to standardized consumer information makes it possible for distant companies and creditors to make rational decisions about doing business with individuals.

The open flow of information gives consumers real choice, in every sense of the word: Choice as to whether to reveal their identities, whether to surf anonymously, whether to disclose information. Choice is taken away if you have legislation that prohibits an activity or makes it unreasonably costly. Direct marketing is a perfect, if mundane, example. I have no particular love for direct-marketing solicitations, but if I am going to receive them I would rather get the ones I am most likely to be interested in. Am I better off if direct marketers are prohibited from accessing personal data so that they send me everything or nothing, rather than offers which are relevant to me? Am I better off if I have to pay more for goods and services because they cannot be target marketed? Am I better off with less choice?—because that is what sweeping privacy laws offer.

THE MEANING OF "PRIVATE"

The Supreme Court has long asked in the context of various constitutional issues, such as Fourth Amendment challenges to government searches and/or seizures: What expectation of privacy is implicated by access and how reasonable is that expectation? When evaluating wiretaps and other seizures of private information, the Court has inquired into whether the data subject in fact expected that the information was private, and whether that expectation was reasonable in the light of past experience and widely shared community values.[23] There should be no interference with information flows to protect privacy interests that are not reasonable.

The US Court of Appeals for the 4th Circuit highlighted this very point in its decision striking down the 1994 Drivers Privacy Protection Act.[24] The court wrote, first, that

> neither the Supreme Court nor this Court has ever found
> a constitutional right to privacy with respect to the type
> of information found in motor vehicle records. Indeed,
> this is the very sort of information to which individuals
> do not have a reasonable expectation of privacy.[25]

Second, the court found it would be unreasonable to prevent the disclosure of such information because "the same type of information is available from numerous other sources....As a result, an individual does not have a reasonable expectation that the information is confidential."[26] Finally, the court concluded that "such information is commonly provided to private parties....We seriously doubt that an individual has a...right to privacy in information routinely shared with strangers."[27]

As the appellate court's language suggests, one long-standing corollary of the principle that the law should protect as "private" only information that one actually and reasonably believes is private, is the concept that private should necessarily mean "nonpublic." No expectation of privacy is reasonable if it involves information that is routinely disclosed or available publicly. This reflects not only the Supreme Court's interpretation of the Fourth Amendment, but also the common sense that the law should not impose costly or burdensome impediments to the collection and use of information that consumers willingly disclose and that is widely available in the marketplace. To do otherwise results in privacy protections that are nonsensical because they are hopelessly ineffective, contrary to the wishes of individuals, and unnecessary barriers to commerce and customer service.

THE LIMITS OF PRIVACY

The requirement that privacy interests must be reasonable, like the focus on open information flows, reflects an understanding that in a democracy and a market economy privacy is not an unmitigated good. Protecting privacy of information imposes real costs on individuals and institutions. Judge Richard Posner has written:

> Much of the demand for privacy...concerns discreditable information, often information concerning past or present criminal activity or moral conduct at variance with a person's professed moral standards. And often the motive for concealment is...to mislead those with whom he transacts. Other private information that people wish to conceal, while not strictly discreditable, would if revealed correct misapprehensions that the individual is trying to exploit.[28]

Privacy facilitates the dissemination of false information, protects the withholding of relevant true information, and interferes with the collection, organization, and storage of information on which businesses and others can draw to make rapid, informed decisions. The costs of privacy include both transactional costs incurred by users seeking to verify the accuracy and completeness of information they receive, and the risk of future losses due to inaccurate and incomplete information. Privacy, therefore, may reduce productivity, lead to higher prices for products and services, and make some services untenable altogether. The protection of privacy may also interfere with other constitutional values, such as the First Amendment protection for expression and the Fifth Amendment protection for private property.

As a practical matter, virtually none of us want as much privacy for others as we do for ourselves. When we hire people to take care of our children, few of us are very interested in the caregivers' privacy rights. When we board an airplane, we don't want the pilots to have extensive privacy rights. The Supreme Court has long said that politicians have effectively no privacy rights. There are areas in which each of us intensely believes that we should have privacy rights, but few of us are seriously willing to accord those same privacy rights to others. Across-the-board privacy rights create a situation that is both undesirable and unworkable.

THE CONCEPT OF HARM

The fourth of these six principles is the concept of harm. We have long recognized that the law should restrict information flows to protect privacy only when a specific harm is actually threatened. When information poses a demonstrable harm, we measure the value of that flow of information against the severity of the harm threatened, and in some instances allow the legal system to restrict the flow of information to protect against that harm. Those instances are actually few and far between, but they nonetheless exist—but only where a specific harm is threatened. This was the view of the US Court of Appeals for the 10th Circuit in *U.S. West, Inc. v. Federal Communications Commission* (which the Supreme Court in June, 2000, declined to review), when it struck down the FCC rules requiring telephone companies to obtain affirmative consent from their customers before using data about their customers' calling patterns to market products or services to them. The court wrote:

In the context of a speech restriction imposed to protect privacy by keeping certain information confidential, the government must show that the dissemination of the information desired to be kept private would inflict *specific and significant harm* on individuals such as undue embarrassment or ridicule or intimidation or harassment or misappropriation of sensitive personal information for the purposes of assuming another's identity. Although we may feel uncomfortable knowing that our personal information is circulating in the world, we live in an open society where information may usually pass freely. A general level of discomfort from knowing that people can readily access information about us does not necessarily rise to the level of substantial state interest under *Central Hudson* [the test applicable to commercial speech] for it is not based on an identified harm.[29]

The harm principle has largely been lost in the flood of privacy legislation. This is a very significant issue, for at least three reasons. The first is that we have historically required a realistic possibility of harm to justify regulation. If there is no harm threatened, then what is the justification for the regulation, especially if the regulation interferes with the free flow of information?

The second concern is that if you don't know what the harm is, you don't know what type of law is necessary to address it or whether a proposed law does in fact address it. For instance, one widely cited example of the need for greater financial-privacy regulation involves Minneapolis-based U.S. Bancorp, which has been accused of selling customer data to MemberWorks, a telemarketing company, for $4 million. The sale allegedly violated both U.S. Bancorp's promise to its customers not to sell such data and the Fair Credit Reporting Act. Some of U.S. Bancorp's customers also reported fraudulent charges for MemberWorks' products. In July, 1999, U.S. Bancorp settled a suit brought by the Minnesota attorney general, without admitting wrongdoing, by agreeing to new disclosure policies and paying about $3 million to the state and charitable organizations.[30]

But as the outcome of that case shows, what U.S. Bancorp was charged with doing already violated both the federal and state consumer-protection laws. U.S. Bancorp paid $3 million in fines. This case is not a poster child for why more regulation is needed, but rather a shining example of how well existing law works.

Another example of the supposed inadequacy of current privacy law is the fear that information, particularly medical information, will be used to discriminate in a financial or employment context. The merger of Citibank and Travelers Insurance has been widely cited as a key example of the "potential for the risky sharing of financial and medical information for marketing or underwriting purposes."[31] But remember, legitimate, lawful business activities routinely involve using personal information to discriminate among potential consumers. Only consumers meeting certain financial criteria are offered pre-approved credit cards. Only consumers likely to be interested in a given direct-marketing opportunity are targeted to receive a solicitation.

Medical information may be more sensitive, but even its use, provided that such use is within the law, raises similar issues. "Discrimination" is the business of insurance underwriting. So we should hesitate before assuming discrimination is always bad. It is not intrinsically unreasonable for a lender to want to know whether a borrower is likely to pay off a loan, or to require insurance for the loan if she is reasonably unlikely—for whatever reason—to be able to. This is especially true if the borrower possesses, but does not disclose to the lender, relevant information about her health. Even if discrimination is clearly harmful, the most efficient and practical response is to outlaw the discrimination. Restricting information flows to protect against unlawful discrimination is like using a hammer to swat a fly: It may get the job done, but it causes a lot of collateral damage, especially if the fly is resting on your head. Restricting information flows to protect against *lawful* discrimination is nonsensical.

The third concern in this harm concept is that if you cannot identify a specific harm, it raises the specter that there may be some other, undisclosed purpose—unrelated to protecting privacy—motivating the regulation. Privacy, as some public officials have already demonstrated, is often an effective lever to use to obtain some other, unrelated concession from companies.

THE IMPORTANCE OF BALANCE

As suggested by the discussion of a number of principles above, the fifth core principle is the concept of balance. As important as open information flows may be, there are occasions when a sufficiently great harm is threatened if information that is reasonably believed to be private is disclosed, that the law will properly protect against its disclosure. But efforts to enhance personal privacy must be weighed against the costs that those efforts impose on the free flow of information, the election and supervision of governments, the development of efficient markets, and the provision of valuable services.

Put simply, privacy protections must be proportional to the interest they are designed to serve. This principle is not only suggested by a common-sense regard for the benefits that flow from open information, but also is mandated by the First Amendment to the US Constitution. When the government restricts information flows—for whatever purpose—it must do so as narrowly or, in some cases, in the least restrictive way possible. For example, when information is true and obtained lawfully, the Supreme Court repeatedly has held that the state may not restrict its publication without showing that the government's interest in doing so is "compelling" and that the restriction is no greater than is necessary to achieve that interest.[32] Under this standard, the Court has struck down laws restricting the publication of confidential government reports[33] and of the names of judges under investigation,[34] juvenile suspects,[35] and rape victims.[36]

Even if the information is considered to be "commercial," its collection and use is nevertheless protected by the First Amendment. The Court has found that such expression, if about lawful activity and not misleading, is protected from government intrusion unless the government can demonstrate a "substantial" public interest, and that the intrusion "directly advances" that interest and is "narrowly tailored to achieve the desired objective."[37] In *U.S. West, Inc. v. Federal Communications Commission*, the US Court of Appeals for the 10th Circuit specifically found that (1) the FCC's privacy rules limiting the use of personal information about telephone subscribers restricted speech and therefore were subject to First Amendment review; (2) under the First Amendment, the FCC bore the burden of proving its rules were constitutional; and (3) constitutional burden required the FCC to demonstrate that the rules were "no more extensive than necessary to serve [the stated] interests."[38] Specifically, the appellate court found that the government's choice of means to protect privacy must reflect

> a "careful calculat[ion of] the costs and benefits associated with the burden on speech imposed by its prohibition." "The availability of less burdensome alternatives to reach the stated goal signals that the fit between the legislature's ends and the means chosen to accomplish those ends may be too imprecise to withstand First Amendment scrutiny."[39]

Balance is therefore a constitutional obligation.

Moreover, it is important to note the strong historical preference—also reflected in the 10th Circuit's decision in *U.S. West*—for sensitive balances that result in no more information than necessary being restricted in order to protect privacy. Consider just one specific example: The Commonwealth of Massachusetts had a statute which required trial-court judges to close all criminal trials when minor victims of sexual offenses testified. In 1982 the Supreme Court struck down the statute as unconstitutional.[40] It is difficult to imagine a stronger privacy interest than that of minor victims of sexual offenses who are having to testify at trial. But even in that instance the Supreme Court said the state may not enact an across-the-board rule closing trials:

> In individual cases, and under appropriate circumstances, the First Amendment does not necessarily stand as a

bar to the exclusion from the courtroom of the press and general public during the testimony of minor sex-offense victims. But a mandatory rule, requiring no particularized determinations in individual cases, is unconstitutional.[41]

Laws that put in place broad restrictions on the flow of information, rather than requiring sensitive balances to prevent specified harms, are constitutionally problematic.

DISTRUST OF GOVERNMENT AND PREFERENCE FOR SELF-HELP

Finally, the sixth of these principles at issue in the current rash of legislation is the concept of self-help and a distrust of government. The new quest for government intervention to protect privacy is ironic, because privacy protection in the United States, probably the greatest level of protection in the world, has historically focused on *government* access to information. We have restricted the government from coming into our homes, from invading our cars, from searching our places of work, from tapping our phones. We are now turning that principle on its head, asking the government to intrude into our lives to protect our information. According to Jane Kirtley, former executive director of the Reporters Committee for Freedom of the Press, the expectation that the government will protect privacy

> ignore[s], or repudiate[s], an important aspect of the American democratic tradition: distrust of powerful central government....[W]hen it comes to privacy, Americans generally do not assume that the government necessarily has citizens' best interests at heart.[42]

This is not only ironic, it is unprecedented in the United States. Remember, constitutional rights in the United States are generally "negative" and apply only against the government, not private parties.[43] Those rights do not obligate the government to *do* anything, but rather to *refrain* from unnecessarily interfering with individuals' freedom to act. This also explains the very high protection in US law for private agreements. Citizens do not have to make promises to one another, but when we do, the government makes available valuable resources to enforce those promises.[44]

This preference for private action and individual responsibility is especially clear when information is involved. The US Supreme Court has repeatedly interpreted the First Amendment to deny plaintiffs aggrieved by even false and harmful speech any remedy, stressing instead, in the words of Justice Brandeis, "the remedy to be applied is more speech, not enforced silence."[45]

The focus on individual and collective private action inevitably restrains the power of the government to pass sweeping privacy laws. But it also facilitates considerable privacy protection through the use of technologies, markets, industry self-regulation and competitive behavior, and individual judgment. Many companies are actively competing for customers by promoting their privacy policies and practices. If enough consumers demand better privacy protection and back up that demand, if necessary, by withdrawing their patronage, virtually all competitive industry sectors are certain to respond to that market demand. In fact, consumer inquiries about, and response to, corporate privacy policies are an excellent measure of how much society really values privacy.

Many industry associations have adopted privacy standards and principles. Corporate compliance with privacy standards constitutes an increasingly important accolade in competitive markets. Moreover, industry associations can help persuade member organizations to adopt and adhere to industry norms for privacy protection. The majority of the individual-reference-services-group industry has agreed to abide by the IRSG Principles, which not only establish data-protection standards, but also require annual compliance audits by third parties and a commitment not to provide information to entities whose practices are inconsistent with the IRSG Principles.[46]

These more flexible, more contextual, more specific tools often provide better privacy protection than broad laws, and that protection is achieved at potentially lower cost to consumers, businesses, and the society as a whole. These responses are exactly what we would expect from the market if consumers value privacy protection in the private sector.

What makes this even more ironic is that the very technologies that we are so worried about, such as the Internet, are precisely the tools that make it possible to shop anonymously, to browse anonymously, to visit a web site without being identified. Even direct marketing, the business we love to hate, allows shoppers to stay at home and buy from offers preselected to be of interest. More than two-thirds of US consumers took advantage of direct-marketing opportunities in 1998,[47] accounting for more than $1.3 trillion in sales of goods and services.[48] Think about that from a privacy point of view. Those 132 million adults didn't even have to expose their faces to the light of day in order to engage in this activity. Information technologies, and the services they make possible, make privacy realistically available for many Americans for the first time ever. Unlike archetypal small-town America, where everyone knows everyone's business, these technologies offer the promise of real anonymity and, as is discussed in further detail below, real control over what personal information to disclose, and to whom. Yet this is what we are trying to regulate, and we are asking the government to do it for us.

Laws and regulations designed to protect privacy may actually weaken it by ignoring, and even interfering with, the power of new technologies to protect privacy. For example, technological innovations such as adjustable privacy-protection settings in both Netscape and Microsoft Explorer, encryption software, anonymous remailers, and, in fact, the Internet itself all facilitate privacy and individual control over the information we disclose about ourselves. The widespread availability, increased power, and decreased price of many technologies also facilitate a vibrant market for privacy protection, whether in the form of online privacy certifications like BBB*Online* and TRUSTe, or complete privacy-protecting services like the recently unveiled iPrivacy, which makes it possible for an individual to browse, make purchases online, and even ship goods to her home or a drop-off location without ever disclosing her real identity, address, e-mail address, or credit-card number to anyone.

If privacy enactments make the Internet an inhospitable place for businesses to offer services and for consumers to shop, those opportunities for technological privacy protection will no longer exist. If the law creates a disincentive for developing privacy-protection tools, then consumers will be left with less protection, not more. Remember, technologies can actually and completely protect privacy; law cannot. At best, the law can create disincentives for data collection and use, and then impose penalties for engaging in prohibited practices. However, this is only effective if *all* of the following are satisfied: (a) the illegal use is discovered; (b) the user is identified; (c) the user is subject to the law or regulation and within the jurisdiction of an appropriate court or administrative agency; (d) the aggrieved data subject has the wherewithal or obtains the cooperation of a government agency to pursue the data user in court; (e) the aggrieved data subject can prove her allegations in court; (f) a judge or jury finds the user guilty and assess a fine or other penalty; and (g) the penalty can be enforced. As this litany makes clear, while privacy laws and regulations can cause considerable damage to society and the economy, they often provide very little privacy protection and none whatsoever against data users outside of the country. I would rather have the real privacy that technologies make possible than have a legal right to sue. To the extent we eliminate the incentive for the development of technological protections for privacy, not just online but in many other settings, we diminish the availability of real privacy for everyone.

THE FAILURE OF PUBLIC POLICYMAKING

We are increasingly witnessing Congress and state legislatures responding to a politically popular issue with poor policy and with poor process. There are regrettably many examples of this. Absence of preemption is perhaps the best one. If Congress really cared about privacy, it would not have allowed every state to enact its own set of privacy standards. This is especially true in view of the increasing globalization of information and information technologies like the Internet. The hundreds of state and local privacy laws adopted in the past year alone are merely the most recent evidence of an expanding phenomenon: the effort to use national or subnational law to deal with fundamentally global issues. Information is inherently global. It is because of its inherently global character that information has been the subject of some of the earliest multinational agreements, treaties, and organizations—dating back to 1601.[49] In fact, the Postal Congress of Berne in 1874 established a multinational postal regime—administered today by the Universal Postal Union—74 years before the General Agreement on Tariffs and Trade was opened for signature.[50]

Today, when data processing is wholly dominated by networked computers, information is difficult to pinpoint and almost impossible to block, through either legal or technological means. Digital information not only ignores national borders, but also those of states, territories, and even individual institutions. Not surprisingly, the inherently global nature of digital information poses extraordinary challenges to the power of national—much less state—governments, and efforts to use national—much less local—law to regulate information in one jurisdiction often pose substantial legal and practical issues in another. At a time in which we are looking at increasingly global activities—global business, global mergers, global shopping, global travel— Congress' most recent decision on privacy is nonsensical. With the Gramm-Leach-Bliley Financial Services Modernization Act,[51] states are expressly permitted to enact their own, more restrictive privacy laws, devolving privacy regulation to the local level. Inconsistent, local regulation at a time when everything else is moving toward centralization and globalization is, by definition, ineffective and imposes high costs while providing poor privacy protection.

The Drivers Privacy Protection Act provides another sad example. Supposedly enacted in response to the 1989 murder of actress Rebecca Schaeffer, who was stalked by an obsessed fan using information provided by a private investigator from her California Department of Motor Vehicles record, the law restricts the public's access to motor vehicle records, but not the access of private investigators.

California provides another all-too-common example. In an effort to protect privacy, California enacted a statute that prohibited the use of arrestee addresses obtained from law-enforcement agencies for marketing products or services, but explicitly permitted such information to be used for "journalistic" purposes.[52] It is difficult to take seriously the state's claim that sending a letter to an arrestee offering the services of an attorney or private investigator would invade her privacy, while publishing her name and address in the newspaper would not. This "overall irrationality," as Justice Stevens called it in his dissent from the Supreme Court's decision upholding the constitutionality of the statute, "eviscerate[s] any rational basis for believing that the Amendment will truly protect the privacy of these persons."[53]

The flood of legislation and regulation suggests this important subject, which touches on core values at the heart of our democracy and economy, is not getting the thoughtful consideration it needs. As a result, everybody suffers. Privacy suffers because these ill-considered laws do not provide effective protection, while their proponents falsely encourage the public to believe that they do, thereby discouraging the development and use of self-help privacy protections. The economy suffers because these restrictions act as a tax, slowing the economy and eroding the benefits of open information flows. And, most importantly, we as individuals and as a society suffer.

THE VIEW FORWARD
TAKING PRIVACY SERIOUSLY

We need to take privacy seriously. My point is not at all to suggest that privacy is not a real issue; rather, it is to suggest that the political process thus far has not treated it as one. Where the collection and use of nonpublic, personal information poses a real risk of a serious harm, Congress should enact well-drafted, carefully targeted legislation. For example, rather than worry about the use of public information to market valuable products and services, I would like to see Congress consider the issue of whether the mass of information stored in commercial databases is used on an individual basis, as when one enterprising snoop obtained Judge Robert Bork's video-rental records following his nomination to the Supreme Court. This type of individual use of information, as opposed to broad use for marketing, raises serious issues that Congress has not yet addressed.

Moreover, not all privacy issues require government action. As discussed above, nongovernmental solutions, which are often best facilitated by government *in*action, are the most effective and appropriate protections for privacy. But there can be no doubt that privacy involves real issues and we must consider them seriously, whether or not that consideration ultimately leads to legislation or regulation.

PUTTING PRIVACY IN PERSPECTIVE

Privacy is important, but it is not the only value the public and this society treasure. Privacy is always in tension with other values—the benefits that come from the open flow of information, freedom from government intrusion in private markets and private lives, the prevention and detection of crime, consumer convenience, and countless other values we seek and increasingly expect every day. If protecting privacy means we no longer enjoy these and other benefits, the cost of privacy may simply be too great. And if the means we use to protect privacy are overly broad or intrusive, much of the cost of that protection will have been unnecessary.

The goal of all privacy law and regulation, therefore, should be achieving a balance between the value of open flows of information and the value of enhanced privacy protection, to guarantee for consumers the maximum practicable benefit. This balance is most likely to be reached if each consumer defines that balance for himself or herself. Consumers who value rapid, convenient service more highly than absolute privacy should be free to make that choice. Therefore, privacy-protection tools should give maximum control to individual consumers rather than decide an appropriate level of privacy protection for all. Maximizing consumer benefit, then, requires not only that privacy protection be balanced against the benefits that flow from accessible information, but also that the government avoid substituting its judgment for that of individual consumers.

Most privacy advocates regard "choice" as the foundation of consumer privacy protections. Unfortunately, the current privacy debate has largely reduced "choice" to the issue of whether a consumer consents to the collection and use of personal information and the method by which that consent is sought. While choice certainly includes consent, the choice principle is actually much broader. It includes the consumer's right to make his or her own choice about the proper balance between the value of the open flow of information and the value of enhanced privacy protection, and to act on that choice by choosing among businesses offering different privacy protections. As we have already seen, choice is most often facilitated, not restricted, by the open flow of information. Choice requires that consumers have the right to choose among competing privacy policies, and obligates the government to preserve to the greatest degree possible a competitive market offering a variety of levels and means (and corresponding costs) of privacy protection.

Legislation that proposes a one-size-fits-all approach to privacy should therefore be avoided as posing constitutional problems, interfering with consumer choice, and taking privacy out of its proper perspective.

THE NEED FOR EDUCATION

We have done a poor job of educating the public, the press, and policymakers about privacy issues and the significant ramifications of regulating information flows inappropriately or unnecessarily. Researchers and organizations that work with information and study its use and regulation have sat back and allowed privacy extremists to come forward with horror stories which often have little to do with privacy or which involve the clear violation of existing laws. The pro-information community has remained lamentably silent or has merely reacted to these anecdotes. As a result, privacy extremists have largely defined the agenda for political and public debate.

It is time that the users of information and the people who study information step forward and begin educating people about the value of open information flows, the danger of letting the government protect your privacy, and the risks posed by overly broad privacy laws and regulations. Some new educational initiatives are underway—such as the Privacy Leadership Initiative[54] and Privacy Partnership 2000[55]—but we need to do more to refocus attention on the core values that have historically undergirded this information society and demonstrate the continuing vitality of, and need for, those principles, before we lose them entirely.

The Need for Research

We need to develop more and better data to demonstrate the value of open information flows and quantify the costs of restricting those flows to protect privacy. One of the reasons that Congress and state legislatures have done such a poor job balancing privacy with open information flows is that both industry and academia have done an even worse job providing the data necessary for crafting that balance. I recognize this is always the academic's cry: We need more data. But this is an area where we have surprisingly little, and the stakes of policymaking in the absence of those data are, as we have seen, very high. What is the value of information in the economy? What does a privacy bill cost? How much does an accessible public record contribute to the economy? There is some exciting new research just beginning, but there is much more work to be done and it needs to be started now, *before* further legislative and regulatory action, not after.

Standing Firm

Finally, while many businesses do and must make the political compromises necessary to survive, it is essential that the business community and other institutions recognize that core values and principles are at stake, as well as the health of the most robust information economy in the world, in the debate over the government's role in protecting privacy. It is vital that we stand firm on these key issues—that we not give away these

114

basic rights, not compromise these constitutional values, not cut a deal to stave off one particularly bad bill that ultimately erodes our entire information infrastructure.

I believe that today we are looking only at a tidal swell that will ultimately turn into a giant wave of privacy legislation, regulation, investigations, and lawsuits. We think the 356 state privacy bills enacted in 1999 is a large number, but I fear that it will pale in comparison to the number to come. Today we are debating "opt-in" versus "opt-out." It won't be long before we are facing restrictions on any use of personal information whatsoever. Today, we are fighting over grocery stores' use of their frequent shoppers' data; it won't be long before we are fighting laws that restrict the right of grocery stores to even identify frequent shoppers or to offer them discounts—laws that have precious little to do with privacy, but that will be carried along, caught up in its powerful rhetoric.

I am not arguing against meaningful discussion of important privacy issues, or efforts to understand better the privacy risks posed by new technologies and applications. But the stakes are simply too great to compromise away the core values and principles that undergird our economy, our democracy, and our society.

Notes

[1] Gramm-Leach-Bliley Financial Services Modernization Act (S. 900), 106 Pub. L. No. 102, 113 Stat. 1338, 1436-1450, Title V (1999).

[2] Department of Transportation and Related Agencies Appropriations Act, 2000 (H.R. 2084), Pub. L. No. 106-69, 113 Stat. 986, 1025-1026, § 350 (1999).

[3] Standards for Privacy of Individually Identifiable Health Information, 64 Fed. Reg. 59,918 (November 3, 1999; HHS, proposed rule), 64 Fed. Reg. 69,981 (December 15, 1999; extending deadline for comment), 65 Fed. Reg. 427 (January 5, 2000; correcting original notice).

[4] Children's Online Privacy Protection Rule, 64 Fed. Reg. 59,888 (November 3, 1999; FTC, final rule; codified at 16 C.F.R. pt. 312).

[5] In 1998, NationsBank, without admitting fault, paid $7 million in civil penalties for sharing information about maturing-CD holders with an affiliate, which then marketed risky derivative funds to those customers without disclosing the risks and other material terms of the transaction. See In the

Matter of NationsSecurities and NationsBank, N.A., Securities Act of 1933 Release No. 7532, Securities Exchange Act of 1934 Release No. 39947, Admin. Proceeding File No. 3-9596 (May 4, 1998; SEC, finding and order), available at http://www.sec.gov/enforce/adminact/337532.txt. In July, 1999, U.S. Bancorp settled, without admitting wrongdoing, a suit brought by the Minnesota attorney general which accused the company of illegally selling customer data; U.S. Bancorp agreed to new disclosure policies and payed about $3 million to the state and charitable organizations. See Holden Lewis, "The devil you *don't* know: Strange banks are selling your private information, too," bankrate.com, October 8, 1999, available at http://www.bankrate.com/brm/news/bank/19991008.asp; Jeff Leeds, "Bank Sold Credit Card Data to Felon," *Los Angeles Times*, September 11, 1999.

[6] Robert O'Harrow, Jr., "A Postscript on Privacy; Bank Bill's Late Change Gives States Last Word," *The Washington Post*, November 5, 1999; Marcy Gordon, "States Challenge Information-Sharing in New Banking Measure," *The Commercial Appeal* (Memphis, Tennessee), November 6, 1999.

[7] Issuance of Safe Harbor Principles and Transmission to European Commission, 65 Fed. Reg. 45,666, July 24, 2000 (International Trade Administration, Department of Commerce, Notice), available at http://www.ita.doc.gov/td/ecom/menu.html.

[8] "White House Hires Aide To Guide Privacy Policy," *The New York Times*, March 4, 1999.

[9] "Privacy Legislation in the States—1999 Trends," *Privacy & American Business* (September/October 1999), pp. 1, 3.

[10] Federal Trade Commission, "Online Profiling: A Report to Congress (Part 2)—Recommendations" (July 2000), available at http://www.ftc.gov/os/2000/07/onlineprofiling.pdf; Federal Trade Commission, "Privacy Online: Fair Information Practices in the Electronic Marketplace: A Report to Congress" (May 2000), available at http://www.ftc.gov/reports/privacy2000/privacy2000.pdf.

[11] Christine Harvey, "American Opinion (A Special Report): Optimism Outduels Pessimism," *The Wall Street Journal*, September 16, 1999.

[12] Only five years after its creation, it reached more than 50 million homes in the United States. By comparison, it took 38 years for radio to reach 50 million US homes, 13 years for television, and 10 years for cable.

[13] Anne W. Branscomb, "Global Governance of Global Networks: A Survey of Transborder Data Flow in Transition," 36 *Vanderbilt Law Review* 985, 987 (1983).

[14] Board of Governors of the Federal Reserve System, Report to the Congress Concerning the Availability of Consumer Identifying Information and Financial Fraud, p. 2 (1997).

[15] 5 U.S.C. § 552.

[16] 5 U.S.C. § 552b.

[17] Fred L. Smith, Jr., "Better to Share Information," *Desert News* (Salt Lake City, Utah), October 14, 1999.

[18] Financial Privacy Hearings before the Subcommittee on Financial Institutions and Consumer Credit of the Committee on Banking and Financial Services, House of Representatives, 106th Congress, 1st Session, July 20, 1999 (statement of Edward M. Gramlich), available at http://www.house.gov/banking/72199gra.htm.

[19] Letter from Alan Greenspan to Edward J. Markey, July 28, 1998, available at http://www.house.gov/markey/980728letterr.htm.

[20] Walter F. Kitchenman, *U.S. Credit Reporting: Perceived Benefits Outweigh Privacy Concerns*, p. 7 (The Tower Group, 1999).

[21] See Fred H. Cate, *Personal Information in Financial Services: The Value of a Balanced Flow* (2000).

[22] Fred H. Cate and Richard J. Varn, *The Public Record: Information Privacy and Access—A New Framework for Finding the Balance*, pp. 10, 13 (1999).

[23] *Katz v. United States*, 389 U.S. 347, 361 (1967) (Harlan, J., concurring); *Terry v. Ohio*, 392 U.S. 1, 9 (1968); *Smith v. Maryland*, 442 U.S. 735, 740 (1979).

[24] Pub. L. No. 103-322, 108 Stat. 1796 (1994) (codified at 18 U.S.C. §§ 2721-2725).

[25] *Condon v. Reno*, 155 F.3d 453, 464 (4th Cir. 1998), reversed on other grounds, *Reno v. Condon*, 120 S. Ct. 666 (2000).

[26] Ibid., p. 465.

[27] Ibid.

[28] Richard A. Posner, "The Right of Privacy," 12 *Georgia Law Review* 393, 399 (1978).

[29] *U.S. West, Inc. v. FCC*, 182 F.3d 1224, 1235 (10th Cir. 1999) cert. denied, 120 S. Ct. 1240 (2000) (emphasis added).

[30] Lewis, "The devil you *don't* know."

[31] Financial Privacy Hearings (statement of Edmund Mierzwinski).

[32] *Florida Star v. B.J.F.*, 491 U.S. 524 (1989); *Smith v. Daily Mail Publishing Co.*, 443 U.S. 97 (1979); *Landmark Communications Inc. v. Virginia*, 435 U.S. 829 (1978); *Cox Broadcasting Corp. v. Cohn*, 420 U.S. 469 (1975).

[33] *New York Times Co. v. United States*, 403 U.S. 713 (1971).

[34] *Landmark Communications, Inc. v. Virginia.*

[35] *Smith v. Daily Mail Publishing Co.*

[36] *Florida Star v. B.J.F.*; *Cox Broadcasting Corp. v. Cohn.*

[37] *Central Hudson Gas & Electric Corp. v. Public Service Comm'n*, 447 U.S. 557, 566 (1980); *Board of Trustees v. Fox*, 492 U.S. 469, 480 (1989) (emphasis added).

[38] 182 F.2d, p. 1235, quoting *Rubin v. Coors Brewing Co.*, 514 U.S. 476, 486 (1995).

[39] Ibid., quoting *Cincinnati v. Discovery Network, Inc.*, 507 U.S. 410, 417

(1993), and *44 Liquormart, Inc. v. Rhode Island*, 517 U.S. 484, 529 (1996) (O'Connor, J., concurring) (citations omitted).

[40] *Globe Newspaper Company v. Superior Court*, 457 U.S. 596 (1982).

[41] Ibid., p. 611, n. 27.

[42] Jane E. Kirtley, "The EU Data Protection and the First Amendment: Why a 'Press Exemption' Won't Work," 80 *Iowa Law Review* 639, 648-649 (1995).

[43] Only the 13th Amendment, which prohibits slavery, applies to private parties. *Clyatt v. United States*, 197 U.S. 207, 216-220 (1905).

[44] See *e.g.* 15 U.S.C. § 57b-1.

[45] *Whitney v. California*, 274 U.S. 357, 377 (1927) (Brandeis, J., concurring). See *44 Liquormart, Inc. v. Rhode Island*, 517 U.S. 484, 498 (1996); *Texas v. Johnson*, 491 U.S. 397, 419 (1989).

[46] Federal Trade Commission, "Individual Reference Services: A Report to Congress" (1997), available at http://www.ftc.gov/bcp/privacy/wkshp97/irsdoc1.htm.

[47] Direct Marketing Association, *Economic Impact: U.S. Direct Marketing Today*, 4th ed. (1998).

[48] Financial Privacy Hearings (statement of Richard A. Barton).

[49] Ludwig Weber, "Postal Communications, International Regulation," 5 *Encyclopedia of Public International Law* 238 (1983).

[50] Ibid.; General Agreement on Tariffs and Trade, opened for signature January 1, 1948, 61 Stat. (5), (6), T.I.A.S. No. 1700, 55 U.N.T.S. 188. See generally Fred H. Cate, "Introduction—Sovereignty and the Globalization of Intellectual Property," 6 *Ind. J. Global Leg. Stud.* 1 (1998).

[51] Gramm-Leach-Bliley Act, §§ 507, 524 (1999).

[52] Cal. Govt. Code § 6254(f)(3).

[53] *Los Angeles Police Department v. United Reporting Publishing Corp*, 528 U.S. 32, 120 S. Ct. 483 (1999) (Stevens, J., dissenting).

[54] The initial members are AT&T, Compaq Computer, Dell Computer, DoubleClick, E*TRADE, Eastman Kodak Company, Engage, Experian, Ford Motor Company, Harris Interactive, IBM, Intel Corporation, Network Solutions, Procter & Gamble, Sony, Travelocity.com, and US Bank.

[55] The Partnership is comprised of 36 companies including America Online, Intel, AltaVista, Microsoft, Excite@Home, IBM, and Yahoo.

The Economic Benefits of Balanced Information Use

Marty Abrams

In olden days, before computers and the Internet, local merchants met face-to-face with their customers and knew exactly what they wanted to buy. In today's marketplace we've lost the intimacy of that old neighborhood shopping district, but we are trying to replace it with more knowledge about consumers, so that their specific service and value needs can be met. Information technology allows us to do that in ways that are revolutionizing the market. For example, Jacques Nasser, CEO of Ford, told *The Wall Street Journal*, "I want to know the watch you wear and the coffeepot you use, so I can produce the right car for you."[1] In essence, he believes that the more Ford knows about consumers' preferences, the better it can design their cars. Ford envisions an interactive system that allows a buyer to go online to order a customized vehicle, and exchange information on financing, insurance, warranty, and repairs. This information will be linked to the production, marketing, and distribution processes, which should result in improved efficiency, reduced cost, and greater customer satisfaction. It also means fewer inventory shocks, giving us longer economic expansion.

The Ford example illustrates the shift from a production-based to a service-based economy. Modern economies are becoming demand-driven rather than production-driven. The sum of individual demands drives economic processes, from shopping for the right product or service to delivery and customer service. To make the system work effectively, information must flow smoothly between consumers and suppliers. But the imposition of rigid data rules gets in the way. In a speech at the Chicago Federal Reserve Bank in May, 1999, Chairman Alan Greenspan maintained that the application of information technology has increased the level of productivity in the United States. "This use of information creates great wealth," he said.[2]

Such positive changes would not have occurred without the free flow of information. The US is the only country that has successfully made the transition from a production-based to an information-based economy. The free flow of information between sectors and the application of technology have fueled economic growth while keeping inflation in check.

A recent study using Fannie Mae data defined the role of information in fueling the growth of the mortgage market.[3] Every mortgage is created to be resold, therefore the market for mortgages is always liquid. Mortgage buyers must know the risk related to each mortgage, and robust data flows make that possible. Interest rates are lower than they would be without information and knowledge that leads to liquidity and greater home ownership. That means that the typical consumer saves about 200 basis points, or $4,000 a year, on a $200,000 mortgage. For the economy as a whole, that's $85 to $100 billion in additional income that people have to spend, save, or invest. Such savings are not available in economies where information is more restricted.

The information culture in the US has made a vibrant service economy possible. The four cornerstones of our information economy are: freedom of speech; a robust, usable public record; shared data; and the intolerance of information use. The fourth cornerstone acts as a check-and-balance on inappropriate information flows. Information that is used in an egregious fashion will result in a public backlash. Companies that misuse customer information are compelled to change their behavior by market forces or by legal action. This unique information infrastructure facilitates the information economy.

The concerns of privacy-sensitive individuals about information collection and use, and extensive media coverage of real or alleged privacy abuses by businesses and government agencies, have spilled into the political arena. Consequently, legislation has been enacted to require companies to ask for a consumer's consent (opt-in) before using certain public-record information. Other laws give consumers the right to opt out of having their financial records used for marketing purposes. A number of states have established privacy commissions, and more privacy-protection legislation is expected at both the state and federal levels.

To understand the growing concern over privacy, we should look at the "tri-deficits" of knowledge, trust, and decision making. The knowledge deficit means that consumers, policymakers, and companies don't understand the linkage between value they receive and flexible information use. Not only do most consumers not realize that they save money on their mortgage because of the free flow of information, they also don't understand that our more competitive information-driven economy has increased the value of their 401(k)s. Policymakers don't understand the economic growth that is generated by information flows, or the effects on the economy of restricting such flows. Finally, most companies don't understand how information fuels their growth and profitability, so they can't make persuasive arguments to politicians, the public, and the media on the importance of free information flows.

The second deficit is trust. Unfortunately, many consumers, who are privacy pragmatists, don't believe information collected and used by business is serving their purposes. They don't trust data users to know where the limits are, and many people believe that data use is out of control. There are two components of the trust deficit, actual harm and consumer expectations. Laws and regulations are available to remedy the use of information that harms consumers. But, to build and retain trust, companies must change their behavior to not go beyond consumer expectations of appropriate information use.

This leads to the third, decision-making deficit. Data users don't understand how to judge how far to go with information. Some companies are so afraid of privacy backlash from consumers that they won't use information, leaving value on the table. Others don't know how to draw the line on use of information, so they will take the risks of a push-back by the public or lawmakers if they go too far. This means that organizations don't know how to find the decision-making equilibrium between the two extremes. Nor do policymakers know how to regulate or legislate privacy. That's not all bad, since premature restrictions on information have been avoided. Unfortunately, the political attractiveness of privacy-protection legislation is driving Congress and state legislatures to propose new and potentially onerous restrictions on information flows without understanding the consequences. And, finally, consumers don't know how to empower themselves to control the use of their information: They can say no, and they can refuse to do business with companies they don't trust to safeguard their information.

The Internet has made the information equation more complex, because it blends physical privacy (*e.g.* surveillance or keystroke monitoring) with informational privacy, which deals with databases and personal histories. Consumer profiling is an example of such blending, which has raised concerns among consumers and policymakers that the public has lost control over the use of personal information. Personal autonomy is an important issue in the digital age, because people want to feel that they have some sense of independence and control over their lives. A lack of autonomy leads to the erosion of trust.

There are two elements of trust. The first is value, that the products and services are right for the consumer, and that price and quality meet customer expectations. Consumers around the world want value to come from information use. The second is the privacy bundle, which includes security. Privacy is about appropriate information use, while security deals with safeguarding information from unauthorized access and change. Trust means privacy, security, and value. Because these elements are interrelated, privacy regulation can have an adverse affect on value, and decreased value reduces trust. Therefore, the good intentions of legislators to protect privacy may have unintended effects on consumers.

There are two fundamentally different approaches to privacy. There is data protection, which guards against wrongful processing, and information balance, which protects against harmful use. Wrongful processing means that companies use information in ways that are inconsistent with the notice to, and consent received from, the consumer.

Information balance means that companies are free to use the information, as long as they do no harm to consumers. The economic effect of each of these approaches is very different. Discussions of opt-in versus opt-out are about the difference between the sense of a contract that comes with data protection, and the sense of protecting against harmful use that is obtained with information balance. Information balance is the preferred approach, because it is the least disruptive to an ever-changing information economy. For example, identifying information from credit histories makes the Internet safer by authenticating consumers. This use is not consistent with the notices given consumers, but brings them great value.

The free flow of information in a vibrant economy is similar to the free flow of capital in a productive industrial economy. Data protection limits information flows and dampens the growth of services. For example, the European services sector is not growing as rapidly as the US services sector, because of data-protection constraints on the former.[4] In contrast to the European system of data protection, the US approach, which favors the free flow of information, stimulates a healthy service-based economy.

Economic growth is facilitated by a system that encourages information balance, which involves some trade-offs between trust and flexible information use. The elements of consumer trust are law, self-governance, industry codes of conduct, company self-restraint, and value. On the other side, companies want to collect and use information as broadly as possible. But, if companies become too aggressive in using information, and go beyond consumers' expectations, public reaction forces a bounce-back in the form of new laws or regulations, or stricter self-regulatory measures. However, too much emphasis on trust results in a deflator for the economy and a loss of value for consumers.

So, the central dilemma is that consumers want trust and autonomy, which means restrained information use. Consumers demand value, which requires robust information use. Therefore, a balance must be struck between trust and flexible use of information. The challenge for business is to make the value of information collection and use clear to consumers. Some companies are beginning to realize the importance of the value equation. For example, MyPoints provides consumers with points for helping it to target ads they would like to see. The more those ads are on the mark and are clicked through, the greater the point awards. This company understands that ads have to be tailored to consumer preferences, and that you have to add value if consumers are to buy into the information revolution.

In summary, we are at an early stage of the information revolution. The trust deficit is a critical component of this change. If consumers don't trust information flows, then politicians will feel the need to legislate. Value is not intuitively obvious. Businesses have to help the public understand the value that comes from information. The Internet has contributed to the public's feeling of a loss of autonomy, by combining physical and informational privacy. And lastly, the wrong public policy will depress the economy by restoring trust through non-productive means.

Notes

[1] Fara Warner, "Engine of Change: Making Bold Strokes, Fine Points, Nasser Puts His Mark on Ford," *The Wall Street Journal*, April 7, 1999.

[2] Alan Greenspan, "The American Economy in a World Context," address at the Federal Reserve Bank of Chicago *35th Annual Conference on Bank Structure and Competition*, Chicago, Illinois, May 6, 1999.

[3] Walter F. Kitchenman, *U.S. Credit Reporting: Perceived Benefits Outweigh Privacy Concerns* (The Tower Group, 1999).

[4] "Putting Services to Work," European Union publication, November 27, 1996.

The Future of Money and Financial Privacy

Richard W. Rahn

People do not want money—what they want is the ability to acquire goods and services. Money is only useful as a means to facilitate trade. Fortunately, new technologies will enable people to acquire the goods they want without holding or handling cash, which is a troublesome, nonearning asset. In the future, trade will be executed by instantaneous and simultaneous debiting and crediting of liquid-wealth accounts, held by both banking and nonbanking institutions. The new electronic digital-payments technology will enable property-rights claims on real assets, such as stock and bond funds, or gold, to be utilized as the medium of exchange for virtually all transactions.

In sum, when businesses or individuals wish to purchase a good or service, they will provide an electronic instruction, directly or indirectly, to their bank or other financial intermediary. The instruction will state that an amount equal to the nominal value of the purchase should be transferred immediately (with no time lag) to the account of the seller of the good or service. As a result, there will be no loss of interest earned, nor will there be any need for a traditional wholesale interbank clearing system. The buyer and seller will have transferred wealth almost instantaneously and without risk of nonpayment. By avoiding the use of government-produced fiat money, with all of its uncertainty and instability, some of the curse of inflation and payment insecurity that plague the world will disappear.

Conventional money will disappear because it is costly and cumbersome. Paper currency and coins can easily be lost or stolen. Conventional money is also bulky to transport and time-consuming to use in business transactions. It requires merchants to keep a monetary "inventory" in order to make change. (When used to buy merchandise from machines, such as a soda vending machine, costly coin- and bill-handling mechanisms must be installed. These mechanisms are subject to frequent mechanical breakdown and theft from both employees and outsiders.) All of this "inventory" of currency and coins is at risk and does not earn its owners any return.

A glorious age is beginning in which people will not have to endure episodes of sustained inflation. People can have a choice of both government issued and privately issued monies, which will enable them to escape from unstable money. If a governmental central bank, such as the US Federal Reserve Bank, engages in inflationary monetary policy, users of its money will switch to a different currency or will hold other assets. People will still be forced to use government money for the payment of taxes and for the receipt of payments from government; but for private transactions people will increasingly move away from government money.[1] Governments that produce money with a stable value (little or no inflation) will find their money may be used as a unit of account and medium of settlement, even though it may not be used as a store of value or a medium of exchange.

There are a series of technological and regulatory changes underway that will eventually make privately issued digital (electronic) money the norm. These changes will alleviate the many problems experienced with conventional central-bank issued money, and particularly with paper currency and coins, which were noted above.

If people could avoid holding any (non-interest-bearing) currency or coins at all, and still have the same, or greater, ease and ability to spend, they would probably choose to do so. Further, if people could keep their assets in a form where they make higher rather than lower rates of return, commensurate with the level of risk they are willing to accept, they probably would choose to do so. Finally, if they could take their liquid assets, such as stock portfolios, and their illiquid assets, such as homes, and turn part of their value into money only at the moment of purchase of some good or service, they would also probably choose to do that.

In fact, people soon will be able to do all of the above. Many business firms and some individuals are already partially turning their assets into money only at the moment they need to make an expenditure. They do this by obtaining a line of credit from the bank, using their assets as collateral. When they need to purchase something, they write a check or have an electronic transfer made against the line of credit. In this case, the bank credit performs many of the functions of money. It makes economic sense for the business to operate in this way when the rate of return it receives on its assets is greater than the cost of the line of credit from the bank.

Debit cards often are issued against interest-bearing accounts. Smart cards, which combine the capabilities of a prepaid and debit card, can also be interest bearing. (This is only true with some smart-card systems; it is not necessarily applicable to those systems that allow anonymous card-to-card transfers.) Almost all electronic money will be interest bearing. Therefore, central-bank money almost certainly will decline in importance because of its lack of competitiveness.

What is most likely to develop is that the primary issuers of electronic money in the future will be mutual funds. Mutual funds, by having diverse and liquid assets, can offer less risk than traditional banks. With a mutual fund, holders can cash in all or part of their ownership at any time, but not at a fixed price. Thus the mutual-fund account is as liquid as a demand-account deposit at a bank. (There are some exceptions, such as a "hedge fund"—in which the participants cannot withdraw their capital or capital obligation before a specified time or only with permission of the fund management.) In some countries, mutual-fund shareholders already can write checks and request electronic transfers to third parties against their share balance.

Mutual funds also have the advantage that they are not subject to bank runs resulting from a loss of confidence in the bank. A bank can find itself in a position where the obligations to depositors are greater than the assets of the bank. Given that bank deposits have a par value, the first people in the withdrawal queue receive 100 percent of their deposits, and the ones left in the queue after the bank's funds run out get nothing if there is no deposit insurance, or get their funds only after a long wait if deposit insurance exists.

Under the mutual fund, increases and decreases in share values in the underlying securities portfolio of the fund are distributed (actually, "marked to market") on an equal pro-rata basis to all of the holders of the fund. The value of the fund may decline, and so each fund holder shares the same percentage decline, as contrasted with the bank deposit "all or nothing" par-value system. What this means is that a holder of a mutual-fund share has more risk than a holder of an insured bank account, but this risk is offset by the greater returns the mutual-fund holder normally receives. So-called money-market mutual funds (which hold highly rated government and corporate debt obligations) are available for those seeking little risk but still higher returns than normal demand accounts.

Another major financial innovation that will accelerate the movement to nongovernmental money is securitization. This is the process by which previously illiquid assets are made liquid. An example of securitization would be a financial company that pools a group of loans and then sells claims on these loans to borrowers. In the United States, organizations like Fannie Mae pool home mortgages and sell them to financial institutions, mutual funds, and wealthy individuals. An increasingly wide variety of assets are now securitized. For instance, the expected stream of royalties from singer David Bowie's recordings have been securitized. In theory, virtually all marketable assets could be securitized. In sum, the new electronic-payment technologies allow holders of assets to earn interest or other returns on these assets up to the moment when they transfer the ownership of a portion of the assets to pay for a good or service.

As more "money" becomes interest-bearing electronic money, there is less risk of inflation because there exists no incentive for private banks or other financial institutions to overissue interest-bearing currency, since it increases the institutions' own liabilities. (This is because the issuance of interest-bearing "money" makes the issuer not only liable for the principal, but also for the interest. Governments producing non-interest-bearing money, such as currency, do not have this liability for the interest, and therefore in the first order they seem to be getting something for nothing. Thus, there is an incentive for the government to produce more non-interest-bearing currency than they would otherwise.) The unit of account (*e.g.* the US dollar) will probably continue to be set by the central bank, even though the use of government money as a transaction medium will decline. But the government will only be able to hold on to its function of establishing a unit of account if it operates in a noninflationary or deflationary manner.

Governments increasingly are being disciplined by the market because, in the age of instant global communications and financial institutions, any increase in inflation immediately causes a capital and currency flight. The Asian financial crisis of 1997 is a good example of how rapidly capital can move from an economy once investors lose faith in a government. Capital flight has a strong negative effect on the real economy, which then causes a political backlash.

Governments increasingly have to compete with other governments and private providers of monetary numeraires (*e.g.* the US dollar, Japanese yen, British pound, Swiss franc). Eventually, some governments probably will define their currencies' value explicitly in the form of a tradable basket of goods and services. Commodities traded on organized commodity-futures exchanges, having one world price, are prime candidates. For example, the dollar might be defined as x amount of gold, plus y amount of crude oil, plus z amount of corn. This would be nothing more than a modern version of the gold standard, but the basket will be one which more clearly reflects what the world both produces and consumes, and whose characteristics are easily measured—metals, agricultural products, energy products, and even such things as insurance rates.

The Federal Reserve Board under Chairman Alan Greenspan is known to have implicitly followed sensitive commodity prices, such as gold and oil, in the determination of US monetary policy. When the Fed deviated from this policy in 1998, by letting the price of the "basket" of sensitive commodity prices fall, including gold in dollar terms, it was forced to play "catch up."[2] These implicit rules most likely will become more explicit over time.

If governments fail to develop explicit definitions for the value of their currencies, the private sector will. Commodity and securities indexes that are presently traded are a step in the direction of producing definitions that could serve the unit-of-account function of money.

In the economy of the future, most wealth will become both divisible and liquid, and instantaneously transferable, and hence will be usable as transactions media. Since there will be no need to withdraw wealth-producing assets to provide purchasing power, as in a monetary economy, and assuming the unit of account is defined by a specific additive quantity of goods and services, there will be no pressures to produce inflation or deflation. All of the requirements to facilitate trade will still be met, and improved upon.

In this new digital world, transaction costs will be sharply reduced, leading to higher income levels for the world's people. Now that the technological problems have been solved, the speed at which people acquire the benefits of the nonmonetary economy will depend largely on how fast governments get out of the way. The new technologies will not be widely accepted unless people believe they are secure in their transactions, and know that they have the financial privacy and anonymity that cash now provides. This means that governments will need to abolish their controls on encryption (which cannot be enforced anyway) and get away from the notion that they have a right to monitor people's spending and investing behavior.

In a world largely without "money," the notion of money laundering as a crime becomes absurd. Tax evasion and such other criminal activities as drug dealing are the real crimes (if society chooses to outlaw them), not the use of money from these activities. Trying to monitor these crimes by monitoring the use of money is difficult, and harmful for the efficiency of money. New technology increases the difficulty of monitoring, so other less destructive and more direct means of fighting crime should be developed. The fact is, whether well-intentioned or ill-intentioned, government policymakers and bureaucrats who defend the encryption controls and money-laundering statutes are denying the peoples of the world better living standards and a higher level of freedom.

Financial privacy is about the ability, and what many consider the right, to keep confidential the facts concerning one's income, expenditures, investments, and wealth. Without financial privacy, many other fundamental freedoms, such as freedom of religion and speech, are endangered. Invasions of financial privacy are common characteristics of virtually all abusive governments. In the digital age, the government can attempt to have a detailed record of every financial transaction and of everyone's complete financial status, or it can accept the reality that it will know only what people want it to know.

Government officials around the world have provided a number of rationalizations to justify their intrusions into the financial privacy of citizens. These rationalizations can be put into two broad categories:

- the need to obtain private financial information in order to insure payment of all taxes due; and
- the need for law-enforcement agencies to have access to private financial information in order to detect and prosecute drug dealers, terrorists, spies, kidnappers, money launderers, and other assorted reprehensible folk.

In addition, governments have found a profitable side-business of selling data about their citizens—such as information about their automobiles and driving practices—to commercial companies. These companies in turn sell the data as market intelligence and research to vendors of goods and services.

Under totalitarian regimes, free speech and a free press are prohibited. Those who write and speak about things the state does not like are branded as criminals, and punished. As technology changes, however, it becomes increasingly difficult for state authorities to regulate what is published and what people hear.

Economic development has come to depend on the wide dissemination of information. The tools of dissemination—the printed word, radio and television, telephones, movies, and most recently the Internet—have become cheaper and cheaper, and therefore far more available, leaving residual totalitarian regimes in a dilemma. They need to allow their populations to have access to the information-dissemination tools if their economies are going to improve, but these same tools can be used to receive and transmit politically prohibited ideas.

If people have computers with printers and modems, copying machines, telephones, radios, and televisions, how can anyone long prevent them from using these devices for nonapproved political communication? The short answer is that no one can.

The reason that free-market democracy largely has triumphed around the globe is, despite its imperfections, it works far better than any alternative economic system. More people benefit in more ways, and fewer are abused under free-market democratic capitalism. When government allows it to properly function, capitalism delivers both the goods and liberty. The same cannot be said of activities managed by government. Over time, governments tend to devolve into inefficient bureaucratic tyrannies.

The greatest threat to future prosperity and liberty comes not from business and the private sector, but from government. The world's people will be neither truly prosperous nor free unless governments retreat from their seemingly never-ending desire to control the production and use of money.

Digital technology enables people to do for themselves what governments attempted to do in the past. The computer, global communications, and the Internet are destroying governments' monopolies on information and money. A person with an inexpensive device able to access the Internet can learn practically anything that is known by just about anyone. Almost any individual or institution that has an asset that can be securitized will soon be able to create financial instruments that can provide most of the functions of money.

A major and growing portion of foreign trade is in services—financial services (such as banking and insurance), business services, engineering and architectural services, legal services, etc. Many of these services can be provided over the Internet, and hence the providers can be located almost anywhere in the world. Many service providers can easily move their places of business to jurisdictions that have a favorable tax and regulatory environment. Free trade in services increasingly will become a necessity, because governments will find they can neither regulate nor tax such transactions, because consumers will receive much of the "product" by way of the Internet in digitally encrypted form. Governments that fail to move to free trade in services will find they are faced with the digital equivalent of trying to sweep back the sea.

Any country with a tax code that has high marginal tax rates on labor and capital, particularly financial capital, will see its tax base shrink, as people increasingly seek and acquire goods and services abroad and invest in low-tax jurisdictions through the Internet. For instance, if a person wishes to hire someone to write computer software, he may consider competent professionals anywhere in the world, because the instructions, work output, and payment can be transferred over the Internet. Professionals living in high-tax jurisdictions either will have to reduce their hourly wages or forgo the opportunity for the work. Purchasers of software are interested in getting the best product for the lowest delivered after-tax price. Many professional software writers may choose not to pay income tax to their governments when their clients are in foreign countries.

Tax evasion will be easier since they will be able to send their products over the Internet in encrypted fashion; hence, the government will not know of the untaxed export, and the seller can instruct the purchaser to make payment to the seller's account in a no-tax jurisdiction.

Holders of financial capital (*i.e.* stocks and bonds, currency, gold, etc.) also will find it increasingly easy to move their portfolios to low-tax jurisdictions. Again, they will do this in an encrypted format so that their own government will not know where the capital has ultimately gone. When tax evasion becomes this easy, like the purchase of whisky in a 1920s speakeasy, many currently law-abiding citizens will find the temptation too great to resist.

The correct response from governments to these new tempta-tions will be to redesign their tax systems. High-marginal-rate tax systems are destructive to economic growth to begin with, and they do not maximize tax revenue. The taxation of capital is particularly destructive, because it has the same effect as eating the "seed corn." Most capital has been taxed at least once—when it was first earned—if not again thereafter. Taxation of capital reduces the amount available for new investment, yet capital is what increases productivity and creates new jobs. The fact that people will have the ability to avoid destructive taxation is a net plus to economic growth, opportunity, and freedom.

Governments that do not modify their tax systems, but try to respond to the new technologies by so-called tougher enforce-ment, will succeed only in criminalizing the actions of a much larger portion of their populations, while at the same time reducing economic growth and freedom.

Benign governments will face the digital age by legalizing financial privacy, redesigning their tax systems, and shrinking their own economic and social roles. Oppressive governments will face the digital age by attempting to abolish financial privacy, and then drown in a sea of corruption and disrespect.

Privacy is a precious commodity. People should be able to live their lives largely as they see fit, provided they do not impinge on the rights of others. As Justice Louis Brandeis said, the makers of the Constitution "conferred, as against the govern-ment, the right to be let alone—the most comprehensive of rights and the right most valued by civilized men."

Most people do not want to have total privacy about their financial affairs because without some disclosure it becomes almost impossible to obtain credit. There is no right to credit; it is a privilege. To obtain it, people must convince someone that they have both the means and the honest intention to pay back the money that is lent to them. Usually the reason that people are unable to obtain credit is because they have a poor history of repayment or no credit history at all. Young people frequently are unable to get credit because they have no payment history, a

"Catch 22." People have been taught to borrow some money or apply for a credit card, even if they do not need it at the time, in order to establish a payment history—which is still good advice. Indeed, in the current economy, those who think they have no need for credit find that it is difficult to rent a car or make a hotel or airline reservation without a credit card.

But while most people voluntarily give up some financial privacy in order to obtain credit, this voluntary act should not imply that their rights to privacy about anything other than what they have freely chosen to disclose should be abridged. As debit cards and smart cards become more widespread, this problem should be partially remedied. But the fact remains, those who choose not to use some form of bank card will find it difficult to make certain types of purchases.

Businesses have an interest in knowing the buying habits of customers, as well as their credit ratings. This legitimate commercial need has spawned a huge data-collection business. Data-collection companies acquire records of virtually any purchase made with a check, debit, or credit card. Magazine publishers sell their subscription lists, a practice that has now spread to most other forms of commerce where potential-customer lists are useful. For example, when a person makes a purchase at the local garden shop, he can almost be assured the shop will sell his name and address to the seed-catalog companies.

Much of this is to the consumer's advantage, because it enables vendors to target their promotions to customers with particular interests. That in turn makes it easier for those with particular interests to obtain information about products they may wish to purchase, because the vendors know who is likely to want to receive specific product information. One can be assured that information about a purchase will not be recorded and sold only if it is paid for in cash and no personal information is provided to the seller.

Even though most purchase and credit reporting is inoffensive or even desirable, abuses take place. Everyone is bombarded by targeted telephone solicitations. In far worse cases of abuse, identities are stolen, and incorrect information gets into data banks, which can do great harm.

The promise that cyberpayments and smart-card systems hold for legitimate business transactions is immense. It would be a very sad fate if the implementation and widespread use of such systems were impeded in a fruitless attempt to regulate against the possibility that criminals would also use such systems. Although there is a possibility that criminals would exploit these same systems to their advantage, there is no reasonable way to prevent this without the wholesale destruction of the beneficial uses of new technologies.

Consider, for instance, the Justice Department's proposal in 1999 to get the US Congress to pass the Cyberspace Electronic Security Act, which would have granted it authority to break into individuals' home or office computers in order to collect private information, including e-mail. The Justice Department argued it needed this authority to combat drug trafficking, terrorism, white-collar crime, and child pornography. If Congress had passed the proposal, the government would have been able to obtain a great deal of information people believe to be protected and private. It might even have proved useful in prosecuting some guilty individuals. But any criminals who might have been caught would necessarily have been the small fish, because those engaged in serious crime could use any number of techniques to warn them that their computers' security had been breached. They would then have been able to foil the government's data-collection plans.

While the proposed legislation stated the Justice Department's well-meaning intentions, it is worth remembering that those who would have been involved in the everyday execution of the searches might have been the same officials who were sworn to protect the FBI files that ended up in the White House political office; or those at the IRS who were sworn to protect citizens' income-tax returns. The fact is that government, like all sectors of society, has its share of bad apples.

In 1998, the US government had 932 convictions for money laundering. These convictions cost a few billion dollars directly, and their enforcement cost on the financial system runs in the hundreds of billions of dollars. This is an enormous burden for banks and others to do all the kinds of record keeping and spying on their customers that the Financial Crimes Enforcement Network requires. Any kind of reasonable cost-benefit analysis will show it to be absurd. The costs run clearly into the tens of millions of dollars per conviction.

And for all the well-meaning intentions of those in government seeking to fight crime, the fact is that crime would be reduced by *ending* government's opposition to the coming digital age. The overmonitoring of paper transactions enshrined in our money-laundering statutes, though designed to thwart crime, instead help feed it.

If one truly were interested in greatly reducing crime, it would make sense to move totally to digital money, and give up paper money altogether. But the only way to do this is through anonymous digital money. A large portion of all crime occurs when criminals try to steal someone else's paper currency. Almost all robberies, and most larceny thefts, take place as a result of criminals attempting to steal cash. Approximately 18,000 murders are committed in the US each year, a significant number of which are motivated by the desire to steal cash, and hundreds of thousands of people are severely injured each year as a result of theft attempts. These crimes would be sharply reduced if there were little or no cash to steal. Criminals steal wallets, hold up convenience stores and gas station attendants, and rob banks to get cash. No cash equals less crime. Digital money could quickly largely replace cash if people were assured of the same degree of anonymity they have with paper currency.

Many in government wish to squelch the developments of the new digital age, either because they fear the loss of their own roles as economic gatekeepers, or because they genuinely believe that the new technologies will make life easier for drug dealers, money launderers, and other assorted criminals. To be sure, these technologies do make a criminal's life easier—as do the telephone and automobile. Yet it is also true that the digital age has given law enforcement many more tools to observe and detect criminal activity. Law-enforcement officials must learn to adapt new technologies to their purposes, rather than outlaw them in the futile hope that they will simply go away.

As the digital revolution takes hold, laws that were written for another era will become increasingly difficult to enforce. Americans and citizens of other countries can choose either to jettison these laws and take advantage of new technologies and the opportunities they create, or keep the laws and pay the price in economic inefficiency, technological backwardness, and government intrusiveness.

Notes

[1] Those who use money-like instruments other than the legal tender of their own government may be subject to capital-gains liabilities, which in turn may slow the movement away from government money.

[2] The Fed attempted to increase the supply of dollars through interest-rate reductions in order to stop the commodity-price deflation. Given that commodity prices are flexible and wages are far less so, when commodity prices drop, the ratio between wages and prices increases, thus causing an apparent rise in wages. This apparently rapid increase in the relative price of labor causes businesses to slow hiring or engage in layoffs, which in turn slows or even reverses economic growth. Thus, deflation can be as harmful to economic growth as inflation, because both cause unanticipated changes in relative prices and distort the price signals the economy needs to operate efficiently. In the digital world, private producers of monetary numeraires will gain acceptance for their products if the producers of government monies fail to maintain constant measures of purchasing power—that is, if they allow their money to either "inflate" or "deflate."

Some Practical and Theoretical Thoughts about Privacy and Banking

Julius L. Loeser

When Comerica Bank earlier last year distributed privacy principles to its retail customers and gave them the right to opt out from information sharing, it not only gave them the right to opt out from information sharing with affiliates, which most banks have done, but it went further and also gave them the right to opt out from sharing of information with third parties, which is what the Gramm-Leach-Bliley Act now requires.

EXPERIENCE WITH THIRD-PARTY OPT-OUT

Our experience, admittedly in a "pre-U.S. Bancorp" environment when privacy in banking did not have as much notoriety as it does today, was that less than 1 percent of the customers opted out. However, the intensity of the feeling of the people who did opt out was considerable. The word "appalled" or a variation of it was in virtually every letter, *i.e.* customers were appalled that a bank would consider transferring customer information to other parties.

I believe that illustrates a need for banks to communicate to their customers that there are innocent transfers of information, such as to printing firms for the preparation of statements or to facilitate a merchant's acceptance of a check written by the customer; that banks generally maintain customer information confidentially; that when information may be transferred to third parties for marketing purposes details of customer transactions are not transferred; and that there can be benefits to permitting transfer of information to third-party marketing firms. Some of those benefits are discussed below.

MORE SIGNIFICANT INTRUSIONS

It is ironic that, while what I sense are antibusiness interests criticize bank sharing of information, they seem oblivious to much greater threats to personal privacy emanating from government intrusion. Banks are required by federal law to file currency-transaction reports with the government whenever a customer engages in a transaction using $10,000 or more (in some geographic areas, as little as $3,000) in cash.[1] Banks are also required by law to keep records of wire transfers and to disclose those records to the government on request. Banks are required to file reports or keep records of purchases of money orders over a certain amount and are also required to file suspicious-activity reports whenever they observe anything suspicious on the part of any of their customers.

Under a recently adopted rule of the US Department of Health and Human Services (HHS) that is known in the industry as "Data Match" and is intended to help the government locate "deadbeat parents,"[2] HHS periodically will deliver to banks lists of deadbeat parents, *i.e.* parents who are not paying child support. Banks are to deliver to HHS or its agents a computer tape listing their account holders so that the government can garnish the funds in any corresponding accounts. Alternatively, a bank may compare HHS's lists against its list of depositors and report to the government any accounts held for persons on the lists, thereby preserving the confidentiality of most of its customers. Most banks are delivering their customer lists to HHS, as this is a less costly way of complying with this requirement.

AFFILIATE SHARING

Ironically, privacy activists do not appear to focus on intrusions like Data Match, yet focus not only on third-party sharing, but also even sharing of information among affiliates. From the perspective of any business, the concern over affiliates sharing information seems particularly misplaced. The very existence of affiliates often is an accident of corporate structure. The way a corporate organization is structured is a function of a number of variables unrelated to information sharing, including tax laws and even personalities, as an executive may wish to be CEO of his or her own operation so that a business is set up as a separate affiliate. In a perfect world one might merge all affiliates together into a single corporation which would eliminate any affiliate-sharing issue whatsoever. However, because of vagaries of corporate structure, an affiliate-sharing prohibition would block the flow of information in an organization, because of the accident of corporate structure.

BENEFITS OF THIRD-PARTY SHARING

IBM Corporation recently has televised two commercials that, intentionally or not, illustrate some of the benefits of third-party information sharing. In one, a gentleman in a focus group complains, "I get catalogues for toys, and I don't have kids." Why does he get catalogues he does not want? It is because no business has shared information about him with the toy-catalogue issuer enabling the catalogue issuer to target market, and so he receives unwanted catalogues for toys. A second person responds, "I get discount coupons for car repairs, and I take the subway." Again, businesses have not shared information about this person and so a marketing firm has been unable to target market, and thus this second person receives nuisance marketing communications. A third person adds, "I get calls for aluminum siding, and I live in an apartment." Again, failure to share information has led to needless intrusions into a consumer's private life. Someone then turns to the two-way mirror from behind which the focus group is being observed and angrily shouts, "You've got all the databases in there, but you don't know who we are." This television commercial illustrates one of the benefits of permitting sharing of information. It spares people from unwanted, potentially intrusive marketing efforts.

The second commercial highlights another information-sharing benefit. In it, a pair of grocery-store clerks is cleaning up late at night, and one picks up what apparently is particularly odoriferous cheese and comments on the smell. The other asks, "Who buys that smelly stuff?" The omnipotent voice of the off-screen store manager, who apparently, with the viewer, is sitting in an office above the store watching, responds over a loud-speaker, "The people who buy that smelly stuff also buy 90 percent of the baby vegetables over in produce. Have you ever looked at the markup on baby vegetables?" This illustrates another benefit of what some might consider an intrusion into personal privacy, *i.e.* tracking what particular individuals buy. A store's ability to track who is buying what, and what other things they buy, enables the store to meet customer wants and to increase profits, in theory potentially even to lower prices. This is precisely the benefit of supermarket discount cards. Such cards provide discounts to customers who permit their purchases to be tracked by the issuer, enabling the store to learn that customers who buy smelly cheese also tend to buy baby vegetables.

A free-market economist might observe that, if a business wishes to share information from customers, it ought to pay customers for that information or for the right to share that information. That is exactly the case with supermarket discount cards. Supermarkets are paying people for being willing to sell information. The supermarket will give a customer a discount on its products because the customer is willing to let information be collected.

That theoretically raises a question about the new legislation under which banks have to give consumers the right to opt out. Following the lead of supermarket discount cards, might a bank increase deposit interest rates or reduce loan fees for customers who do not opt out? If that would be permissible, could a bank conversely increase prices to people who opt out? In essence, that is what grocery stores are doing.

BEYOND BANKING

While, for some reason, policymakers concerned about privacy have focused on the banking industry despite its long tradition of customer confidentiality, the new privacy legislation applies to many other industries as well. It applies to any business engaged in activities in which banks or their affiliates will be permitted to engage under the new law. Under the new legislation, that includes businesses as varied as real estate development and wire transfer, automobile dealers that finance cars, department stores and other retailers that issue credit cards, as well as stock brokerage firms, insurance underwriters and agents, and even travel agencies. Businesses in each of those industries will be required to adopt privacy policies and provide them annually to customers, to permit their customers to opt out of information sharing with third parties, and then to track those who have opted out.

"MARXIST" ANALYSIS

To the extent that, as discussed above, one of the customer benefits of sharing information is to facilitate target marketing and thus spare consumers the nuisance of receiving marketing communications in which they would not possibly be interested, one might see a clash of two competing, admittedly ill-defined, consumer-interest groups when it comes to the issue of privacy; *i.e.* the interests of those who wish to be marketed for products and services in which they might be interested, but who do not wish to be bothered by marketing solicitations for unwanted products and services, clash with the interests of those who want to prevent information sharing because they see it as an intrusion upon their privacy.

A recent National Public Radio broadcast presented what I think of as a class-warfare, almost Marxist, analysis of these types of competing interests. It reported that some argue that impeding the free flow of marketing information to customers informing them of the availability of products and services they desire hurts low-income persons. The premise is that, while the rich have ready access to information about products and services, perhaps through the Internet or by subscribing to *Consumer Reports*, the poor do not have such ready access to information about products and services and cannot afford to purchase such information. Under this analysis, it is thought that lower-income persons therefore benefit most from targeted marketing that information sharing facilitates, and, thus, those who would impede information sharing are advocating a course of action that would harm the less fortunate.

THEORETICAL THOUGHTS
THE FIFTH AMENDMENT

The premise of privacy advocates is that information about a person is a property right of that person. However, information that one person gleans about another person based on the former's experience with, or observation of, the latter can hardly be deemed a property right of the latter, but may well be a property right of the former. Admittedly, it may be a different issue whether information about someone given to a business by the person who is the subject of the information remains the property of the person or becomes the property of the business; however, it is not absurd to argue that a recipient of information from a person who is the subject of the information, absent some other contractual understanding with the giver of the information, acquires a property interest in the received information. In either case, a constitutional issue would appear to be raised whether legislation restricting the use of the information that is property constitutes a Fifth Amendment "taking."

THE FIRST AMENDMENT

There may also well be First Amendment issues that need to be considered in this area. Some states have prohibited the release of arrest records to persons who would use the records for commercial purposes (*e.g.* publishers, attorneys, insurance companies, drug and alcohol counselors, religious counselors, driving schools) while permitting the release of such records for other purposes (*e.g.* scholarly, journalistic, political, and governmental). This may not be substantially different from the Gramm-Leach-Bliley Act's permitting the sharing of customer information for many purposes (*e.g.* to bank regulators, law-enforcement agencies, and judicial authorities) as well as admittedly for some commercial purposes (*e.g.* servicing, securitization), but not other commercial purposes. (Note the act's paternalistic prohibition against sharing account numbers for use in marketing, even with the consent of the customer.)

Some federal courts have held that, in enacting arrest-record statutes like those described above, state legislatures have drawn a line based on the "speech use" of such records, disallowing release to those wishing to use them for commercial speech, while allowing their release to those having a noncommercial purpose. One example of such a ruling is *Lamphere & Urbaniak v. Colorado*, 21 F.3d 1508 (10th Cir. 1994). (In my analogy to the Gramm-Leach-Bliley Act, the person whose free speech is being infringed might well be the third-party marketing firm from which the information is being withheld, not the free speech of the bank holding the information.) Such courts have gone on to conclude that, because commercial speech is protected under the First Amendment (albeit less than "core" First Amendment speech), and because speech includes direct-mail solicitation (Q: even the despised telephone solicitation?), the restriction constitutes a content-based restriction on protected speech. See *Speer v. Miller*, 15 F.3d 1007 (11th Cir. 1994).

A similar principle was invoked when the state of Minnesota imposed a use-tax on paper and ink only on producers of periodical publications. See *Minneapolis Star & Tribune Co. v. Minnesota Commissioner of Revenue*, 460 U.S. 575 (1983).

More pertinent is *U.S. West, Inc. v. Federal Communications Commission*, No. 98-9518 (10th Cir., August 18, 1999) which held that it is not permissible to curtail commercial speech unless it is to protect substantial rights and the protective measure is narrowly tailored. In that case, the Federal Communications Commission had adopted regulations requiring customer opt-in before telecommunications firms could lawfully share information concerning to whom, when, and where a customer places a call. The regulation implemented a provision in the Telecommunications Act entitled "Privacy of Customer Information." The 10th Circuit held that the commission failed to consider adequately the First Amendment.

In discussing the First Amendment issues, the court stated that, for the government to be found to have the requisite substantial interest in privacy to pass First Amendment muster, it "must show that the dissemination of the information desired to be kept private would inflict specific and significant harm on individuals." The court questioned whether undue embarrassment or ridicule, intimidation or harassment, or misappropriation of sensitive personal information for the purpose of assuming another's identity give rise to a sufficiently substantial interest. The court also suggested that an opt-out procedure is more narrowly tailored than an opt-in procedure and, thus, more likely to withstand First Amendment scrutiny.

LOOKING FORWARD: THE NEXT PRIVACY-POLICY DEBATES

Privacy activists believe that, not only should a consumer be able to control the use of data about that consumer, but also the consumer should have a right to correct erroneous or incomplete information about him or her, and that requires access to the data by the consumer. Certainly, this policy is codified in the Fair Credit Reporting Act in areas in which the availability of credit, insurance, and employment may be affected by information. It is not clear that there is a similar compelling need to ensure information accuracy in the area of marketing, however. Nonetheless, the Federal Trade Commission must think that the need to ensure accuracy of information for marketing purposes is fairly compelling, as "access" is one of five information principles it has adopted. The Department of Commerce, in negotiating with the European Union, also has established access as a requisite element in a program that meets the requirements of the EU directive prohibiting a member country from permitting the sharing of information with persons in any other country that does not have adequate privacy protections in place. The business community, perhaps predictably, normally does not provide access because of the costs involved.

Undoubtedly, the next frontier in the privacy debate will be state legislatures. The Gramm-Leach-Bliley Act reserved authority to states to legislate in this area, and various state attorneys general have been active in pursuing what they deem to be misuses of customer information by banks. Legislation is already pending in some states, and legal scholars are already debating whether the Fair Credit Reporting Act, which permits information sharing with affiliates in cases in which customers have been given the opportunity to opt out and not done so, may preempt any state laws that are eventually enacted purporting to restrict affiliate sharing.

THE BIGGER PICTURE

Finally, it would not be proper in closing a piece such as this to fail to take a step back and consider the bigger picture, and that is how the banking industry is very cognizant that what sets it apart from other financial-services industries is the trust that it has engendered from customers. Bankers realize and, in their cloistered conversations about policymakers' sudden, new-found interest in privacy, often dwell on the fact that the basis of the customer trust the industry enjoys is that, for many decades, the industry has guarded the privacy of its customers. It is not idle bombast to say that, over the years, the banking industry has led American business in protecting customer privacy and expects to continue to do so.

Notes
[1] 31 CFR 103.22.
[2] 42 U.S.C. 666(1)(a)(17)(A).

Credit Information Reporting, Social Accountability, and Consumer Opportunity[1]

Daniel B. Klein

SOCIAL ACCOUNTABILITY MECHANISMS

"Gossip" has a bad name. But everyone gossips to some extent, because everyone chats with coworkers, neighbors, and friends, often about other people. Gossiping can be a crucial part of performing one's job, and an important source of information on goods and services, employment opportunities, neighborhood problems, and other daily concerns.

In fact, gossip is vital to society because it serves the indispensable function of creating accountability. Usually, when people interact, if one party fails to meet his or her obligations the other party is the only person who sees the failure. Reporting it helps to form a reputation on the chiseler and creates pressures against chiseling. No one wants a reputation as a chiseler, and an excellent way to avoid acquiring one is not to chisel.

Civilized society depends on accountability mechanisms, including gossip. No one denies that many individuals will meet their obligations even if no social mechanisms exert accountability; people do have a conscience and a sense of honor. But an external system of accountability encourages people to cultivate the practices and habits necessary to develop internal accountability. Moreover, the extent of our obligations is often unclear to us. Knowledge of what is appropriate in any particular situation depends on the signals sent to us by accountability mechanisms when the spirit is willing but the mind is uncertain which actions would be regarded as good.

And, of course, social-accountability mechanisms not only police our own scruples, they protect us against predation, because there will always be people who act irresponsibly and fail in their obligations.

Society has many social-accountability mechanisms. The media is one. Scholarly peer review is another. Both the criminal and civil justice systems are accountability mechanisms. All of these work to reward good behavior and punish bad, and to function effectively they must obtain information about who did what to whom, when, and why. They ask questions, assess the validity of responses, and judge the credibility of character. All accountability mechanisms collide with privacy, with the human desire to keep things secret, especially things that, in the common phrase, "are not to one's credit."

The credit-reporting agency (or credit bureau) must be seen within this framework, because it is an important social-accountability mechanism. Lenders, employers, landlords, and insurers are interested in making opportunities available to consumers (in their role of prospective credit users, employees, tenants, and insurance policyholders), but only if they can obtain information on trustworthiness. These groups pay credit bureaus for information about consumers, especially information about whether they have met past credit obligations.

In America, the credit-reporting business is dominated by three large companies: Equifax, Experian, and TransUnion. They work through more than 500 local offices and contracted affiliates. Through their local offices and affiliates, they receive information from virtually every creditor. Hence, the flow of information is two-way.

As a by-product of this primary function, credit bureaus use the information generated to assemble marketing lists for companies and organizations which need to identify consumers likely to be interested in their products. The gamut of purchasers ranges from L.L. Bean to the National Braille Press to the Children's Television Workshop (Sesame Street Magazine) to the Sierra Club.

Both these functions—credit reporting and the facilitation of targeted marketing—are now under attack in the name of "privacy."

POLICY ISSUES CONCERNING CREDIT-REPORTING AGENCIES

Consumers in general know very little about how credit reporting works, and tend to be suspicious. The range of information included on credit reports is smaller than many suppose. Credit reports usually include only the following kinds of information:

- consumer's name, address, Social Security number, place of employment, and spouse's name;
- open credit lines, outstanding credit balances, credit limits, history of timeliness of payments, and amount of last payment;
- bankruptcies, liens, and public judgments against the consumer.

Reports do not include information about life style, religion, political affiliation, driving records, medical history, or other dimensions of the consumer's life, dimensions that might well be known even to a casual acquaintance.

Nor does the information circulate freely. The Fair Credit Reporting Act (FCRA), passed in 1970 and amended in 1996, specifies that credit reports may be purchased only by those with a "permissible purpose," notably creditors, employers, landlords, and insurers. Terms of strict confidentiality surround the use of reports by these parties. One need not fear that neighbors are reading one's credit report.

About 10,000 creditors supply information to credit bureaus each month. The bureaus virtually always report that information faithfully. In rare cases, faithful reporting is erroneous reporting because creditors occasionally supply inaccurate information. The creditor may have failed to record or update actual payments or delinquencies by consumers. The errors of others surface in reports assembled by the bureaus, who bear the brunt of complaints. Errors in the broadest sense occur for many reasons: public records are faulty, consumers neglect to have their mail forwarded, consumers misplace bills, outgoing mail fails to find its way to the mail box, mail is improperly delivered, mail is improperly forwarded, and so on.

When a consumer disputes information in a credit report, a verification process begins. The dispute is usually submitted in writing. The verification process flows from the consumer to the bureau to the creditor and back again. Consumers with valid complaints have good cause to feel some frustration, but one must realize that credit bureaus do not know beforehand whether a complaint is valid or spurious. If they revised their records to satisfy every complaint received by phone, scam artists would claim to be the victim of errors. The 1996 Amendments to the FCRA require the bureau to verify disputed information within 30 days or delete it from the records. Barry Connelly, president of Associated Credit Bureaus, claims that in most cases disputes are verified or resolved within two weeks. When adverse information is verified and the consumer feels that there is more to the story, he may enter a brief statement to be included in the record (usually limited to 100 words). Also, when a consumer disputes information with the creditor, the creditor must report the account information as "in dispute."

Some consumer activists, journalists, and public officials charge that credit bureaus violate people's privacy, report false or incomplete information, share information with inappropriate parties, and fail to respond to consumer inquiries and disputes. Critics claim to be protecting consumers from losing out on opportunities such as mortgages or car loans.

Partly as a result of these charges, credit-reporting services are restricted by state and federal laws. Restrictions either on the books or on the agenda include measures to do the following:

- impose penalties or assign liability to credit bureaus for errors in reports;
- require credit bureaus to notify or get permission from consumers before using information about the consumer;
- specify rigid procedures for credit-bureau operation, including how long information may be retained on reports, how credit reports are to be written, who may use the reports, how consumers are to be notified of credit decisions, and how consumer inquiries and disputes are to be handled;

- provide consumers with their credit reports at no charge or reduced prices;
- require credit bureaus to respond to consumer inquiries within a specified time period or face penalties;
- create government bureaucracies to police the credit bureaus and formulate new regulations on their operations.

The lengthy 1996 Amendments to the FCRA included many of these restrictions. Credit reporting has been made into a major public issue only in the last 10 years, but now the issue is here to stay. Critics continually seek to add further restrictions, and lawsuits and policy initiatives concerning credit bureaus are multitudinous and can be expected to continue.

The critics only dimly recognize that credit bureaus are important social-accountability mechanisms. Any infringement on privacy or propagation of erroneous information ought to be compared to that of other social-accountability mechanisms: gossip, the media, the courtroom. In such a comparison, the credit bureau may serve as a paragon of reliability and discreetness. It conveys only the most pertinent information to only the most relevant parties in a highly standardized, impersonal, and professional manner.

An understanding of accountability illuminates the far-reaching benefits made possible by credit bureaus. Credit bureaus make opportunity—in the form of credit, employment, housing, and insurance—more available and more affordable to everyone in society. These things cannot exist without accountability in society. Because institutions such as credit bureaus are part of the foundation of civil society, the policy debate over their operation is of paramount importance.

Once we understand the importance of credit bureaus as social-accountability mechanisms, we are more inclined to regard the criticisms leveled against them as unreasonable and, often, self-contradictory. In particular, some critics want to require not only greater accuracy, but agreement from the consumer before certain bits of information are included. Accountability mechanisms can always be honed to greater precision, but a tension must exist between making information more accurate and making its availability dependent on the consent of its subject. Because people have an incentive to suppress the bad, the two goals conflict. If laws guaranteed complete privacy, the freedom to warn others about those who fail to meet their obligations would be destroyed. (And imagine a parent's reaction if victims in his or her neighborhood had to respect the privacy of a babysitter who molested children.) People would be inauspiciously silenced. The need for accountability mechanisms in credit is underscored by the startling increase in filings for personal bankruptcy, which tripled between 1986 and 1997.

ORIGINS AND HISTORY OF CREDIT BUREAUS

Before credit bureaus existed, creditors, merchants, and landlords relied on word-of-mouth, letters of reference, and other forms of gossip to assess the trustworthiness of a consumer. Everyone had to be his own credit bureau, gathering, interpreting, formatting, storing, retrieving, and transmitting information. Creditors and others could monitor information on regular customers and local parties, but their information, and, hence, their confidence were limited. In consequence, they made opportunities available only to those who were known. Prior to World War II, few retailers sold on credit, and those that did confined it to well-known customers.

Creditors could exchange information with each other, sharing lists of names known to be poor credit risks. But crisscrossing systems are inefficient. Far better is a centralized agency that serves as a hub for all creditors and merchants, collecting information from all, dispensing it to all, and reducing redundancy, inconsistency, and variability in communication.

"Commercial" credit reporting on the reliability of merchants and companies in meeting obligations to wholesalers and suppliers developed as a private business during the 19th century, culminating in the now-dominant firm of Dun & Bradstreet. "Consumer" credit reporting developed primarily in the form of community cooperative or nonprofit associations operated for the benefit of the users. The reason for the difference is the more personal nature of consumer credit information. Retailers fear that customers will be offended by questions, and unsettled by the thought of an investigation. In dealing with consumer information, a cooperative organization, such as a merchants' association, arouses less suspicion and resentment than does a for-profit business. Furthermore, at its inception a credit bureau may face a significant collective-action problem in getting businesses to participate, and cooperative appeals may be an especially effective method of securing cooperation.

Only after decades of development by cooperative organizations was consumer credit reporting ready to operate on a commercial, for-profit basis. During the 1950s, 60s, and 70s, with the boost of new technologies in communications, big companies entered the field by buying up the operations of regional organizations, eventually integrating them into a highly uniform, nationwide service.

Although most credit bureaus today operate on a for-profit basis, their fundamental function has not changed: providing information so that two parties, who may be perfect strangers, can trust each other enough to engage in mutually advantageous exchange.

TWO TYPES OF ERRORS

Imposing on credit bureaus a liability to pay large damages to consumers for inaccurate, adverse information in credit reports could well result in information that is less complete and less accurate, and reduce the extent to which credit is available to consumers.

If a bureau faces legal penalties for including adverse information that is incorrect, it will err on the side of excluding adverse information, even that which is accurate. Users of the reports would soon learn that they were getting watered-down information, and would have less confidence in transacting with strangers. They would make opportunity less available even for consumers who had used credit responsibly. Restrictions on free speech would eliminate opportunity for the trustworthy and the untrustworthy alike.

When they focus exclusively on one type of error—inclusion of inaccurate information—critics are thinking asymmetrically. If bureaus are made to pay heavy damages to consumers harmed by the inclusion of inaccurate information, why shouldn't bureaus also be made to pay damages to businesses harmed by the exclusion of accurate information? Yet if *this* liability were imposed, then credit bureaus would be in a no-win situation, which would strangle the goose that lays the golden eggs.

Another asymmetry in the complaints against credit bureaus exists: Given that credit bureaus make possible much of the opportunity that consumers enjoy, why should consumers be able to sue credit bureaus when reports have errors, but not be required to pay rewards to credit bureaus when reports do not have errors? Critics are asserting, in essence, that consumers are entitled to have their credit report maintained without serious inaccuracies, but, symmetrically, one could assert that credit bureaus are entitled to rewards from consumers when reports are accurate. Such paradoxes of the entitlement mentality recommend that we reject entitlement in favor of the cogent alternative: obligations by contract.

CONSUMER OPPORTUNITY DEPENDS ON ACCOUNTABILITY MECHANISMS

Restrictions on free speech and free commerce have many consequences. In *Economics in One Lesson*, Henry Hazlitt writes that those like the consumer activists "are presenting half-truths. They are speaking only of the immediate effect of a proposed policy or its effect upon a single group." The great challenge is to supplement and correct "the half-truth with the other half." But to consider all the consequences of a proposed policy, Hazlitt says, "often requires a long, complicated, and dull chain of reasoning." Only by seeing consequences that are unintended and nonobvious can policymakers really serve consumers. The art of economics is elucidating these consequences.[2]

Consumer activists propose safeguards to protect the consumer from unfair outcomes resulting from erroneous information. But they overlook the influence of the proposed safeguards on the system as a whole. If the cost of credit reports rises, then fewer will be requested, and more customers will be granted or denied credit based on arbitrary factors, such as appearance or zip code. The deteriorated quality of credit reports in general will reduce credit opportunities in the future.

The reduced utility of credit reports will have other unfortunate effects. If obtaining credit becomes less dependent on consumers' credit history, consumers will become less vigilant in meeting their obligations, knowing that doing so will not cost them future opportunity. As the social-accountability mechanism becomes less effective, consumers in general will become less trustworthy.

As we trace the effects further, we find that the harm caused by "protection" widens. If credit reports become more expensive, more costly to handle, and less informative, businesses that have been giving credit might stop doing so. Furthermore, in rare cases it will happen that the business shuts down operations altogether and no longer provides goods and services to consumers or jobs to workers.

There are yet other ways that hardship befalls consumers because of restrictions. If credit reports are more expensive or less informative, then businesses that trust consumers will be operating at higher cost and suffering more losses from delinquencies, defaults, and other failures to meet obligations. Increases in the cost of doing business translate into higher prices for consumers. When consumers get credit—which will be less often—they will pay higher interest rates. When they get housing, they will pay higher rental rates. When they get employment, they will receive lower salaries. The injury to each consumer may be small, but that small injury must be multiplied by the great number of consumers who are affected. And increased business costs may affect the prices of any of the items a creditor sells.

In advocating restrictions, consumer activists do not attempt to demonstrate that their proposed restrictions will do more good than harm. They tend not even to acknowledge harm. The social-accountability mechanisms that serve consumers and businesses alike depend on layers of institutions and practices. Consumer activists pretend that those institutions and practices will go on keenly serving consumers even when hamstrung by restrictions. They take for granted many of the blessings of the modern economy.

Nor do they seem to understand that the system already has substantial incentives to create accurate information. It is not to the advantage of a business that a trustworthy consumer be wrongly denied credit. And it is not to the advantage of the credit bureau to furnish reports that contain errors. All parties have clear incentives to make the information correct. Do not believe the drumbeat of animadversion on this point that issues from activist organizations and is replayed in the press.[3]

PRIVACY AND THE ISSUE OF MARKETING LISTS

Many companies, especially those conducting business on the Internet, now accumulate information about their customers and sell marketing lists to other businesses. Activists have long attacked credit bureaus for making personal information available to marketers, who then annoy the consumer with "junk mail."

The activists, citing practice in Europe, seek to restrict free speech in the name of privacy. In European Union countries, consumers have to "opt in" in order to be included in list-making services. Instead of the European opt-in rule, credit bureaus in America practice an "opt-out" rule, whereby consumers can exclude themselves from mailing lists generated by a credit bureau by notifying the bureau of their wish not to be included. Since there are three major bureaus, three notices suffice. (For full instructions on opting out of mailing lists and telemarketing, go to the Direct Marketing Association's web site at http://www.the-dma.org/consumers/consumerassistance.html.)

Thus, activists play upon the paranoia of consumers and voters, who know little about the system's actual workings. The proposed restrictions would hurt consumers, as they do in Europe.

What does L.L. Bean or the Sierra Club really find out about consumers from credit bureaus? Practically nothing. Such marketers specify consumer characteristics and request a list of individuals who match those characteristics, or some combination of them. For example, the characteristics may be number of credit cards, zip code of residence, or positive payment history. The characteristics may be refined and detailed, but the marketer never sees credit reports.

Indeed, the marketer usually does not see even the list. The credit bureau is not eager to share its stock-in-trade, and it guards the exclusivity of the information. Most lists go to a third-party fulfillment house, which sends the marketer's catalogs out to consumers on the list. In those cases, only the fulfillment house sees the list. The credit bureau seeds each list with decoy names and addresses, and if catalogs other than those associated with the original order show up at the decoy address, the credit bureau knows that the fulfillment house cheated on the contract. The fulfillment house is then subject to penalties or loss of repeat business from the credit bureau—notice how reputational mechanisms cascade throughout the system to assure promise-keeping and discreetness. The suppleness of contract allows men and women in commerce and industry to overcome problems in ways far more creative than dreamt of by interventionists.

It is annoying to find our mailboxes stuffed with advertisements and catalogs. But opt-in requirements (à la Europe) would impose a burden on consumers who gain from commercial information. Because opting in would call for added time, attention, and effort, many consumers would miss opportunities they would like to have, opportunities that would improve their condition. Indeed, it is the prescreening services of credit bureaus that make the credit-card industry so competitive.

While everyone has a certain disdain for junk mail in the abstract, catalogs are actually a great boon, helping consumers discover and acquire products without leaving home. They are especially valuable to the disabled, the elderly, parents with families, and people without cars. In 1991, the Consumers Union noted that the ability to narrow the market reduces costs, and has spawned some 10,000 specialty catalogs, selling everything from apples to automobiles to waders to wine.[4]

Given the narrow range of information used in compiling mailing lists, concern over "privacy" is mainly a red herring. But even if infringements were serious, we should be wary of the privacy activists. They are peddling restrictions that do not provide coherent principles and which upset other vital principles. The activists often suggest that consumer information should be treated as the property of the consumer. But people cannot rightly be said to own information about themselves. Pure information is not a form of property and hence cannot be owned. As Solveig Singleton says,

> [I]f someone buys a lawn mower from Sears...two parties engage in the transaction—the customer and Sears. Why should the information about the sale belong only to the customer and not to Sears as well? If the customer were to complain about the transaction to Consumer Reports, he would not have to ask Sears's permission. Why cannot Sears boast of the transaction to its creditors?[5]

Information exists only in as much as a thinking human mind reacts to certain external events. External events may be influenced by legal rules, but it is incoherent to think of information itself as someone's property, which they should somehow be able to dole out, as they dole out their money. The same incoherence characterizes the concept of "privacy" as the term is used in these debates, where it seems to mean a right to have others not have information about you.

Legal rules may govern the external events that go into the creation and conveying of information. But before restricting freedom with arbitrary regulations, let us ask whether freedom of contract might not provide an effective framework for dealing with privacy issues, one that is far superior to regulatory requirements. People can form contracts that specifically forbid their trading partners to reconvey information. Illegitimately reconveying the information would then be a breach of contract—a failure to live up to a promise—not a misuse of someone's property. Contract provides a coherent principle. A system based on freedom of contract would accommodate consumers' preferences about receiving junk mail and learning of products.

If activists Europeanize information services in America, they will also work to Europeanize consumption opportunities and living standards. American consumers are much better served by the safeguarding and revitalizing of the American customs of free speech, free enterprise, and opportunity, along with a tort system that responds to errors arising from negligence or contract breach.

CONCLUSION

In a vast society like the United States, our opportunities depend crucially on our ability to persuade strangers to trust us. But this will happen only if we give them reasons. Credit bureaus respond to this need by collecting and collating information. They create the reputation necessary to convince strangers that we can do business, that social accountability is working.

The secondary function of helping marketers reach efficiently the subsets of consumers likely to be interested in their offerings is also an opportunity-enhancing activity. Without the benefits of niche marketing, each of us would have more difficulty discovering the options available to us.

The activists are using privacy as a red herring. They are promoting slogans and agendas that do not rest on coherent principles of law and that do not reflect people's legitimate expectations. They seem to remain rather ignorant of the affirmative uses of information collection. They seem to dislike free speech, free enterprise, and freedom of contract. Their interventionist agenda kills opportunity and breeds litigation. To the extent they succeed, consumer opportunity and well-being will be reduced.

Notes

[1] This article is an adaptation of a chapter in the author's *Assurance and Trust in a Great Society* (Irvington, New York: Foundation for Economic Education, 2000).

[2] Henry Hazlitt, *Economics in One Lesson* (San Francisco: Laissez Faire Books, 1996), p. 6.

[3] For a detailed analysis of this issue see Daniel B. Klein & Jason Richner, "In Defense of the Credit Bureau," *Cato Journal*, vol. 12 (1992), pp. 393-412, and Solveig Singleton, "Privacy as Censorship: A Skeptical View of Proposals to Regulate Privacy in the Private Sector," *Cato Institute Policy Analysis*, no. 295, January 22, 1998.

[4] *Consumer Reports* (1991), p. 643.

[5] Singleton, "Privacy as Censorship," p. 15.

The Money-Laundering Conundrum: Mugging Privacy in the Assault on Crime?[1]

Lawrence B. Lindsey

The nature of the money-laundering conundrum is inherently one of finding a balance, a balance of reason. The crux of the lesson I learned at the Federal Reserve was that we need to restore some reason and balance to the discussion of privacy. As a country, we have a strong commitment to privacy. We have discovered in our Constitution that we actually have a right to privacy—although the Founding Fathers never wrote that down—and yet we see constantly an assault on our privacy, an erosion of our privacy, both by the state and also by the private sector.

There is no question the threats posed by international terrorists and drug cartels are a serious threat to our national security and to our individual liberty. But it is also true that threats to our individual liberty by a potentially abusive government exist as well. As citizens, we must use what was recommended to us— eternal vigilance over our government, not a one-time, fix-it solution—to make sure that the right balance is being struck.

Why is it an issue of balance? Consider the issue of money laundering. Using the term "crime" loosely, in the sense of something that is socially harmful, the use of money is not the crime. The reason we are interested in it is because it's the flip-side of a criminal transaction that is socially harmful. The government has a temptation because it is very hard to enforce the laws it has on the books against the real criminal activity. It finds it much easier to track the money trail and use it as a proxy for the criminal activity. Whenever you are going to use a proxy, a nonsocially harmful proxy, you had better raise the issue of balance and reason.

In his speeches, Richard Rahn raises the issue of Japanese internment during World War II. Although in some ways an unfortunate example because of its emotional force, it is also an appropriate one. The Supreme Court wrestled with taking an innocent characteristic, believing it to be correlated with a real or potential threat, and using that characteristic to enforce the law. That's exactly what is happening with money-laundering laws: The government is using the otherwise innocent characteristic of spending money, which it believes may be correlated with criminal activity, in order to enforce the law. In the case of Japanese internment, history suggests that where balance and reason were struck then differs from what we would find today. The justices of the Court at the time found the balance they struck appropriate. This underscores the point of why we are going to need eternal vigilance: Circumstances are going to change.

Another important point to understand about money laundering is that, because we are dealing with an innocent characteristic, the law can be overly broad. The Financial Crimes Enforcement Network (FinCEN) argues that standards of conviction under the money-laundering statutes are in fact quite narrow. FinCEN maintains that one must know when using currency that it was obtained through the fruits of illicit activity. This is one reason why we are not seeing a lot of convictions for money laundering.

But it also raises a real problem, because of the issue of fungibility. For example, suppose a cabinet nominee who wasn't confirmed due to failure to pay nanny taxes—a potentially criminal activity—spent money. Was the precise unit of currency spent the same dollar saved by not paying the nanny taxes? No, of course not. That is not what is meant by the law. In fact, money is fungible. So, because of the fungibility of money, any time you use currency, assuming you have ever committed any criminal activity in the past, you theoretically could have engaged in money laundering. Again, what is necessary is to find the place of balance and reason.

Prosecutorial discretion and juries are what we now rely upon to decide where that balance and reason exist. But even under the supposedly narrow definition of the law that FinCEN uses, we have a literally unlimited application of that law to anyone engaging in any transaction who has ever committed a crime, or knows that they have committed a crime. And given that we are not a society of saints, but rather one of minor sinners, that unfortunately is probably most of us.

It is important to look at the issue of costs. We no longer require a reasonable basis to try to track the money flows. The government has implicitly decided that it needs to trace all money flows and be able at its leisure to look at that great collection of data and see if it can detect any suspicious information. Take, for example, what happens with currency-transaction reports, the main way in which the government gathers information. The government requires us to file a form any time we use currency to what it considers an excessive amount, typically any deposit over $10,000.[2]

Between 1987 and 1995, the government collected 77 million currency-transaction reports, something on the order of 62 tons of paper. Out of that, it was able to prosecute 3,000 money-laundering cases. That is roughly one case for every 25,000 forms filed. In other words, entire forests had to be felled in order to prosecute one case. But it gets worse: Of the 3,000 money-laundering cases prosecuted, the government managed to produce only 580 guilty verdicts.[3] In other words, in excess of 100,000 reports were filed by innocent citizens in order to get one conviction. That ratio of 99,999 to one is something we normally would not tolerate as a reasonable balance between privacy and the collection of guilty verdicts.

There is another angle: Since banks are used as enforcement agents, the Treasury Department engages in sting operations to monitor compliance. FinCEN officials go to a bank and tempt it to commit a crime. Between 1990 and 1995, 290 defendants were charged as a result of sting operations, with 29 convictions.[4] That's one in 10. And that's out of thousands of sting operations. By any standard of cost-benefit analysis, we are asking for a lot of compliance to catch a few people. Merely analyzing the situation from the viewpoint of the use of scarce government prosecutorial resources, this practice does not make the grade.

But there should be more in the calculus besides scarce government resources. There is the invasion of our privacy, which doesn't seem to enter into the calculation.

It is worth remembering that the people being caught are on the money side. It is impossible to imagine the counterfactual here, but we also are forced to live with the existing level of global terrorism, the existing level of drug lords. How much hypothetical reduction we get is supposedly the benefit. But if you actually look at the people we've managed to prosecute, it looks kind of small compared to the burden of paperwork and the number of people who have to engage in required activity to comply with the law.

This compliance burden is only getting greater. For example, in my last year at the Federal Reserve we approved a rule that if you wish to transfer or "wire" more than a certain amount of money domestically, a report needs to be filed. This covers all sorts of situations, often seen in TV ads—"Hey Dad, I need $200 to pay the rent, can you wire it to me?" Any time that figure exceeds $750, the people who provide you with this service are required to keep records on you. They have to know who you are; they have to keep information on you in their files, all for having allowed you to wire $750. That's just the starting point.

The number of tangible pieces of paper that have to be filed may be shrinking, largely because records can be kept on magnetic tape. But whether we're talking about pieces of paper, computer bytes, or reels of tape, lots of reports are being filed. For example, consider the Suspicious Activity Report. According to FinCEN, suspicious activity is defined as any suspicious transaction involving possible violations of law—a definition no doubt helpful if you are trying to enforce the law. Regulations issued under the Bank Secrecy Act require banks to report their customers as "suspects" whenever the banker has "reason to suspect" that a large transaction is unusual for the customer and the "bank knows of no reasonable explanation for the transaction."

In 1993, of the roughly 10 million currency-transaction reports filed, 63,000 were marked suspicious[5]—a number that should give an idea of the level of overcompliance. The 0.6

percent share resulted in a 1 percent rate of criminal charges. But the banks had produced an important degree of filtering for the law-enforcement professionals. It was therefore the regulators' hope that a more sophisticated screening of the data would produce an even more efficacious ratio of "suspicious" to "probable cause" than 100 to one. The requirement that banks monitor all their customers' transactions could conceivably be advanced as making government more efficient, not nosier. Hence, the "Know Your Customer" rules proposed—and withdrawn under intense pressure—in early 1999.

The number of reports labeled suspicious has roughly doubled, because banks are becoming much more concerned about getting it wrong. If a financial institution does get it wrong, it is subject to penalties. That is the nature of what could be termed overly broad enforcement. We don't know where to draw the line—we don't know if it is $750 for a domestic transfer or $3,000—but it is important, given our obligation for eternal vigilance, to keep these numbers in mind.

Another concern too seldom considered is the disproportionate impact of these rules on the least fortunate people in society. I never appreciated this issue until I was on a community tour in Denver in the Five Corners neighborhood of the city. I was visiting the first bank to open in Five Corners since World War II. It is a low- and moderate-income area, now predominantly African-American. A lady came up to me and said, "You folks in Washington think we are all drug dealers, don't you?" I asked what she meant by that and she replied:

> I had saved money for a down payment on a house and, of course, there being no banks, I saved it at home. I brought in the cash to the bank for the closing and they didn't believe me. They wouldn't accept it. They wouldn't accept US currency for the down payment on this house that I'd saved all my life for.

This is the chilling effect that these laws have on a society in which roughly 15 percent of our citizens are unbanked.[6] And that percentage climbs to nearly 25 among lower-income families. They do not have access to the traditional mechanisms that much of the rest of society uses to engage in financial transactions. They are the ones who must use cash; they are the ones who must use those wire services to transfer money so the daughter can pay the rent. Just watch or listen to the commercials; individuals who are unbanked are exactly those being targeted. With our rules, the government is actually creating an impediment to commerce for those who need access the most.

But when FinCEN considers making exceptions, it makes exceptions like, "You don't have to file a report if you are a company traded on the New York Stock Exchange." This does nothing for the people who really bear the burden of this law, who are those in the low- and moderate-income populations of America.

Indeed, the enforcement mechanism here is rather troubling. Consider, just as a random example, a Treasury Department release from May, 1997, announcing the results of a Geographic Targeting Order. Under the Bank Secrecy Act, FinCEN can tell any group of people that any set of transactions is subject to particularly close monitoring. And the particularly close monitoring in this situation was any wire order going to Colombia. The people who were covered by it, which included 3,500 different sources of wire transaction, were largely located in the Colombian neighborhoods of New York City. If any bank in the US had pursued such a policy, it would immediately have been hit with civil-rights complaints, probably justified. But that was not a problem for FinCEN because that was, in fact, the target population.

Suppose, though, that you are a bank caught in this net. You have a problem, because the activity reports are confidential. If you deny performing a wire transfer for someone based on the activity report, you might be sued. But you are not allowed to use the Suspicious Activity Report in your defense, even though the report is the reason the government told you that you couldn't perform the service. So you are subject to a violation of civil-rights law, and you cannot use something in your defense which the government ordered you to use in the first place.

How did this work out in this instance? The banks were caught in the middle. The government trumpeted as a success the fact that there was a 30 percent drop-off in money being transmitted to Colombia. They particularly noted that business to Colombia dropped off even at money remitters not subject to the Geographic Targeting Order, suggesting that much of the money remitted to Colombia was controlled centrally by high-level cartel money brokers. But that doesn't necessarily follow. If I hear that the government is looking at all money going to Colombia, and I am planning to remit my $800 to my family after working all month to earn it, I might get nervous fearing I might go to jail. Not to mention the fact that the banks executing the transmission might decide to say no.

This is the unspoken other cost. I am not for money laundering; I am not for drug trafficking; I am not for gun running. The question is, how do we most effectively enforce the law? The answer, returning to our central premise, is eternal vigilance. Balance and reason will decide. And we have over-stepped the bounds of balance and reason today.

The difficulty of striking a balance between stopping criminals and safeguarding privacy is not a new one. America's founding fathers faced a similar dilemma. It is interesting to recall how they saw the balance when they wrote the Fourth Amendment:

> The right of the people to be secure in their persons, houses, papers, and effects, against unreasonable searches and seizures, shall not be violated, and no Warrants shall issue, but upon probable cause, supported by Oath or affirmation and particularly describing the place to be searched and the persons or things to be seized.

The presumption was that a search warrant would be issued, and it would specify who was targeted for search and what information was to be seized. It would seem to be clear that current money-laundering-enforcement practices are the kind of blanket search that the writers of the Constitution sought to prohibit.

Somehow "probable cause" does not seem to mesh with the one in 25,000 odds that the currency-transaction reports provide.

The reason all of this has passed constitutional muster may say more about the circumscription of our privacy than we care to admit. The government has argued with a straight face that it is not carrying out the search—the banks are. In examples such as the currency-transaction reports, the government claims that all it is doing is requiring an informational document from entities (that is, banks) which it has the power to regulate.

So the government has gone too far. But I don't think that we can politically separate invasions of privacy by the government from invasions of privacy by the private sector. Many of us may think that the erosion of privacy by the state and by the private sector are separate issues. In fact, they probably are not. They certainly are not separate in the minds of the public. A fine, theoretical case why that should be so can be made. After all, when I give information to my bank, it is a contract and we can negotiate the contract and the market can dictate the solution, and I can be there if you want me to be there. But that's not a very useful political argument, despite its useful rhetorical value. The real political problem is when the bank uses that information to call me at 6 o'clock at night, just when my family is sitting down to dinner, to market some additional service to me. I find that a much more intrusive invasion of my privacy than I do if the government is theoretically collecting currency-transaction reports, and so I resent it more.

The financial-services industry obviously wants to be able to use information for marketing purposes much more, particularly as it is developing into a more comprehensive industry from a balkanized one. But it should be very careful to resist the temptation to invade people's privacy. It is joining not the side of the angels, but the side of the state. Obviously, there is an incentive for the financial-services industry instead to line up on the side of the individual citizen, to affirmatively resist invasions of privacy, both by the state and by the private sector.

The key point is that the financial-services industry today should be very careful who it makes a deal with. It has every interest to be on the side of privacy. When it makes deals in the interest of marketing, which result in erosions of privacy, it is in the end undercutting its own base.

Notes

[1] This article is a compilation of Dr. Lindsey's views principally derived from remarks he gave at CEI's conference on financial privacy, held on November 30, 1999.

[2] Bank Secrecy Act, Public Law 91-508.

[3] "Clean Getaway for Money Launderers," *The Journal of Commerce*, December 10, 1996.

[4] Ibid.

[5] "Money Laundering: Needed Improvements for Reporting Suspicious Transactions Are Planned," GAO report GGD-95-156.

[6] "Banking Relationships of Lower-Income Families and the Government Trend Toward Electronic Payment," *Federal Reserve Bulletin* (July 1999). The actual number is 12.6 percent.

Personalization, Privacy, and the First Amendment[1]

Eugene Volokh

Does personalization jeopardize our privacy, and, if so, what should the law do about it? This is related to two broader questions: Do we have a legal right to "control the flow of information about ourselves" by stopping others from speaking about us? And should we have such a right?[2]

People constantly learn information about us: They see what we do, what we buy, what we look at, and the like. If they know who we are, and if they have enough financial incentive, they can record this information under our name. If we engage in computerized transactions with them, such recording becomes very easy, as does combining this information with still other information that is tied to our names. If the transactions are personalized—if we voluntarily turn over information about ourselves that facilitates our business arrangement—then they will have even more information to record. And once they've recorded this information, they can easily communicate it to others (usually for money).

A lot of people don't like this. To be more specific, a lot of people don't like to have others learn information about themselves; they are usually quite happy to learn information about others, and sometimes resent it when legal barriers block them from learning such information. Nonetheless, many believe we should have (in the words of various privacy advocates) a legal "right to control information about ourselves."

INFORMATION PRIVACY UNDER CURRENT AMERICAN LAW

Let me begin by asking: Do we currently have such a legal right? The answer, as is usual in the law, is "sometimes." The one thing that is *not* helpful here is to talk generally about our "right to privacy." The law does recognize certain things that one might call a right to privacy. First, the Supreme Court has interpreted the Bill of Rights as securing a "right to privacy" that limits the government's power to interfere with certain personal decisions related to family life—contraception, abortion, child-rearing, and the like. Calling this a right to privacy is probably a misnomer, but more importantly this right has little to do with the right to informational privacy that we're discussing.

Second, the law protects our physical privacy in a variety of ways. The Fourth Amendment limits the government's power to search us, our homes, and our papers. Trespass law imposes even broader limits on the power of private parties to break into our homes and rifle through our papers. Some other laws, for instance the so-called "intrusion upon seclusion" tort, further protect us from unwanted spying, for instance barring people from looking into our homes with high-powered cameras. Computer-trespass laws generally bar people from accessing our computers without our authorization.

All these may properly be called "privacy" rules (in fact, the intrusion tort is often called an "invasion of privacy" tort), but they only limit others' ability to learn things about us by access-ing our property. They do not limit others' ability to communicate things that they have lawfully learned about us.

Third, the Supreme Court has suggested that the Bill of Rights may stop the government from revealing certain poten-tially embarrassing information that it might have about us, for instance our medical histories. This is closer to a right to information privacy, but it is limited in a critical way: Like virtually all other constitutional rights, it applies only to the *government's* actions. The Constitution says little about what private persons or businesses may or may not do; recall that the Bill of Rights starts with "Congress shall make no law..." and the 14th Amendment, which applies most of the Bill of Rights to state and local governments, starts with "No state shall...." Whatever rights we might have against our business partners, none of these rights flow from the federal Constitution.

Fourth, Congress has specifically enacted some laws that bar the *government* from revealing certain information about people, for instance the Privacy Act, which applies to a variety of federal agencies, special laws that apply to the census department and the IRS, and the Driver's Privacy Protection Act, which generally bars state governments from revealing driver's license information. Many states have likewise enacted similar laws that apply to their own state and local government agencies. Again, though, these laws, while they are important tools for stopping the government from compromising our information privacy, say nothing about what private parties can do.

Fifth, a few laws genuinely do aim to stop certain private parties from disclosing certain information about people. Federal laws bar cable companies and video stores from disclosing information about customers' viewing habits. State professional-licensing laws bar lawyers, doctors, and other professionals from revealing certain confidential information learned from the relationship. More controversially, the so-called "disclosure of private facts" tort bars anyone—including newspapers—from publicizing highly embarrassing and supposedly unnewsworthy information about anyone else. (This is also sometimes called an "invasion of privacy" tort.) Note, though, that all these laws apply to only a narrow range of revelations; none of them stop a business (either an e-business or a bricks-and-mortar business) from revealing which kinds of food, shoes, or books you bought from it.

CONTRACTS AS TOOLS FOR PROTECTING INFORMATION PRIVACY

So we see that people's search for legal protection of their information privacy cannot rely on some currently existing, broad "right to privacy"; American law just does not recognize such a thing. On the other hand, information privacy does get considerable protection from a source that to some is unexpected—the law of contract.

Contracts are tools for you and your business partners to make your own law for your own transactions. If you have a great new product idea and you tell it to me, there'd be nothing illegal in my revealing it to the whole world, even if that would lose you a lot of money. But if I promise to keep it secret, then my revelation becomes a breach of contract, and opens me up to a damages lawsuit. By our contract, we have given you a right to insist that I keep certain information private.

Likewise, a customer and a seller can create a sort of right of privacy, if the seller promises not to communicate data about the customer, or promises to communicate it only under certain conditions. True, in contracts it takes two to tango—if the seller isn't willing to undertake such a promise, the customer can't make the seller do it. But the customer can just go to another seller, and in a hotly competitive economy many companies would be happy to attract more customers by promising privacy. And such a privacy contract doesn't require any special formalities, like a signature on paper; if the site says "We promise to keep your data private," and people act in reliance on that promise, that promise becomes a binding contract.

Of course, some businesses may breach their contracts, but the law offers significant remedies for such breaches—customers can file a class-action suit, and can often ask the Federal Trade Commission (FTC) or other regulatory bodies to take action on their behalf. Moreover, the scandal created by a lawsuit can cause businesses more loss than the lawsuit itself would. Also, as I'll discuss below, Congress can make these contracts easier to enforce, require the privacy terms to be clearly specified, and set default contractual terms that protect information privacy in transactions where there are no explicit contractual provisions on the subject. These contractual rights will never be perfectly enforced, but no law is ever perfectly enforced.

Contracts, however, have one important limitation: They legally constrain only the parties to the contract. If a business breaches (intentionally or inadvertently) a privacy-protection contract with you, and communicates the information to some other business, you can sue the first business for breach of contract—but you can't sue the second business, since it never agreed to be bound by any contract. So if some information about you leaks to some centralized database, to a newspaper, or to anyone else with whom you have no contractual relationship, you can't stop those third parties from communicating it further. At best, you can sue the original entity with which you had the privacy agreement and which leaked the information, if you can figure out which entity it is.

PROPOSED EXPANSIONS OF INFORMATION-PRIVACY LAW AND THE FREEDOM OF SPEECH

So that's what the law is today; but what should it be? Well, to begin with, Congress (and possibly state legislatures) could strengthen the protections offered by contract law. Most importantly, they can define default privacy-protection rules; for instance, they can say that sellers of medical supplies *implicitly* promise not to reveal information about their customers, unless they explicitly and prominently disclaim this default provision.

This explicit disclaimer will alert customers to the site's refusal to agree to keep transactions confidential—then, those customers who care enough about their information privacy would know that they should go to the competition. Congress could also authorize special remedies for breaches of information-privacy contracts, and could give the FTC extra authority (or extra funding) to prosecute businesses that breach these contracts, rather than just relying on injured customers to bring suit themselves.

Congress could also impose mandatory information-privacy rules that go beyond what parties explicitly or implicitly promised. To take an extreme example, for instance, Congress might bar any person from communicating any information about another's purchases or other transactions without the subject's permission. Alternatively, it might just bar people from communicating such information for money.

Is it permissible, however, for Congress to do this? After all, there's another term for "barring any person from communicating any information about..."—and that's a speech restriction. This is clearest if we start with one application of this hypothetical law: a newspaper reporting that someone, for instance, a politician or a celebrity, was seen buying some product or engaging in some transaction. The newspaper, after all, is communicating information about another's commercial transactions, and it's doing so for money. But stopping the newspaper from publishing such stories raises pretty clear First Amendment problems.

And the First Amendment doesn't just protect the media (a good thing in the cyberspace age, when the line between media and others is blurrier than ever). It generally lets all of us communicate to each other on a wide variety of topics, without the government restricting our speech based on its content. True, the First Amendment doesn't provide absolute protection to all speech, but it does provide very broad protection, outside of a few relatively narrow exceptions. And none of the existing First Amendment exceptions justify the government banning speech that reveals supposedly private information, in the absence of an express or an implied contract not to reveal it.

To begin with, it's pretty clear that information-privacy speech restrictions can't be justified on the grounds that "they don't restrict speech, they only restrict the sale of information." Speech often *is* the sale of information—consider *The Wall Street Journal*, *Encyclopedia Britannica*, and Amazon.com, the contents of which are fully constitutionally protected against government suppression even though they're sold for money. Commercial advertisements indeed get less constitutional protection than other speech does, under the "commercial speech" doctrine, but this principle is limited to commercial ads and doesn't cover other communication, even if it's done for money.

Nor can information-privacy speech restrictions be defended on the grounds that they merely create a "property right in personal facts." Traditional intellectual-property law generally does not allow property rights in facts as such; one reason that the Supreme Court gave for upholding the constitutionality of copyright law is precisely that copyright law doesn't interfere with the free communication of facts. (Copyright gives people a monopoly in their particular expression of ideas or facts, but never in the facts or ideas themselves, even if the facts or ideas are originated by them.) Under current intellectual-property and free-speech law, facts about people are owned neither by the subject nor by their gatherer; they are "free as the air to the common use." And that's a good thing—suppression of facts, whether done in the name of intellectual property or otherwise, is a troubling matter.

But isn't information about people's transactions of relatively low constitutional value? Isn't it something that's really not of legitimate public interest? After all, "Volokh bought a lawnmower" isn't "We hold these truths to be self-evident...." It isn't commentary on political issues, or debate about high philosophy. Shouldn't we balance the rather modest constitutional value of this speech against the important interests supporting suppression of this speech?

This is a powerful point—but before we urge the legal system to accept it, we should think about all its implications. This, after all, is exactly the argument made in favor of the Communications Decency Act (CDA), which the Supreme Court nonetheless struck down in 1997. Sexually themed speech (whether you call it "pornography" or "art"), the CDA's proponents argued, isn't really that constitutionally valuable, and the right to communicate such speech had to be balanced against the government's interests. Likewise for flagburning or the famous "Fuck the Draft" jacket that the Supreme Court held in 1971 to be constitutionally protected; though these are at least politically themed, they're hardly of the highest constitutional value. If such expression were excluded from public discourse, the Republic wouldn't fall. Plenty of people have urged that the right to engage in such speech should also be restricted.

If the Court were to accept the notion that personal information is of "low constitutional value," this would provide powerful precedent for further restrictions on other categories of speech which some (including some Justices) are prepared to call "low-value." Conversely, if we think even pornography, profanity, and nonrational vituperation are speech, and as such deserve protection under the free-speech clause, we might ask why the same wouldn't apply to (accurate) speech about our neighbors' behavior, habits, and purchases. And if we wouldn't approve of the Supreme Court balancing away constitutional rights in favor of government interests with the CDA and other laws, we might worry about this for information-privacy speech restrictions, too.

Moreover, information about what others are doing often can be of significant value. Sometimes, it can even be of political relevance, for instance when it discusses the behavior of political figures. In Europe, where information-privacy speech protections have taken greater hold, and where the government generally has more power to restrict speech than it does in the United States, there is already talk about forbidding journalists from publishing supposedly "private" information about public officials' sexual affairs. Even in the US, the "disclosure of private facts" tort mentioned above—one of the few currently existing information-privacy speech restrictions—has already led a court to hold that a newspaper may be punished for speaking about a political official's past sex-change operation. I personally wouldn't care about such a fact in deciding whether to vote for someone, but other voters might, and in a democracy the media shouldn't be gagged from informing them about it.

At other times, information about people can be valuable to us in our daily lives, for instance when someone—in the media or not—reveals that one of our acquaintances has a criminal record, or a bad credit history. Should we trust the person in business? Should we trust him to watch our children? We can't decide unless we're informed about this. And while obviously the other person might not want us to have full information on this score, it's not clear why the government should have the power to use its coercive force to ban people from speaking this information.

Here, the experience of the private-facts tort is illustrative. Several cases have actually held that newspapers can be punished for revealing people's criminal pasts, even if the revelations are entirely accurate. For instance, in one case a court held that a publication could be held liable for running a story that revealed that a particular person had committed an armed robbery eleven years before. Naming the criminal, the court said, served no "public purpose" and was not "of legitimate public interest"; there was no "reason whatsoever" for it. The person was "rehabilitated" and had "paid his debt to society." "[W]e, as right-thinking members of society, should permit him to continue in the path of rectitude rather than throw him back into a life of shame or crime" by revealing his past:

> Ideally, [the person's] neighbors should recognize his present worth and forget his past life of shame. But men are not so divine as to forgive the past trespasses of others, and plaintiff therefore endeavored to reveal as little as possible of his past life.

But appealing as the court's rhetoric might sound, there's considerable danger in the government deciding which speech is of "legitimate public interest" and which isn't, or which things "right-thinking members of society" would want to know and which only the wrong-thinking ones would care about. Maybe we shouldn't assume that someone who committed armed robbery eleven years before might still be dangerous (though many criminals in fact do go on to commit more crimes). Maybe we ought to forgive and forget. But in a free society, we are entitled to decide this for ourselves; and under a regime of free speech, the government ought not forbid others from informing us about the things that can inform our decisions.

And if we and not the government should be the ones who decide what is said and what is listened to about people's criminal records, perhaps the same should apply as to other speech. Many might indeed say that certain kinds of speech, for instance speech about someone's food or clothing purchases, aren't of legitimate interest (though as it happens this is also information that is least embarrassing, and the very information that people would most want to conceal is also often the information that others would like to know about them). But perhaps freedom-of-speech principles should be understood as leaving it to speakers and listeners to decide what information they should find interesting, and as denying the legal system the power to make this decision for us.

More importantly, even if a narrow restriction on speech about a person's innocent shopping habits might do more good than harm, the danger with accepting any legally enforced system of control over factual information is that it may eventually go far beyond its roots. As I mentioned, in Europe the concept of information privacy is already being urged as a justification for controlling media reports about politicians. The experience with the private-facts tort shows that some forces in America would urge the same. And accepting the notion that certain facts may be suppressed because they are of "low value" or because they lack "legitimate public interest" creates a precedent in favor of broader suppression of other speech that is supposedly likewise of "low value."

CONCLUSION

US law today generally imposes few restraints on private parties communicating information about people. The chief legal protection people have is contract: If a business promises to keep information private, consumers can hold it to that promise—and they can threaten to withhold patronage from businesses that refuse to undertake such obligations, a powerful threat in today's competitive marketplace. Many businesses will realize that to lure customers they must provide both personalization and a promise that the personal information they learn will stay confidential. The government can put extra teeth into such promises, by providing supplemental enforcement (for instance, through regulatory bodies such as the Federal Trade Commission).

The government may, of course, go beyond enforcing people's promises of confidentiality, and impose broader, categorical obligations on them not to speak about certain things. It's important, though, to recognize such obligations for what they are: speech restrictions, which raise serious constitutional problems.

One can argue that courts should carve out a new First Amendment exception to justify such restrictions, and perhaps the courts will be sympathetic to such arguments. But there are costs to such new exceptions. In a legal and political system that is built on precedent and analogy, one speech restriction can easily lead to other, broader ones. Relying on admittedly imperfect contractual protections may ultimately prove to be the safer bet.

Notes

[1] This article is based on "Freedom of Speech, Information Privacy, and the Troubling Implications of a Right to Stop Others from Speaking About You," forthcoming in the *Stanford Law Review* and available at http://www.law.ucla.edu/faculty/volokh/privacy.htm; please see that article for further details on most of the points made here, and for detailed citations to the relevant legal authority.

[2] Important *caveat*: I am an expert on US law, and am writing only about US law. As to foreign law, I know nothing about it and, despite that, have no opinion.

Privacy and Human Rights: Comparing the United States to Europe

Solveig Singleton

One premise shaping the debate about privacy law in the United States is that the European Data Protection Directive is a more advanced model than any so far developed here. A headline in the *Government Computer News* for October 26, 1998, reads "Europeans Lead US in Data Protection Policies."[1] Under Europe's Data Protection Directive, the United States is considered to have inadequate protection for personal information, such as that which data companies might keep on consumer transactions. This finding touched off lengthy negotiations between Europe's guardians of data and the US Department of Commerce, to determine whether and when US companies may store information about their clients, employees, and customers in Europe. In June of 2000, European officials and the Commerce department finally reached an agreement, setting out policies US firms doing business with European clients and customers may follow to obtain a "safe harbor."

But why is the US regime considered unacceptable, as opposed to merely different? To answer these questions, it is important to compare the European approach to privacy with that of the United States, with particular attention to financial services. This analysis concludes that the US approach to privacy—a general rule of freedom of information coupled with a constitutionally limited government—is actually superior to that of Europe.

THE EUROPEAN APPROACH TO PRIVACY—AN OUTLINE

The basic ground rules for privacy for members of the European Union are laid down in the European Union Data Protection Directive (95/46/ED), which applies to both electronic and old-fashioned paper-filing systems, including (obviously) financial services. The "data" covered by the directive is information about an individual that identifies the individual by name or otherwise. Each EU nation's government is to implement the directive in its own way.

The Data Protection Directive begins by laying down basic privacy principles, starting with the idea that information should be collected for specific, legitimate purposes only, and be stored in individually identifiable form no longer than necessary. Central to the European approach is the notion that people are entitled to control data and information about themselves as a fundamental human right.

The European Directive creates specific rights for the person the information concerns—the "data subject." The entity collecting the information must give the data subject notice explaining who is collecting the data, who will ultimately have access to it, and why it is being collected. The data subject also is given the right to access and correct the data. Financial data is not treated in any special way by the Data Protection Directive, but is governed by these general principles.

The rules are stricter for companies wanting to use data in direct marketing, or to transfer the data for other companies to use in direct marketing. The data subject must be explicitly informed of these plans and given the chance to object.

Stricter rules also govern sensitive information relating to racial and ethnic background, political affiliation, religious or philosophical beliefs, trade-union membership, sexual preferences, and health. To collect this information the data subject must give explicit consent. The law admits several exceptions, including exemptions for employment contracts, nonprofits, or the legal system.

SOME INTERESTING EXEMPTIONS

Musing over the principles laid down by the directive—the idea that one has the right to be notified of, and consent to, the use of information about oneself, and to access and correct this information—one might well ask whether such broad principles can be reconciled with many vital or convenient human activities. May one, for example, take a client's business card out of the country without providing him explicit notice of exactly how it will be used and stored? Send an old roommate a mutual friend's address? At first glance the rules taken literally would turn generations of ordinary human behavior into a regulatory riddle. Thus, for practicality's sake, the directive has come to be riddled with exceptions.

These include an exemption for data kept for personal and household use—so that one may keep an address book with the names of college friends and distant uncles. Synagogues, trade unions, churches, and other nonprofits are permitted to keep even "sensitive" information about their members. Indeed, it is hard to imagine how they would operate if they did not.

The European idea of privacy and controlling information about oneself as a human right thus has peculiar characteristics. Ordinarily, a fundamental human right would not be so riddled with broad exemptions. It would be decidedly peculiar, for example, to announce that the right not to be tortured was a human right, except when it came into conflict with the government's need to collect taxes. But governments in Europe naturally exempt themselves from the directive when it comes to the state's own monetary or financial interests (*e.g.* taxation) or criminal matters. The human right to privacy simply gives way to fiscal convenience or a general need for public order.

While that result is natural enough and probably essential, the breadth and number of the exemptions to the Data Protection Directive threaten to swallow the "human right" itself. This in turn indicates that this "human right" is on shakier philosophical footing than the regulatory consensus in Europe suggests. In particular, the Data Protection Directive recognizes at least one conflict with another basic right, free speech, providing that national governments may exempt journalists from provisions of the directive when *in the government's view* the interest in free speech outweighs privacy interests. This level of deference to government on a question of free speech would be constitutionally unacceptable in the United States.

THE ORIGINS OF THE EUROPEAN DATA PROTECTION DIRECTIVE

The horrors of the Holocaust inspired many Europeans to give renewed attention to the problem of privacy in the years following World War II. National-socialist governments in several countries used census data to identify households of certain ethnic, religious, or other targeted groups. In the United States, around the same time, census data was used to identify Japanese-Americans for relocation.

This shameful history yielded the lesson that information collected for innocent purposes can become a tool of oppression in the hands of a powerful government. As various welfare states swelled in size and power in Europe, the first "data protection" laws sought to guard against this danger. The German province of Hesse passed such privacy laws in 1970 in reaction to the computerization and centralization of personal information. Sweden passed the first national data-protection law in 1973—during the period that it adopted national identity cards. Support for data-protection law grew in Britain when the country began to use a centrally administered system of national driver's licenses.

As each country developed its own national privacy regime, trade disputes arose. For example, Sweden denied a British company a contract to make magnetic-stripe cards, finding Britain's laws failed to give Swedes enough protection. To prevent such trade disputes, data-protection laws were harmonized across Europe, first with the Council of Europe Convention for the Protection of Individuals with regard to Automatic Processing of Personal Data. The EU's Data Protection Directive followed, ratified in 1995.

Swiss banks meanwhile offered a contrasting lesson in privacy and its relation to human rights. The banking secrecy offered by the Swiss banking system allowed hundreds of refugees from war-torn Europe to secret their savings in pseudonymous bank accounts (although this was not the purpose for which banking secrecy in Switzerland was established). Swiss bankers have taken criticism for making it difficult for survivors to find those funds. But this is partly a consequence of secrecy, without which no money would have been saved at all.

DATA PROTECTION AND THE PRIVATE SECTOR

Privacy laws in Europe apply to data held in the private sector as well as data held in the public sector. Indeed, given the breadth of exemptions that give government the freedom to manipulate data for tax and criminal powers, the directive poses scarcely any challenge to the heart of government power, and applies far more stringently to the private sector. Given that the logic of the privacy laws is rooted in concern about the expansion of government, why target the private sector? Two reasons are commonly put forth:

- fear that governments will gain access to data held in the private sector; and
- the view that the private sector itself violates human rights by using information for direct marketing or other purposes without notice and consent.

This analysis concludes that the former argument is impressive, though ultimately insufficient to justify restraints on the freedom of information in the private sector. The latter argument barely makes it off the ground.

PRIVACY LAW IN THE UNITED STATES

Privacy has not been the focus of much political attention in the United States since Vietnam, until recently. Perhaps this is because the welfare state has not progressed as far or as fast in the United States as it has in Europe. US citizens and policymakers are less suspicious of big business—and downright supportive of small business—compared to their counterparts in some European countries. On an issue with a close nexus to privacy, the need for "protection" of consumers from advertising and direct marketing, the United States takes a far less regulatory approach than Europe. Even many left-wing or moderate policymakers in the United States would find a German court's ruling that Lands' End's advertising of a lifetime guarantee is "unfair competition"[2] something of a head-scratcher. Whatever the reasons, the recent debate in the US on privacy certainly has been driven by events in Europe. However, the overall health of the US economy, especially the service-industry sector, gives opponents of top-down privacy regulation good reason to push back.

PRIVACY AND THE FEDERAL GOVERNMENT

The Fourth Amendment to the Constitution does not limit what information the government may collect. It does limit the means by which that information may be collected, making information collectors accountable to the judiciary. Lax judicial scrutiny has somewhat eroded this protection. The courts have held, for example, that the Fourth Amendment does not protect businesses from "regulatory searches."

Historically, concern about privacy has flared up from time to time in response to proposed government programs. The public was mollified at the time of the creation of Social Security with the promise that Social Security numbers would only be used for Social Security purposes. More recently, public resistance to the idea of a national ID card blocked the implementation of this idea. In the financial-services area, the FDIC's proposed "Know Your Customer" regulations were defeated after a public outcry in early 1999.

During the 1970s, concern over privacy reached new heights, spurred largely by surveillance of Vietnam War protestors and abuses of wiretapping powers and tax, bank, and telephone records during Watergate. In the words of one commentator, "All of these show what government can do if its actions are shrouded in secrecy and its vast information resources are applied and manipulated in a punitive, selective, or political fashion."[3]

These concerns gave birth to the Privacy Act of 1974. The act applies only to records of personal information held by federal agencies, stipulating that the government create no secret files, and provide the public with a right to access and copy their own files. Agencies are obligated to keep reasonably accurate records, and to keep records only if "relevant and necessary." Federal agencies are not supposed to sell or rent records. Agencies are supposed to obtain an individual's consent before disclosing the content of his records—except within the agency, for "routine use," or to law enforcement. CIA records and other law-enforcement offices are exempt from the right of access and correction. Other exemptions cover materials prepared in anticipation of litigation.

Subsequent privacy concerns were addressed on the federal level by the Electronic Communications Privacy Act of 1986, which protects private electronic communications from unauthorized surveillance by the government, as well as the Computer Matching and Privacy Protection Act of 1988.

Privacy protection on the state level is a different story. In contrast to federal efforts, many states permit the sale of state-held records such as driver's license information, and a variety of public records are available to commercial enterprises. As of this writing, many bills to regulate privacy are under consideration in various states, some of which would adopt the European model.

Privacy and the Private Sector

In the United States at the federal level, the freedom of information remains the rule for many transfers of information between private companies. There are a handful of statutes governing the private sector's use of data in health care, the video-rental industry and the cable-television industry, and a few other areas. Generally, actors in the private sector are bound by state common law, which offers basic and minimal privacy protections in the form of privacy torts. These torts are narrowly defined, often closely linked to a violation of property rights. Courts recognize that these torts are tightly confined by the rights of free speech, especially as applied to media defendants.

Several federal statutes create privacy-related laws for financial services in the United States. In this sense, financial services are the regulated exception, rather than the unregulated rule, for information held in the private sector in the US.

Credit-reporting laws applicable to the private sector include the Fair Credit Reporting Act (FCRA), passed in the 1970s. The main purpose of this act was to allow consumers to access and correct mistakes in their credit reports. Consumers can sue for damages if the law is violated. They may also insert explanatory comments in their own credit report concerning disputed information. Information over seven years old may not be included in a report. Particularly detailed reports, known as investigate reports, may be released only with notice to the consumer. The FCRA also limits the uses of credit information, and requires that measures be taken to limit the dissemination of reports. Under the 1996 Amendments to the Fair Credit Reporting Act, businesses can share certain consumer information with their affiliates, but they must first give customers the choice of opting out of the sharing.

The Financial Services Modernization Act of 1999 took regulation of financial information a step further. The new law applies to any entity that engages in financial activities, including not only traditional banks but a merchant or manufacturer that offers credit, stored-value cards, or money orders. It applies to personally identifiable financial information about consumers. Essentially, the law requires that consumers must receive notice of a privacy policy and a chance to opt out of information sharing with third parties. The law will take effect in November of 2000.

Government is not the only guarantor of personal privacy. The market also weighs in, as evidenced by the self-regulatory requirements of some banking associations. The Consumer Bankers Association's guidelines, for example, state that financial institutions should not reveal specific information about customer accounts to unaffiliated third parties for marketing purposes unless the customer has been informed and can opt out.

OLD WORLD VS. NEW WORLD
PRIVACY AND HUMAN RIGHTS

US and European principles on privacy share one key similarity. Europe's data-protection law and America's Privacy Act of 1974 both attempt to reign in dangers to human rights from the expansion of government. Both, however, do little or nothing to check the growth or scope of government databases or information-collection powers. Neither cuts to the heart of government powers—taxation and law enforcement.

Since so much of the privacy debate is conducted in the terminology of human rights, it is worth noting that the fundamental danger to human rights stems from the growth of government *power*—not simply from the growth of *databases*. As long as we assume that federal authorities should take responsibility for regulating more and more aspects of our daily lives, from education to health care, from labor markets to child-support payments, we will be unable to resist authorities' demands for more information. Likewise, governments with huge tax systems that demand more and more of taxpayers will naturally want to keep track of their citizens. It would be downright illogical to argue that yes, we trust governments to help us here, there, and everywhere, but we do not trust them with the information that they consequently require to run these programs more efficiently.

For all the sporadic battles privacy advocates win, whether against "Know Your Customer" or national ID cards, in the end federal databases will remain as threats to individuals' privacy as long as government power remains. Centuries ago, young national governments in Europe and China decided they needed to keep track of who belonged to which family. Thus developed the surname. John, known in his neighborhood as John the Short because of his stature, became John Short, and his son Tom became Tom Short, not Tom, son of John. Tax systems demanded this new system of nomenclature, and got it. Over time, we have all become accustomed to having surnames and even find them useful; privacy protests would be futile if not downright silly. Note, however, the *real* issue is a question of government power, specifically how broad powers of taxation will grow.

Changes in the way governments process information thus follow inexorably from changes in their substantive roles. Unless the state's growth is restrained at a substantive level, it will remain a danger to human rights no matter how it administers data. The growth of government power and its level of involvement in our lives is the fundamental issue—not what information or nomenclature it may incidentally collect.

The answer to the threat of human-rights violations by powerful governments is thus not to impose trifling restrictions on the use of data (from which the governments then exempt themselves), but to restrict the power of governments to regulate our daily lives. If we do not assign government the task of tracking money launderers or dispensing health care, it will not collect from citizens the information needed to do so more efficiently.

ASSESSING THE EUROPEAN MODEL

The European model of data protection is surprisingly weak, because it is premised on the notion that the danger to human rights from the growth of the welfare state can be controlled, *without controlling the power of the welfare state itself.*

Take, for example, France. French authorities rigorously regulate (among other things) the hours per week that one may work. Stories have appeared in the press of how police have been sent into private businesses, appearing at the doors of offices to demand that people stop working immediately, or be ticketed. Inspectors stand outside the doors of office buildings, stopping and searching businessmen as they leave; laptops and cell phones are confiscated to ensure no work will be done at home. The dangers to human rights are obvious and enormous. The violations of privacy are severe and outrageous. But the European Data Protection Directive does nothing to stop this.

On the other hand, the relative secrecy provided by Swiss banks is an excellent example of how to prevent information from becoming a vehicle for human-rights violations. The private sector should remain free to use technology or to negotiate contracts that provide confidentiality. But the data-protection laws simply have not proven to be a check to government surveillance in Europe.

THE HIDDEN POTENTIAL OF THE US MODEL

A cursory glance suggests that the United States, having little omnibus privacy law as such, has no way of preventing the use of information to violate human rights. But a closer look suggests the US constitutional model has the *potential* to protect human rights. The problem in the United States has been persuading the judiciary to take the Constitution seriously—not a lack of laws or principles, but difficulty with enforcing them.

The US Constitution, in a nutshell, describes a system of limited government. The federal government's powers are limited and restricted to those enumerated in the Constitution. Were this principle given teeth, the growth of the federal government would be reigned in, restraining new government demands for more information. The idea behind the US Constitution as originally conceived is to have a government limited in size and substance—a government that will naturally make fewer demands for information, and have fewer powers to abuse.

Another traditional limit on the power of government in the United States is the nondelegation doctrine. When Congress delegates broad authority to administrative agencies, it increases dangers to privacy, because the agency is free to "regulate" without public scrutiny. The recent outcry over the FDIC's "Know Your Customer" proposal shows that agency snooping programs will rarely sit well with the public when exposed to its scrutiny. The FDIC withdrew its *official* "Know Your Customer" proposal in response to public comments. But many banks, cowed by the regulators' broad powers over their economic welfare, continue to comply with "voluntary" "Know Your Customer" rules. The original model of US government would check such "informal" legislation on the part of regulators.

FINANCIAL PRIVACY AND THE PRIVATE SECTOR
THE LOGIC OF REGULATING PRIVATE-SECTOR DATA

As noted previously, one major difference between European data-protection laws and US laws on privacy is that the US private sector remains comparatively free of regulation, even when data is used for marketing. Some freedom remains even where more heavily regulated financial data is concerned. This makes sense. The private sector is not armed with the unique powers to control police, armies, and the courts. It is not a danger to human rights in the sense that governments are.

The view that uses of information for marketing in the private sector violate human rights is a peculiar one. Why should a business not be free to record and use facts about transactions, about real people and real events, to develop products and to identify people who might have an interest in its products? Once a consumer enters into a transaction with another entity, this entity has as much of a right to use the information about the transaction as the consumer. Why would it violate someone's rights to use information about him to sell him something? Junk mail may be annoying, but it is difficult to see it as akin to torture.

A legitimate argument may exist that restraints on the private sector are justified because of the risk that government will seize the information. This is a real risk. But there is little in Europe's data-protection model to prevent this. The data-protection model must exempt many private databases (such as those kept by trade unions or churches) just to allow normal life to continue. These databases remain and can be targeted by police or tax authorities. The data-protection authorities in Sweden have purged from the airline-reservation system information about travelers requesting kosher meals. But what difference does this make if a hypothetical future police state can simply get the information from the local synagogue? Meanwhile, the US Constitution at least makes government seizures subject to scrutiny from the judicial branch.

The most important objection to the argument that private databases must be restricted to prevent government abuse is that it is wrong to restrict private freedoms to prevent wrongs by miscreant public servants. Germany and France, in their desire to prevent the rise of extremist political movements, censor political speech such as Holocaust revisionism, anarchist newspapers, or books about the illness of the French president. There is a tremendous irony in noting that what some European countries have apparently concluded from World War II is that one may restrict government power by increasing controls on the private sector. This approach is simply not consistent with preserving private citizens' rights. If one's concern is abuse by governments, by all means enforce restrictions on governments and their employees. But do not take away the freedom of the private sector in the name of defending it.

ECONOMIC CONSIDERATIONS AND CONSUMER WELFARE

With all of these assaults on personal liberty in the name of protecting privacy, it bears asking: What are consumers losing?

Europe's implementation of the Data Protection Directive offers some clues. We are likely to lose some small businesses (in Britain, bankruptcy rates for small businesses have increased markedly; commentators attribute this partly to data protection and partly to other regulatory initiatives that have fallen heavily on small business). A small business in Britain, for example, might face a devastating fine of thousands of pounds for disposing of a PC without erasing a file of customer names and addresses—even if the stray information is never used for harm.

Consumers could lose big by reducing the free flow of information between banks and affiliates (and/or third parties). The use of this information to target offerings of new financial services in new markets dramatically reduces the costs of getting information out to consumers. Being able to precisely target a marketing offer to likely first-time home buyers, for example, might lower the costs of marketing the offer from as much as $10 or $12 to as low as $2. And this will often mean the difference between whether the offer can or cannot be financed at all. Do we want to assume, as do many European officials, that marketing is not a fundamentally legitimate activity?

Bureaucratizing the information flow between financial-services organizations could mean that many new services cannot be offered, or that many consumers will never hear about a favorable new type of account or loan. This means less competition, with fewer new companies and business models. Extending notice-and-consent requirements to transfers of data between financial-services affiliates would give the advantage to big, integrated firms over smaller ones that contract out for services such as printing accounts.

A grave concern should be that consumers may find it increasingly difficult and expensive to obtain credit. In Greece, for example, even a professional may find a credit card impossible to obtain. Elsewhere in Europe, the cost of obtaining a credit card is much higher than in the United States—with interest rates for an ordinary credit purchase as high as 25 percent.[4] A major problem overseas is that restraints on the flow of verification information make fraud rampant.[5] Consumers with a poor credit history may find it particularly difficult to obtain any credit at all.

Top-down regulation of privacy also conflicts squarely with free-speech rights—not only for journalists and regulated companies, but for grassroots political ventures. In Sweden, for example, a law was passed making it illegal to publish personally identifiable information on the Internet. The prosecutor was embarrassed to realize a literal reading of the law meant a human-rights group could no longer legally have a web site with the heading "Pinochet is a murderer."[6] The prosecutor tried to save the situation by explaining that "minor" violations of the law would not be punished. But reportedly this resort to prosecutorial discretion has not saved animal-rights groups and consumer activists from liability under the privacy law.

DATA PROTECTION AND THE INFORMATION ECONOMY

The data-protection model cannot easily be adapted to information-age technology. The purpose of information technology and innovation is to make the conveyance of information faster and cheaper, while the purpose of data protection seems to be to make the transit of information slower and more cumbersome.

Supporters of the European directive have had to scramble to adapt data-protection laws to new technology. The original premise of the directive was that express consent was to be required (turning normal rules of contract law on their head). But how can this be reconciled with the telephone system? When one makes a call, one's billing information is automatically relayed from switch to switch across many jurisdictions—all without notice or consent. When one sends an e-mail, one's personally identifiable header information often is flung from shore to shore, across many servers in many lands in an unpredictable pattern. It would not be uncommon for an e-mail sent from Brussels to Paris to travel through a server in California.

EU authorities have decided to "deem" the person sending the information to be the person making the call or sending the message. This fiction painfully strains the principles of the directive itself—implicit consent in effect "snuck in" to save the regulations from the embarrassment of technological backwardness.

EU authorities remain uneasy about the Internet's fundamental nature—making communication of all information seamless and cheap. European privacy authorities reported, "Presently it is almost impossible to use the Internet without being confronted with privacy-invading features which carry out all kinds of processing operations of personal data in a way that is invisible to the data subjects." And Dutch regulator Diana Alonso warned, "We just want to let (companies) know when they are making new software and hardware, they should pay attention to [privacy] principles."[7]

As with phone calls, would the EU be willing to abandon the restraints of the directive to permit new technology and innovative business models to go forward? For example, if credit reporting had not been invented yet, would EU authorities allow it to begin? If so, they must reject the rule that it is wrong to use information about consumers without their consent, gutting their directive and implicitly admitting that it will often be an obstacle to consumer welfare. If not, the result would be to "freeze" in time the types of information collected, and the purposes for which they are used, in the late 1990s.

A large part of the wonder of information technology is that it will empower us not just to send our names and addresses around faster, but also to create and store types of information that historically have been lost and wasted. Every event in the life of a human being is a potential source of information—our decisions not to buy as well as those to buy, our idle wanderings as well as purposeful ventures, our casual interactions with coworkers. A top-down regulatory model, the principle of which is that what is not expressly permitted is forbidden, would appear to be fundamentally hostile to such experiments in creating new libraries of data and learning from them.

CONCLUSION

The most effective rules for ameliorating federal threats to privacy are to limit the powers of the federal government overall and restrict the growth of federal programs. So long as such programs grow unchecked and taxes rise unchecked, government demands for more information will prove irresistible.

Top-down regulatory models of how information "ought" to be used are incompatible with innovation in financial services. If we in the US continue to turn the default rule of freedom of information on its head, we will find ourselves trying to operate a modern economy on the principle that what is not explicitly permitted is forbidden. It is only because we have for ages gone by the opposite rule that our economy and people continue to thrive.

Notes

[1] "Europeans Lead US in Data Protection," *Government Computer News*, October 26, 1998, p. 1.

[2] Peter Girard, "Lands' End Winks at German Ruling," *Catalog Age* (January 2000); Carol J. Williams, "Market Forces Loosening State's Grip On 'Germany Inc.'," *Los Angeles Times*, June 11, 2000; Mary Lisbeth D'Amico, "German E-Commerce Faces Legal Tangle," *InfoWorld Daily News*, March 10, 2000; Deborah Hargreaves, "Lands' End to File Brussels Complaint," *Financial Times (London)*, January 11, 2000, p. 8.

[3] Unnamed ACLU representative, quoted in Major John F. Joyce, "The Privacy Act: A Sword and A Shield But Sometimes Neither," 99 *Mil. L. Rev.* 113, 122.

[4] See *e.g.* Sarah Cunningham, "John Lewis Succumbs to Consumer Pressure," *The London Times,* September 18, 1999; "U.S. E-Merchants Fail to Gain Market Share in Europe Due to Differences In Buying Habits," *Business Wire,* June 22, 2000 ("differences in monetary policy and banking regulations in many European countries have severely restricted the availability of credit cards").

[5] See *e.g.* "Online Europe," *New Media Age,* January 27, 2000, p. 12 (quoting merchant Kevin Sefton, "Merchants try to mitigate risk, but we're in an

extremely difficult position...UK credit card transactions are verified against the card number and date only.").

[6] Jacob Palme, "Freedom of Speech, The EU Data Protection Directive and the Swedish Personal Data Act," June 9, 2000, available at http://www.dsv.su.se/jpalme/society/eu-data-directive-freedom.html. See also e-mail from Jacob Palme to Declan McCullagh, June 9, 2000, archived at http://www.politechbot.com/p-01218.html.

[7] Suzanne Perry, "EU Regulators Seek Internet Privacy Protection," *Reuters*, March 4, 1999.

Swiss Views on Financial Privacy

Franz A. Blankart, Jean A. Bonna, and Michel Y. Dérobert

Respect for privacy is a traditional cornerstone of the Swiss legal system. Privacy is considered to be an expression of freedom of the individual. The culture of discretion reveals itself in a number of areas. For example, Switzerland has a law on data protection and imposes an obligation of confidentiality on professions such as doctors, lawyers, and priests, to name just a few. Her banking law has also codified, since 1935, the Swiss banking secrecy that safeguards the financial privacy of Swiss banks' clients.

This article offers insight into the Swiss views on financial privacy, addressing the following subjects:

- How the relationship between a state and her citizens is reflected in her views on financial privacy;
- The origins of the rules of Swiss banking secrecy;
- Financial confidentiality in the Swiss legal system today—the limitations on financial privacy necessary to fight crime, its implications for taxation, as well as its relation to the supervision of banks and financial markets; and
- Future challenges to financial privacy in Switzerland.

HOW THE RELATIONSHIP BETWEEN A STATE AND HER CITIZENS IS REFLECTED IN HER VIEWS ON FINANCIAL PRIVACY

Is Privacy a Person-to-Person or a Person-to-State Issue?

In a recent report, the Organisation for Economic Co-Operation and Development (OECD) Committee on Fiscal Affairs gives the following definition of bank secrecy:

"Bank secrecy" is widely recognized as playing a legitimate role in protecting the confidentiality of the financial affairs of individuals and legal entities. It derives from the concept that the relationship between a banker and his customer obliges the bank to treat all customers' affairs as confidential....Access to such information by ordinary third parties would jeopardize the right to privacy and potentially endanger the commercial and financial well-being of the account-holder.[1]

One may deduce from this text that its authors—tax officials from OECD countries—consider privacy a person-to-person issue, not a person-to-state issue. Financial confidentiality is there to protect individuals and their affairs from each others' indiscretion. The state is another matter altogether, as shown by the rest of the report.

This report shows that the OECD's tax officials adopt views usually advocated by states with a history of strong central power, which do not value highly the respect of their citizens. The structure of power is top-down. Financial confidentiality represents a risk to the state. Citizens cannot be trusted.

But in an essentially federal system such as that of Switzerland, power finds its roots in the citizen. It is he who lends power to the government. The structure of power is bottom-up. The citizen has to watch over the government, which consequently can not be the surveyor of the citizen.

A FUNDAMENTAL HUMAN RIGHT

Despite these historical and constitutional differences in the relationship between state and citizen across different countries, the respect for privacy is nowadays considered a fundamental human right throughout Europe. The right to privacy is expressed in a number of constitutional, public, and private laws.

Article 8 of the European Convention for the Protection of Human Rights and Fundamental Freedoms states clearly the inviolability of the right of personality and hence of personal data. This is also true for the EU directive on the protection of personal data of October 25, 1998. It is up to the subject of the data to give consent to processing a disclosure of his data, even if the free flow of information is the cornerstone of a market economy.

Data protection is the key: The term denotes protection against inquisitive curiosity of the government and protection against the competitive curiosity of third persons. In present times, as technological progress makes it possible to follow a private person's information trail step by step, data protection is all the more necessary. Governments have to earn public trust by confidence-building measures, not by deployment of more police, surveillance, and domestic force.

The Importance of Cultural Values

The right to privacy is nevertheless not absolute, insofar as the justified interest of the state outweighs the interest of the individual. This is generally the case for government engaged in the fight against crime. But countries differ in their conceptions of what is a crime. For most serious crimes, the vast majority of countries share the same values. But in a number of areas, one country might consider a certain criminal law to be in the overwhelming interest of the public, while another country would regard the same law as an unacceptable infringement on individual freedom. Such differences abound: They include laws related to gun control, speed limits on motorways, freedom of information and free speech, and financial privacy. This list of examples is by no means exhaustive.

These differences follow historic and cultural traditions. It seems that a majority of Americans will not give up the right to carry guns, although this seems strange to many Europeans. Germans want at all costs to be allowed to drive their cars at speeds that most of their neighbors consider extremely hazardous. Under the First Amendment of the US Constitution, information that would violate anti-racism law in Switzerland can be freely displayed on US-based Internet sites. Nordic countries in Europe have stripped their citizens of any financial privacy vis-à-vis the tax authorities, but that would never be accepted in Switzerland or Austria.

THE STATE VERSUS THE INDIVIDUAL

The question as to what extent financial privacy should be limited for public purposes depends on the respective roles of the state and the citizen. In Switzerland, the answer is based on the philosophies of Rousseau, de Tocqueville, and Jefferson, which attribute the source of public power to the people and not to government. The state is there to serve her citizens; the citizens are not the state's servants. If the citizens start giving more and more tasks to their "servant"—the state—they will progressively lose their freedom and privacy. As the government is in a dominant position, its use of power could easily shift to the abuse of power.

While safeguarding social justice and public policy (*ordre public*), the state's role is to create an optimal framework within which the citizen may be economically active, fully assuming his own legal and moral responsibilities. Respect for privacy is, in any case, a basic principle, for respect for privacy mirrors the respect for freedom. Consequently, in the banking world, the rules of financial confidentiality do not protect the bank; they protect the customer.

In Europe, no public administration or private person has the right to circulate or publish any data on a private person or a company, with the exception of the press. The press may publish such information if there exists a clear need for the public to be informed on the subject. For example, articles on the private behavior of a public figure (say a politician) would be permitted.

THE ORIGINS OF THE RULES OF SWISS BANKING SECRECY
AN ANCIENT TRADITION

What is widely known as "Swiss banking secrecy," which provides protection for the privacy of both Swiss and non-Swiss bank customers with regard to their financial matters, is nothing else than the duty of discretion that banks, their officers and employees, their external auditors, as well as the Swiss federal officials who are involved with banking supervision, must observe. This principle is very old; it can be traced back to the civil codes that existed in the principalities that form today's Germany, as well as in the cities of Northern Italy.

THE GENESIS OF THE SWISS BANKING LAW[2]

In Switzerland, banking secrecy is formally defined in Article 47 of the Federal Banking Law, which came into force on March 1, 1935.[3] This text codified long-standing practice. Until that date, there was no federal regulation of banks in Switzerland and therefore no codified rules on banking confidentiality. But for centuries a distinctive relationship of confidence had developed between the banks and their clients on the basis of unwritten law, comparable to the client-attorney privilege.

After World War II, Swiss banking secrecy was interpreted as having been designed to protect persecuted citizens from neighboring countries, including German Jews trying to hide their assets from the Nazi regime and French high-net-worth individuals trying to escape the threats represented by the socialist *Front populaire* government. However, the protection that these foreign clients were given in Switzerland was the result, and not the purpose, of the introduction of Swiss banking-secrecy codes.

The origin of Swiss banking law dates from the beginning of the century, long before the Nazi Party seized power in Germany. The genesis of Swiss banking secrecy cannot be linked primarily to political events that occurred outside Switzerland. Various cantons (like Basle) already had regulation of this kind in place.

Until the 1930s, Switzerland, like most countries, did not have a modern banking law. Such a law was introduced during this period because of the massive difficulties that the banking system encountered as a result of economic crisis. Switzerland's banks were badly hit by the German banking crisis of 1931. Almost a billion Swiss francs were frozen in Germany because of its bad currency situation. The total assets of the (then eight) Swiss big banks shrunk by more than half. Five of these banks had to be salvaged from bankruptcy. During the 1930s, a total of 60 banks had to be either taken over or liquidated.

This dramatic situation helped Parliament overcome its long-standing reluctance to pass a Federal Banking Law, although such a law had been under discussion for some 20 years. The first draft had been presented to the federal government as early as

1916. Interestingly, this draft did not contain any provisions for client confidentiality. At the time, the protection offered by banking secrecy was considered obvious.

TAX INFORMATION ISSUES

This fact is documented by the discussion that took place during World War I, when the first "War Tax" was introduced. In December, 1915, the Socialist Party had proposed that banks should provide the state with all information to allow the proper assessment of taxpayers. This proposal was expressly rejected in Parliament by the conservative majority as a breach of the not-yet-codified rules of banking secrecy.

In 1917, the Socialist Party launched a constitutional initiative in order to introduce a new federal tax.[4] This led the conservative parties to accept a second "War Tax" instead. On this occasion, too, the question was raised as to whether the confidentiality of taxpayers' information from the tax authorities should be protected or dropped. Parliament voted against the lifting of banking secrecy.

The question whether banks should be subjected to state supervision, or even nationalized (as demanded in the Socialist Party's program of 1920), remained a current issue during the 1920s. The abolition of the still-unwritten banking-secrecy rules was requested by a coalition formed by representatives from the left and from the farmers—both groups being traditionally critical of "Big Money"—but to no avail.

A further constitutional initiative was launched by the Socialist Party during the 1920s. It aimed at introducing a "Wealth Tax" designed to write off the debt incurred by the federal state during World War I. By then, the farmers were again on the conservative side and the initiative was rejected by a seven-to-one margin. The idea that the fiscal authorities should be given access to clients' bank information was then dropped for a long time. Thus, the discussion surrounding banking confidentiality has always been a state-to-person, and not only a person-to-person, issue; and the debate was a domestic, rather than an international, one.

INTERNATIONAL CONSIDERATIONS

However, the international situation that prevailed at the time cannot be overlooked. Between the two world wars, the political climate in Europe was extremely tense, to say the least. The Russian revolution and the rise of communism in that country; hyperinflation in Germany; the rise of national-socialism and fascism in a number of European countries; and the world-wide economic crisis are but a few of the developments of these hectic days.

These events also had consequences in Switzerland: Social unrest led to a tragic confrontation between the army and left-wing demonstrators in Geneva in 1932; the activities of national-socialist movements had to be prohibited by the federal government in various Swiss cities, including Zurich, Lugano, and Davos; foreign powers' intelligence activities in Switzerland led the government to pass, on June 21, 1935, an urgent decree for the protection of the security of the Confederation.

Spying on Swiss banks by foreign governments was a very real issue during that time. Such surveillance was carried on because of political uncertainty and the fragile currency situation in a number of countries. High war taxes were also leading to capital flight. The situation in Germany was particularly difficult, because of the reparations due after World War I. France, for instance, was interested in obtaining German assets held privately in third countries. From 1931 onwards, there were rumors that German financial authorities had access to illegal information about investments in Switzerland. In 1932, the Swiss press reported openly on Germany's spying on Swiss banks. The Swiss federal prosecutor made no secret of his irritation about these developments.

The national-socialist government in Germany next threatened with imprisonment those who would not declare their foreign assets. Although it was not known at the time to what extremes this regime would go against its own citizens, renewed cases of spying worried the Swiss authorities. So it was only logical that the new Federal Banking Law, introduced mainly to protect depositors and savers, would contain a provision on banking secrecy making it an offence to divulge any matter relating to the affairs of a bank's client.

This formal codification of a long-standing banking tradition was introduced following a proposal put forward by the Office of the Federal Prosecutor "in view of the spying on banks from abroad." By then, no political party seems to have objected.

FINANCIAL CONFIDENTIALITY IN THE SWISS LEGAL SYSTEM TODAY

Since the official beginning of Swiss banking-secrecy policy, the world has changed dramatically. The internationalization of markets, free flow of capital, technological progress, as well as other positive developments have played major roles in making the world a better place.

However, the old problems have not disappeared from the face of the earth: In many places, people may still feel threatened by their government, although these governments would invariably dispute such an allegation. To be sure, there are few regimes left in the Western world that seem even remotely likely to treat their citizens as brutally as the Nazi regime did in Germany before and during World War II. But who could blame the representatives of certain ethnic minorities in a number of countries (which shall remain unnamed) if they set aside some of their savings, just in case something happens, as some European families did during the period discussed above?

Meanwhile, other problems have surfaced. One is the proliferation of criminal behavior, led by two main developments. First, economic progress and globalization made old criminal activities more profitable than before; second, changes in attitude have meant that certain behaviors merely frowned upon in the past (such as trading on insider information, manipulating stock prices, not to mention handing out bribes in order to secure contracts in certain countries) have become criminal offenses. The rules on banking confidentiality have had to cope with these developments.

BANKING SECRECY RULES DO NOT PROTECT CRIMINALS

A closely knit network of legislation keeps the Swiss financial center clean. Switzerland maintains a closely knit network of laws and regulations designed to prevent money of criminal origin finding its way into the country. When criminal activity is involved, these same laws enable criminal investigations to be carried out, and they impose a comprehensive duty on bankers to disclose information as well as provide for international mutual assistance in criminal matters. This is the case, for example, where money laundering or participation in the actions of a criminal organization are suspected.

The condition, however, for granting judicial assistance enabling other countries to access a client's financial information is that the crimes the client is alleged to have committed must be recognized as such both in Switzerland and in the country requesting assistance. This is known as the principle of double incrimination. Any other system would result in the Swiss courts trying to enforce foreign laws on Swiss territory, which would be contrary to this country's culture and tradition.

Swiss banks must know their customers. Swiss bankers are no more interested than their colleagues in other countries in attracting money which has been generated by criminal activities. But, like all other major international financial centers, Switzerland is likely to be considered as an attractive place to invest not only legal funds but also illegal ones. For this reason, the Swiss banking community has developed stringent standards of customer identification to prevent any abuse of the confidentiality rules designed and enforced to protect the privacy of law-abiding clients.

These "Know Your Customer" rules require every bank employee to identify customers and, where appropriate, establish the beneficial owners of the funds in question before opening any account relationship. By signing an "Agreement on due diligence" more than 20 years ago, the Swiss banks pioneered a system which has since provided a model for other financial centers. After a number of revisions and improvements, the Swiss "Know Your Customer" rules are considered the most severe in the world.

Numbered accounts are not anonymous. Despite the picture presented in detective stories, spy films, and sometimes in the media, anonymous bank accounts do not exist in Switzerland. The names of the holders of numbered accounts are always known, albeit only to a small circle of people within the bank. In terms of banking confidentiality, no legal distinction is made between numbered and other accounts.

International judicial cooperation is working. As mentioned above, Switzerland offers international judicial cooperation with other countries in criminal matters. This is particularly true of money laundering and other financial activities of criminal organizations. Recent history has proved that Switzerland cooperates more efficiently than other major financial centers. In conjunction with the Swiss "Know Your Customer" policy, this body of laws is very effective. In one well-known money-laundering case that caused a scandal in the United States, it was from Switzerland rather than New York or London—two banking centers also involved in the story—that the beneficial owner of the accounts was traced to offshore centers.

However, there are limits to what Switzerland is ready to do in the field of international judicial cooperation. The protection of individuals must be ensured, be they Swiss or foreign citizens. This is why Switzerland insists on the principle of double incrimination, which states that cooperation will only be granted if a crime is considered as such in Switzerland as well as in the country requesting cooperation. Other limitations also exist: The courts must respect the principle of proportionality. That is, they must strike a balance between the gravity of the offence and the weight of proof on the one hand, and the protection of privacy on the other. Finally, restrictions exist regarding the use that can be made of the information provided.

BANKING SECRECY AND TAXATION

How the Swiss system works. As regards taxation, Swiss citizens have two inseparable rights:

- They vote on their level of taxation.
- They report their income and wealth, without the tax authorities enjoying extensive powers to spy on them through the banking system.

These rights are consistent with the relationship between the citizen and the state in a federal system, the latter being at the service of the former, not the other way around.

However, to protect the community's fiscal interests, the state has the following mechanisms:

- a 35 percent withholding tax, collected from domestic issuers and debtors on every dividend or interest payment;
- a harsh enforcement system at the administrative level (with fines and a reversal of the burden of proof that criminal law would not allow); and
- criminal proceedings in the case of fiscal fraud.

In short, the Swiss system aims at guaranteeing the privacy of the taxpayer vis-à-vis the state while ensuring safeguards to protect the tax department's interests.

This system works. At any rate, the level of tax avoidance is no higher in Switzerland than in other countries. Although this area eludes, by definition, official statistics and is therefore difficult to assess, two indices point in the right direction. First, the relative weight of direct taxation is higher in Switzerland compared to most other countries, which tends to prove that the collection of direct taxes does not pose a particular problem in this country.[5] Second, it is generally acknowledged that Switzerland is one of the countries where the underground economy is the least widespread.[6]

This tends to show that the Swiss taxation system, whilst it limits the right of the state to access the taxpayers' bank information, takes into account, in a fairly balanced way, the obviously divergent interests of both the individual and the community and is, above all, well-accepted by taxpayers.

Tax competition is good, not bad, for the taxpayer. A number of international organizations (including the OECD and the European Union) have embarked on a crusade against "harmful tax competition." According to their views, this form of competition is ruinous. Tax competition tends to reduce the tax burden on highly mobile production factors such as capital, whilst it increases the tax burden on less mobile factors such as labor. The fact that tax authorities have limited access to bank information is described as a problem in this respect.

It should be noted, at the outset, that competition is always considered harmful by those who are exposed to it. Whilst the fiscal authorities complain about reduced tax revenues, the statistics—also published by the OECD—speak another language. In fact, they show that the tax proceeds in OECD countries have steadily grown over the years.

Despite globalization, liberalization of capital movements, and the use of technology by financial operators (which are the three main developments described as providing taxpayers with new opportunities to escape taxes, legally or not), the rate of taxes levied by OECD countries in proportion to their GDP has increased from 32.8 percent in 1980 to 35.6 percent in 1990 and 37.2 percent in 1997. Of course, when OECD's tax experts write about "vanishing taxpayers," these figures are not mentioned. The reality shows that the allegedly harmful tax competition has not deprived governments of their financial resources.

Interestingly, the pressure felt by high-tax countries does not seem important enough to induce such countries to reduce the tax burden put on their citizens. Sweden, for instance, managed to push her revenues from 51.9 percent to 53 percent of GDP from 1997 to 1998.[7] In Sweden, like most OECD countries, income and wealth taxes represent the main part of state revenues.

A country's ability to withstand tax competition has little to do with the powers given to its tax authorities to access bank information, but a lot to do with the right incentives given to taxpayers. In a recent economic survey on Switzerland, the OECD acknowledges this fact (at least indirectly) when it writes:

> The Swiss tax system appears to be fairly robust in the face of increasing globalization and financial mobility. In contrast to many European countries, Switzerland has not been constrained to shift the weight of taxation from capital towards labour and consumption, which are relatively immobile bases. One factor contributing to this outcome is that tax incentives for saving through pension funds and life insurance companies are very attractive, dimming households' interest in shifting financial assets abroad to evade taxation. Low marginal income tax rates in certain cantons go in the same direction.[8]

In short, each country is responsible for ensuring that she has a fair tax system and that her citizens are subject to a reasonable level of taxation. What can be considered as reasonable depends very much on cultural habits and political priorities, which can only be set at a national level. Governments have to be aware of the fact that an increased tax burden weakens their competitive position in relation to other countries, and this ultimately leads to ever-higher levels of taxation. If taxpayers shun taxes, the reason must primarily be sought in their own country. One can only guess how taxes would soar if competition in the area of taxation was more limited than it already is.

Putting the blame on the insufficient access to bank information in other countries is too simple an answer for a complex problem.

BANKING SECRECY AND THE SUPERVISION OF BANKS AND FINANCIAL MARKETS

Sound banking supervision. The duty of discretion applies in effect to the business relations between banks and their customers. This duty does not hamper an effective system of banking supervision, such as that carried out in Switzerland by the Federal Banking Commission. Swiss legislation concerning bank supervision has three distinct characteristics:

- The Federal Banking Commission, in its capacity as a supervisory body, has the power to call on banks to hand over all information and documents it needs to carry out its function. The Commission's employees can work with this information but vis-à-vis outsiders they are obliged to observe secrecy requirements just as bankers are.
- The Commission is also empowered to pass on to foreign authorities supervising banks and financial markets confidential information or documents not available to the general public according to internationally recognized standards. However, information concerning individual bank customers may be released only under certain administrative procedures under which the customer has the opportunity to defend his rights.
- The Swiss Federal Banking Law gives foreign supervisory bodies the power to carry out on-the-spot checks in Switzerland. These checks can be carried out on risk, systemic, organizational, and behavioral items, but not on individual bank depositors.

Insider trading and stock-price manipulations are banned. It is by now widely agreed that stock markets must be fair. Switzerland has outlawed insider trading (since 1988) and stock-price manipulation (since 1997). The discussion about the legitimacy of anti-insider-trading laws has been settled in most countries, although some economists argue that insider traders in fact improve the information of market participants via the price mechanism. International standards have been set; insider-trading laws are similar across developed countries. So customers of Swiss banks will not be allowed to take advantage of banking confidentiality in order to trade on inside information. But the administrative procedures in place in Switzerland will allow banks' clients to defend their rights to confidentiality to a greater extent than in many other countries.

FUTURE CHALLENGES TO FINANCIAL PRIVACY IN SWITZERLAND

DOMESTIC POLITICAL SUPPORT FOR FINANCIAL PRIVACY

The vast majority of the Swiss people support laws protecting financial privacy, although left-wing parties—in the minority—are traditionally critical of banking secrecy. In 1984, the Socialist Party put forward a constitutional initiative proposing that banking-secrecy requirements be lifted, but it was rejected by 73 percent of voters and by all the cantons. All opinion polls carried out since then on this subject show that the proportion of the population in favor of maintaining this legislation is very stable.

In Switzerland, the protection of financial privacy in person-to-person relations does not seem to pose any serious problems. The Federal Law on Data Protection prohibits companies from misusing their clients' personal data and obliges them to give access, on request, to this data. The generally prevailing culture in the country makes any abusive use of this information unlikely. Privacy violations are more likely to arise in personal relationships or in relation to medical issues rather than with financial information. Today in Switzerland, the level of public confidence with regard to the security of financial data held by banks and companies is generally high. The impression that personal privacy is at risk is not widespread, but the development of information technology could change this situation, as it has in other countries.

With respect to the relationship between the state and individuals, the main area of concern is taxation. As discussed above, Switzerland has set up a system of tax collection that takes a balanced approach toward the collective interests of the state (which must collect taxes) and the individual interests of her citizens (who do not want to allow the state to invade their financial privacy). This system enjoys wide political support.

INTERNATIONAL ISSUES

There is a consensus in Switzerland that banking-secrecy rules must give way in the fight against criminal behavior. Problems created by violations of economic regulations and international organized crime, as well as the need to improve the system of international judicial cooperation, have led Parliament to modify a number of laws in recent years. These laws are being enforced with success, as witnessed by a number of cases that have caught the attention of the media.

These cases are sometimes described as "scandals" by the press. This shows, however, a certain degree of misunderstanding of the real situation. Humans are not faultless; expecting a large international financial center to have only clients that are perfectly honest is mere wishful thinking. The importance is to catch those clients who are dishonest and ensure that they do not go unpunished. Although it is always a disappointment to learn that criminals exist, the fact that the system allows for their prosecution should not be looked at as a defeat, but as a victory.

International taxation will remain a problem because national tax systems will continue to differ from one country to another. In this field, the protection that Swiss banks provide their clients gives rise to a certain amount of criticism, especially from countries that care less than Switzerland about their citizens' privacy. These critics think the tax authorities should have full access to banking information, even beyond national borders. This, however, raises very complex problems concerning the harmonization of tax laws, a difficult issue.

At the level of general principle, taxation is a relatively simple matter about which rational minds can easily agree. However, as soon as discussions reach a greater level of detail, agreement is more difficult. Because of the very sensitive political character of taxation, each country ends up defending her own system and practices, to the detriment of the others. Sooner rather than later, negotiators stumble on questions related to national sovereignty.

No organization has had as much experience in these problems as the European Union, charged with adopting directives that will subsequently have to be transposed into the national legislations of its member countries. In 1998, the European Commission proposed a new directive aimed at solving some of these problems.[9] Nine years earlier, the EC had come up against insurmountable difficulties because of a previous project that had not succeeded in obtaining the necessary consensus. The 1998 proposal is still on the table and the subject of arduous negotiations within the EU. Switzerland, not a member of the EU, has already indicated willingness to negotiate her part in a system that ensures an agreed minimum taxation of the income on savings. But her government has also clearly indicated that it will not surrender the protection of financial privacy guaranteed by the Swiss legal system.

CONCLUSION

Every state under the rule of law protects the privacy of her citizens. In Switzerland, this right to discretion has developed over time, becoming established in the legal system and firmly anchored in the values of the country. Banking confidentiality can be compared to the duty of professional confidentiality to which doctors and lawyers are subject. Swiss legislation meets the highest international standards when it comes to fighting organized crime and money laundering: It offers criminals no protection whatsoever. This is why Switzerland can claim to be one of the "cleanest" financial centers in the world today. The country will, however, continue to protect the financial privacy of legitimate clients—be they Swiss or foreign—who are merely trying to protect their financial assets. Although Europe is, fortunately, no longer the dangerous place that it was half a century ago, there is ample evidence that the need for a safe shelter still exists for minorities in various, less fortunate, parts of the world.

Notes

[1] OECD: Improving Access to Bank Information for Tax Purposes, ref. DAFFE/CFA (2000) 4/Final.

[2] For further information, cf. Robert U. Vogler, "Wie entstand eigentlich das Schweizer Bankgeheimnis?" in *Neue Zürcher Zeitung*, March 18-19, 2000.

[3] Article 47 of the Federal Banking Law makes any breach of banking secrecy a criminal offence punishable by imprisonment for up to six months or by fines up to CHF 50,000 (approximately US $30,000), or both.

[4] Switzerland is a semi-direct democracy. Her citizens may at any time ask to

modify the federal Constitution. To succeed, 100,000 signatures must be collected within 18 months approving the proposed amendment (this is called a "people's initiative"). After examination of the amendment's text, the "Sovereign," *i.e.* the people and the cantons (Swiss equivalent of American states), vote on the initiative. If a double majority accepts the amendment, the Constitution is amended and Parliament must modify federal law to conform. The people may also be asked to vote by referendum on the laws adopted by Parliament. Within three months of the adoption of a new law, 50,000 voters can oblige the electorate to vote on any new law, confirming it or rejecting it as a whole.

[5] According to OECD statistics, direct taxation of individuals (on income, capital gains, and wealth) as a proportion of total tax revenues account for 52.8 percent in Switzerland, 47.9 percent in the US, 41.0 percent in Germany, 29.8 percent in the United Kingdom, and 24.1 percent in France (last available figures: 1997).

[6] According to a study performed by the Johannes Kepler University in Linz (Austria), Switzerland stands (after Austria, the United States, and Japan) at the very bottom of a list of 29 countries ranked by the importance of the underground economy as a percentage of official GDP. Cf. *The Economist*, August 28, 1999, p. 63.

[7] By comparison, the equivalent figure in Switzerland is 34.8 percent of GDP (but rising and many observers—including the authors of this article—consider that she would be well advised to stop that trend).

[8] OECD Economic Surveys 1998-1999: Switzerland, Paris, 1999.

[9] Cf. European Commission's May 1998 proposed directive on taxation of interest payments (COM98 295).

Financial Privacy and Data Protection in Europe

Alfred Büllesbach

INTRODUCTION

This chapter provides a perspective on data protection in Europe, using German laws and the European Data Protection Directive as models for a pan-European financial-privacy and security regime. Section I introduces the principles of European data protection, recognizing the similarities and differences in legal regimes among European Union countries. Section II describes the relationship between data protection and bank secrecy, showing why the two do not conflict. The requirements for processing and using personal data in Germany are outlined in Section III. Section IV discusses the applicability of German law to financial-services providers, while Section V outlines the conditions imposed on financial institutions that collect, process, and use personal data. Section VI describes the conditions for transfers of personal data to third parties, including data exchanges within the credit-protection system. Section VII stresses the importance of the legal entity that conducts data processing on behalf of others. Section VIII discusses cross-border data flows and payment transactions. Additional obligations of financial institutions as data controllers and individuals' rights are covered in Section IX. Section X concerns the distribution of financial services via such new media as the Internet. The supervisory requirements for data-protection activities, and the role of the corporate data-protection officer, are described in Section XI. Finally, Section XII discusses data protection as a self-regulation task and a challenge for global companies.

I. PRINCIPLES OF DATA PROTECTION IN EUROPE

Despite differences among the different countries in Europe, generally, the concept of data protection in Europe: takes the form of a system of regulation governing the collection, processing, and use of personal data; grants specific rights to individuals affected by data processing; and imposes obligations on individuals responsible for data processing. This approach is very different from that of the United States. The objective of European data protection is not the protection of data, but rather the protection of the personal rights of those whose data is being processed. The essential core of data protection in Europe is described in the German Federal Act on Data Protection (Bundesdatenschutz-gesetz—BDSG) as follows: "The purpose of this law is to protect the personal rights of individuals from becoming infringed upon by the use of their personal data."

The development of Europe's approach to data protection stems from specific historical and political experiences with dictatorial systems of power in parts of Europe. But today, the progressive development in the area of information technology plays an important role.

The early phase of electronic data processing was influenced by the use of mainframe computer systems, which instigated the fear of citizens being watched by "Big Brother" during widespread data collection and processing. The progressive technical development in the information-technology area and especially the increasing interconnection of computers will continue to simplify the collection and gathering of information, and intensify its processing and use.

Attempts to regulate these developments resulted in the enactment of data-protection laws in the 1970s. The German province of Hesse adopted the first law in 1972, while Sweden was the first European country to enact a data-protection law, in 1973. In the population-census order of the Federal Constitutional Court in 1983, the highest German court developed the "right to informational self-determination" so that individuals could decide what others, especially the government, were allowed to know about them.

The right to informational self-determination acts as a right of the concerned party to defend himself against those who seek to collect and process data about him. When infringed, this legal construction creates compensation claims for misused information, provisions for rectification, and damages. The law also includes other basic rights that protect the personality. For example, there are legal protections for securing telecommunication secrecy. Parallel to this, extensive data-protection legislation has developed that includes area-specific regulations for processing personal data.

In the past, area-specific regulations mainly addressed the public sector; but now there is a tendency to regulate the private sector, especially in the area of innovative information and communication technology. In this context, the Telecommunication Act is noteworthy, as section 11 codifies data-protection requirements in the telecommunication area. In addition, data-protection regulations in the Teleservices Data Protection Act (Teledienstedatenschutzgesetz—TDDSG) govern institutions that provide "telebanking." The TDDSG is part of the Information and Communication Services Act (Informations- und Kommunikationsdienstegesetzes—IuKDG) enacted in 1997. Credit institutions and financial-service providers must observe effective data-protection regulations when collecting, processing, and using personal data, and they must also provide their services so the right to informational self-determination of the parties affected by data processing is not infringed.

In Europe, the right to data protection is generally recognized as a human right, as described in Article 8 of the European Convention for the Protection of Human Rights and Fundamental Freedoms. The establishment of data-protection requirements in the respective national legal systems can vary. In Denmark, for example, the data-protection law[1] that applies to the public sector differs from the data-protection law for private enterprise.[2] A general data-protection law with regulations for the public sector contained in a special paragraph exists in Luxembourg,[3] the Netherlands,[4] Austria,[5] Switzerland,[6] and Spain.[7]

In Germany, the BDSG provides specific regulations for the public sector while it also regulates the authorization of processing personal data by private corporations. The control of data protection at federal agencies is exercised by the Federal Data Protection Commissioner. Private corporations or institutions processing personal data are supervised by the responsible authority according to national law. Owing to the federal structure of Germany, the individual Länder (states) also have extensive data-protection regulations, which are carried out by the Länder administrations.

There are no distinctions between the rules governing the public and private sector in Belgium,[8] Estonia,[9] Finland,[10] France,[11] Greece,[12] Great Britain,[13] Ireland,[14] Italy,[15] Norway,[16] Poland,[17] Portugal,[18] Russia,[19] Sweden,[20] the Slovak Republic,[21] the Czech Republic,[22] and Hungary.[23]

Besides regional and national data-protection regulations, international regulations also must be considered. These regulations are not represented in the form of directly effective law for lack of direct domestic applicability to financial-service providers. In 1981, the Council of Europe passed the Convention for the Protection of Individuals with Regard to Automatic Processing of Personal Data, which contains suggestions for the formulation of national data-protection laws. Following its ratification in 1985, this international agreement at first was enacted in only the following five countries: France, Norway, Sweden, Spain, and the Federal Republic of Germany.

On October 24, 1995, the Directive of the European Parliament and of the Council on the Protection of Individuals with Regard to the Processing of Personal Data and on the Free Movement of Such Data was enacted. Not all member states have carried out this directive, which was supposed to have been incorporated into the various countries' national laws by October 24, 1998. Parallel to the EU Data Protection Directive, the so-called Telecommunication Data Protection Directive[24] had to be implemented, a process that still has not been successful in Germany. The implementation will become relevant for financial-service providers with regard to Article 12, which regulates the authorization of unsolicited telephone calls.

After complete implementation of the Data Protection Directive, a standardized legal data protection will be created in the member states. Data can then be transferred directly within the EU domestic market, facilitating the cross-border flow of financial data within the EU. But transferring data to so-called third countries remains problematic under legal data-protection standards, and is only authorized when the third country shows an adequate level of data protection corresponding to the EU standard. In June of 2000, representatives of the United States and Europe reached an agreement on privacy principles that US companies operating in Europe could adopt to get a "safe harbor" from liability under EU law.

The Signatory Act[25] establishes general requirements for the secure use of digital signatures in legal and commercial transactions. On December 13, 1999, the Directive of the European Parliament and Council Regarding Common General Requirements for Electronic Signatures was adopted and was ultimately enacted on January 19, 2000. The objective of this directive is to facilitate the use of electronic signatures and to contribute to their legal recognition. While implementing this objective, the guideline distinguishes between "electronic" and "advanced electronic" signatures. For advanced electronic signatures, technical and organizational requirements for "certified service providers" and for producing these signatures are formulated. The directive must be implemented into national law by July 19, 2001, and will result in changes in the signature law.

An additional EU directive regarding distance marketing of financial services is under development.[26] This is designed to provide a smoothly operating and secure domestic market for these services for consumers and financial-service providers. The directive does not affect those rights granted to consumers by community regulations regarding the protection of personal data and the private sphere.

In September, 1999, the European Commission presented an Amended Proposal for a Directive of the European Parliament and Council regarding specific aspects of electronic-payment transactions in the domestic market ("E-Commerce Directive"). The draft, in consideration reason (20), refers to the obligation of member states to create secure communication requirements for the consumer resulting from Community regulations ensuring the protection of personal data and the private sphere.

II. THE RELATIONSHIP BETWEEN DATA PROTECTION AND BANK SECRECY[27]

Under standard business conditions, banks are usually bound to secrecy regarding all customer-related facts and values. This bank secrecy is a product of the contractual relationship between bank and customer, while data protection is imposed by act of law, for example, by the BDSG. The contractual obligation to secrecy does not refer to any special official or professional. Nevertheless, bank secrecy is granted a special position,[28] as it is legally recognized in investigations conducted by the Internal Revenue Service (IRS). It may restrict the investigative authority of the IRS on the one hand and the bank's obligation to disclose information to the IRS on the other hand. The obligation to disclose information is required only in criminal tax proceedings and other exceptional cases found in Section 30 of the Tax Code. The IRS must pay particular consideration to the trust relationship between the credit institutions and their customers when investigating the facts of a case.

Data protection and bank secrecy represent two independent entities that do not oppose one another. Rather, they co-exist as long as they do not overlap. Before a bank discloses customer data to third parties, it must observe both sets of legal obligations, at least when its customers are natural persons, for the BDSG protects, unlike bank secrecy, only natural persons.[29] Unlike bank secrecy, predominately relevant only in connection to third parties, data protection also regulates the collection, storage, changing, or use of data (*e.g.* for marketing purposes) by the bank.

III. PRINCIPLES FOR PROCESSING PERSONAL DATA IN GERMANY

The following central principles must be observed under the BDSG when processing and using personal data:

- ensuring the existence of specific legal authorization or consent by the concerned individual;
- observing the principle that data should not be used for purposes for which it was not collected;

- binding employees to data secrecy;
- observing the rights of individuals with regard to notice, access to their files, the rectification of errors, the timely deletion of files, and objections to direct marketing;
- assuring technical data security.

Several principles of modern data-protection law are found in the new BDSG, such as prevention (the principle of processing as little data as possible) and economizing. Compliance with these principles is monitored. Internal data-protection control is the duty of the corporate data-protection officer. Externally, authorities appointed by national law must exercise supervision, control authority, and monitor compliance with registration obligations (to which specific data-processing centers, especially corporations that process data by order of others, are subject). All parties concerned, including individual consumers, can bring issues before these authorities. A monetary fine will be imposed for violations of the regulations, which could lead to the enforcement of claims for damages.

IV. APPLICABILITY OF GERMAN LAW TO FINANCIAL-SERVICE PROVIDERS
SECTORS OF APPLICATION

The general provisions of the BDSG, as well as specific regulations for the private sector (Sections 27-38), apply to financial-service providers under private law in the absence of special data-protection rights for this sector. The regulations for public institutions (Sections 12-26) apply to federal credit institutions operated under public law, such as the Deutsche Bundesbank. In addition, credit institutions of the Bundesländer organized under public law, the Landesbanken, are subject to the data-protection laws of their respective Land. The following refers to financial-service providers as private enterprises.

TERRITORIAL AREA OF APPLICATION

Unless the data processing occurs within the national territory of the Federal Republic of Germany, the BDSG applies according to the territorial principle. This remains true even if a phase of processing such as storage occurs domestically. The BDSG is also relevant when data are collected through an affiliate branch of a bank in a foreign country, but are stored by a domestic branch.

After the implementation of the EU Data Protection Directive, data collected through a domestic, independent subsidiary in Germany and processed in a foreign country will also be subject to the BDSG. The location of data processing will no longer generally determine which national data-protection right is effective but, rather, the location of the processing officer. A member country should allow the "export" of its citizens' usual data-protection rights within the commercial territory of the EU without being restricted by unfamiliar data-protection regulations of other countries. The BDSG draft[30] formulates this as follows:

> This law is not applicable if the responsible location situated in another Member State of the EU collects, processes or uses personal data domestically, in other words, this is carried out by a domestic establishment. This law is applicable as long as the responsible location situated outside the EU acquires, processes or uses data domestically.

These provisions are not effective if foreign locations have domestic establishments.[31] In such cases, they are required to comply with German data-protection laws. They are also not effective in cases in which data collection, processing, and use are carried out within the EU by financial-service providers with headquarters outside the EU, to avoid making a data-protection standard lower than the EU's available to the regulated parties. In these cases, the territorial principle applies once again.

PERTINENT CONCEPTS AND DEFINITIONS

Only "personal data," defined as "detailed information about personal or factual relationships of a specific or definable natural person," are affected. Information about deceased or legal persons is not covered by the BDSG, but could be covered by other laws, such as those describing general personality rights. The BDSG does not protect aggregated or anonymous data. A person is "definable" when data that does not refer to a person by name can be combined with additional information to supply a personal reference. The account number of a customer, for example, is personal data, since it can assign a numerical sequence of events to an individual person based on its records.

In cashless payment transactions, it can be difficult to clarify the question of personal reference.[32] For example, a retailer participating in an electronic-cash-based procedure based on the promise of payment of a card-issuing institution cannot make any claims against this institution for the release of the name or the address of the card holder, if the data is not available due to an illegible signature or the use of a PIN.

The BDSG applies to specific activities relevant to data protection in private enterprise, such as the collection, processing, and use of personal data, whether these activities proceed automatically or when the data are organized or evaluated in files. "Processing" represents a collective concept, covering storing, altering, transferring, blocking, and deleting.

The law designates as "data controller" each person or organization that stores personal data for its own purposes or has others store the data. The data controller is entirely responsible for the authorization of processing and is the contact partner for the enforcement of rights on behalf of concerned individuals. Consequently, the new BDSG will replace the term "data controller" with that of the "data processing responsible." A bank as a legal entity, for example, is responsible, not the individual employees or the legally independent data-processing agency.

When an employee or agency collects, processes, or uses data under instructions from the controller, these activities do not result in "transfers of data" to "third parties" in the sense of the BDSG (such transfers are only permitted under certain conditions). Since the law is consistent with corporate law, affiliate branches are assigned to the controller; under the BDSG, this will be applicable to domestic branches. Also, the BDSG does not recognize any so-called corporate privileges; associated corporations in a corporate group are considered third parties in relation to one another under data-protection law.

V. CONDITIONS FOR PERMISSIBLY COLLECTING, PROCESSING, AND USING PERSONAL DATA BY FINANCIAL-SERVICE PROVIDERS

The processing and use of personal data is permitted only if a law permits, or when the concerned individual has consented. While the BDSG currently in effect does not subject data collection to this authorization provision, the amendment of the BDSG stipulates that this legal provision will cover all processing phases in the future.

RELEVANT LEGAL REGULATIONS OUTSIDE THE BDSG

The following regulations outside the BDSG are examples of laws that authorize financial institutions to process personal data under legal obligations related to the need for transactional documentation, notice, and information:

- Data collected under Section 31 of the Securities Trading Act about the financial situation of the client should be stored under Section 34 of that act, which regulates recording obligations.
- According to Sections 2 and 9 of the Money Laundering Act (MLA) in connection with Section 154 of the Tax Code, financial institutions must, under their identification obligations, store the acquired data of depositors of cash amounts over 30,000 DM. According to the MLA, this data can be used to fight money laundering, for corresponding criminal-prosecution measures, as well as for information in taxation procedures.
- General accounting or recording obligations (Section 256 of the Commercial Code, Section 319 of the Tax Code) can legitimize data-processing activities according to commercial and fiscal regulations.
- Special data-protection regulations of the Civil Action Code in Sections 915 ff. and the List of Insolvent Debtors Code must be observed when accessing data in the debtors' index at municipal courts and for their further use by credit-information

systems in the credit industry. The SCHUFA,[33] as one of the most important German credit-information systems, is authorized to transfer data from these indexes to establish and manage a private index. The authorized storage duration of such data is restricted.

- The German Banking Act (GBA) requires specific loans, such as large-scale loans of the Deutsche Bundesbank, to be disclosed. Registration obligations under corporate law set out by the GBA may also be relevant.
- In the case of a deceased bank customer, transmission obligations of the bank are applicable to the IRS according to the Inheritance Tax Law (ITL).
- According to Section 45 of the ITL, a credit institution also has informational obligations related to the need for control of investment income-tax payments. The institution also must respect official inspection rights of the GBA and other regulations that impose information obligations in taxation procedures, public-investigation procedures, and criminal proceedings.
- Employment offices have information rights under a means test (Section 315 of the Social Security Code Vol. III) before they agree to pay out unemployment benefits.
- Finally, an institution that acts as an employer towards Social Security carriers also has information-collecting obligations.

In all of these cases, the data must not be used for purposes for which is was not collected. For example, the use of this data for advertising purposes would not be authorized.

Legitimation under the BDSG

Section 28 of the BDSG concerns data processing for an entity's own corporate purposes. Data processing on behalf of other entities and offered as a service, such as credit-information systems or directory distributors, is regulated by Section 29.

Data processing to fulfill a contract with a client.
According to Section 28, storing, changing, transferring, and using personal data under contractual obligation to the con-

cerned customer is permitted. The financial-service provider is authorized to process and use all data required to carry out the services requested by the client. The decisive contractual relationship for the purpose of the requirement may be seen not only in individual contracts, such as processing an electronic-payment transfer or a credit-card transaction, but also in an invested long-term business connection.

Looser contractual-promise relationships are equivalent to contracts, provided a concrete contract initiation is discussed. For example, a financial institution's one-sided appeals or advertisements for new customers would not be relevant. Under a current account agreement (for, say, a checking account), the following information would be relevant in addition to the basic data of the customer such as name and address: credit line, conditions, securities, credit standing, as well as marital status, income, assets, liabilities, and prior convictions. Should the customer only be interested in accumulating assets in a savings account, relevant credit-standing data cannot be retrieved by the financial institution in the absence of the possibility of an overdraft.

The gathering of customer data common in the credit-card industry for the purpose of producing user profiles should be included under specific requirements of credit-card contracts. This gathering is supported by the fact that unusual transactions are quickly recognized, cards are blocked earlier, and the liability risk of the customer is minimized. Based on the earmarking principle, other uses such as a targeted customer appeal in the form of special personalized offers would be excluded; these uses would no longer be covered by the original contract. The disclosure of bank-customer data to third parties for advertising and marketing purposes would also be unauthorized, unless the customer consents to this disclosure and the bank is no longer bound by bank secrecy.

Data processing and use without contract or when exceeding contract. If neither a contractual relationship nor a similar contractual-promise relationship exists, or if personal data is used beyond what the contractual relationship permits, for example, for advertising purposes, data use is permitted according to Section 28 of the BDSG. Such use is allowed when it is required to preserve the justified interests of the financial institution and there is no reason to assume that the protection-worthy interest of the concerned individual regarding the exclusion of data processing or data use predominates.

Justified interest of the financial-service provider not only is considered in the case of legal concern, but also when it concerns a purpose carried out according to the general sense of justice according to economic, social, or cultural needs. This is especially true for the economically important area of marketing.

The establishment of a noncustomer file for expansion purposes, to enable offering target-group-oriented products or services based on these data, would be permitted if the data were legally acquired from another location such as a directory distributor, or when the data originate from generally accessible resources (*e.g.* address and telephone books) and the use does predominate over the protection-worthy interests of the concerned party.

In practice, the balancing of interests required by law is predominately handled in summary. One can simply assert that the processing and use of data for advertising purposes are authorized so long as the opposing interests of the concerned individual do not obviously predominate, as they would if the customer made use of his objection right according to Section 28, Paragraph 3 of the BDSG. Implementing the EU Data Protection Directive will intensify these obligations, as concerned parties must be informed by the time of the first contact[34] about the origin of their data and their right to object to the data being used for the purposes of advertising, marketing, or public-opinion survey.

The use of customer data from a contractual relationship to produce behavioral or personality profiles for general advertising purposes may often represent an excessive encroachment on the informational right to self-determination of the customer. This authorization barrier must be especially observed in view of data-warehouse and data-mining concepts for advertising purposes.[35] A detailed evaluation of personal data that causes the client to become a "transparent" target of advertising measures need not be tolerated.

Credit scoring and "Automated Individual Decisions" under the EU Data Protection Directive.

In the current version of the BDSG, the use of personal data by computer-supported decision processes is not specifically regulated. During a scoring procedure, a score value is generated from a database by mathematical and statistical procedures that give the probability of a specific event occurring. The question of how relevant this procedure is to data protection is controversial.

The banking industry holds the belief that the prognosis summarized in a score value does not represent an appraisal of the credit standing of a concrete customer.[36] But the data-protection supervisory authorities argue that by establishing a score value, the data of the concerned party would be expanded by a value. This value would be based merely on the experiences with credit histories of other customers, and would provide a comparison with other customers by assigning a position within a reference group to the concerned customer.[37]

Article 15 of the EU Data Protection Directive will be included in the German act, which regulates the authorization of "automated individual decisions." Each person will have the right

> not to be subjected to a decision having legal consequences or one that would cause considerable infringement, which is exclusively issued based on an automated processing of data for the purpose of evaluating individual aspects of a person, such as career capabilities, credit standing, reliability or behavior.

While one may argue the scoring procedure is merely a decision tool of loan officers, whose personal evaluation of the overall situation determines the final outcome, the future BDSG explicitly stipulates that credit scoring should be regarded as an automated individual decision. The banking industry will have to adjust to this, perhaps by granting internal complaint possibilities to concerned parties.

THE IMPORTANCE OF CONSENT

The permission standards within and outside of the BDSG are equivalent to a consent by the customer. Customer consent is frequently used to legitimate data processing, especially in the banking area, even when the processing of the customer's data without explicit consent would be legitimized because of the contractual relationship. In such cases, the consent is of declarational importance, especially when it is connected to relevant legal regulations as well as to the type and extent of processing.

The extent of the authorized processing can be expanded with written consent. Verbal consent over the phone or a "mouse click" is not sufficient. An exception allowing "electronic" consent in the area of home banking and only applicable when using digital signatures is contained in Section 3 of the Teleservices Data Protection Act.

Pre-formulated consent statements are usually a component of a contractual agreement and are subject accordingly to content control under the Act on General Commercial Requirements (AGBG). A violation of the AGBG occurs when the pre-formulated consent is too generalized, when consent should be asked for each processing of all data, or if nothing is said in regard to the purpose of processing.

In addition, the customer can be disadvantaged in connection with the use of the consent. For example, when an application to open an account includes a pre-formulated statement saying the customer agrees to the transfer of his data to cooperation partners of the bank in the corporate group (so-called corporate group clause), a violation against the AGBG has occurred in most cases. Since the BDSG does not recognize corporate privileges, but rather considers each legally independent corporation as an independent data controller, such a generic corporate clause would lead to a situation where the group of those able to use his data would not be clear to the customer.

A clause is considered legal when it clearly reveals that the granting of an approval is optional and that the opening of an account is not dependent on whether the customer decides to release his data throughout the corporation. In this connection the "corporate clauses" or the "exclusive financial clauses" developed by the Central Loan Committee in cooperation with the Data Protection Supervisory Authority of the German Bundesländer represented in the "Düsseldorf Group" are an example.

The SCHUFA clause, in which the customer would agree that the financial-service provider may transfer to the Credit Protection Organization data the customer already released by filling out specific applications (for example, for opening an account or granting financing aid), has come under review by Germany's highest court. It was noted in criticism that the consent regarding the transfer of "data of the borrower when processing a loan" disregarded the determination order. The banking industry requires that clauses be distinctly formulated and include a notation regarding the extent of the data transfer.

Still unclear is the question whether this ruling concerns a pre-formulated statement subject to content control according to the AGBG, when the financial institution requests that the customer state whether he agrees to be informed by phone about new products and services by checking either "yes" or "no." Since a high-court decision has not yet been issued regarding this question, the banking industry has refrained from including such a telephone-advertising clause in the General Commercial Requirements.

VI. CONDITIONS FOR TRANSFERRING PERSONAL DATA TO THIRD PARTIES OR DATA EXCHANGE WITH CREDIT-PROTECTION SYSTEMS

The transfer of customer data to a credit-protection organization is not regularly supported by a contract with the customer. Consequently, this requires the balancing of justified interests between the institution, a third party, or the general public,[38] and the protection-worthy interests of the customer. Bank secrecy is not an indication of an opposing interest of the customer, since the customer has released the credit institution by the signature of the SCHUFA clause.

The basic interest of the credit institutions connected to a credit information or protection system is to transfer data regarding the nature, number, and extent of current liabilities, to facilitate the evaluation of the credit standing of a customer interested in obtaining credit. For this purpose, the regional SCHUFA organizations have been established. According to the principle of mutuality, these organizations provide credit information on the condition that corporations requesting their services are obligated to contribute and update necessary data on behalf of the system.

The transfer of data from the database of the SCHUFA organizations is based on the justified interest of associated corporations in the sense of Section 29, Paragraph 2 of the BDSG. Not every economic risk would be a reason for data to be retrieved. While a contractual partnership with SCHUFA is now restricted to corporations granting money and product loans (with an exception for cellular phone providers, whose credit risk is considered comparable), the group of contract partners will be wider in the future due to the development of a new system.[39]

In connection with the cooperation regarding a credit-protection system, the purpose-binding principle must be considered, according to which the receiver of data is allowed to use such data only for immanent system purposes.

Despite the basically justified interests of the institutions connected to the system, it remains necessary to balance others' interests in each incidence. In view of the consequences that the transfer of specific data can have for credit applicants, a distinction must be made between the "hard" and "soft" credit-standing data. Hard credit-standing data, such as the opening of a bankruptcy proceeding or the affidavit of the debtor according to Section 807 of the Code of Civil Procedure (Zivilprozessordnung—ZPO) by which his insolvency is known to the court, can be transferred. But the transfer of soft credit-standing data from or to the credit-protection system must be preceded by a concrete individual-case inspection. A situation where soft data is used is when a lender has cancelled a standing credit and is involved in a lawsuit with the borrower regarding the right of credit cancellation.

Also, the SCHUFA is obligated to document all retrievals from their database. If the data transfer occurs in an automated procedure, the retrieving location (the financial institution) must carry out the recording obligation.

VII. THE LEGAL ENTITY DOING "DATA PROCESSING ON BEHALF OF OTHERS"

When personal data is transferred from one data controller to another, this represents a data transfer according to Section 3 of the BDSG. This processing stage, like others, is subject to authorization conditions. An exception is granted when data is given to an entity such as a service center with the order to process or use such data for the controller, who remains responsible for obtaining legal authorization, especially in the case of information from an external concerned party. Section 3 clarifies that the contractor is not a "third party" in relation to the customer. The following criteria are prerequisites for authorized data processing on behalf of others:

The controller must carefully select the contractor to carry out the order according to instructions. The placing of an order must follow in writing. The individual processing phases must originate with the order; so must technical organizational measures with which the contractor must ensure the requirement to maintain data security is carried out. Furthermore, the controller must make sure the contractor complies with his registration obligation to the supervisory authority. The contractor must also ensure that his employees adhere to confidentiality obligations when handling data and must appoint a data-protection officer. In addition to technical and organizational operation of data-processing centers, typical services of a contractor can also include carrying out market analysis with data prepared by the customer or creating technical requirements for home banking.

When complete corporate functions are outsourced, the legal framework for data processing on behalf of others is no longer applicable. If the contracted corporation acts as the responsible party, taking over the payroll or salary accounting and bookkeeping duties, such a service is no longer designated as a supporting (technical) help function. The necessary data-transfer rules relevant to a *de facto* transfer are then subject to the requirements according to Sections 4 and 28 of the BDSG.

When outsourcing, the Banking Act must be observed, under which the financial institution must obtain the legally required instructional authority on a contractual basis and incorporate the transferred areas of responsibility under control procedures.

Under Section 3 of the BDSG, foreign contractors are handled as third parties. After the implementation of the EU Data Protection Directive, the treatment of foreign contractors must be differentiated from that of domestic contractors as follows: Service providers located in an EU member state are treated like domestic contractors[40] based on the achieved reconciliation of privacy-protection standards. For contractors outside the EU, the general regulations as well as the requirements concerning data transfers in third countries apply.

VIII. CROSS-BORDER DATA AND PAYMENT TRANSACTIONS

So far, the BDSG includes no special regulations governing the transmission of personal data to nonofficial bodies abroad. However, ultimately, the same conditions apply to cross-border as to domestic transmission of data.[41] The person affected by the transfer must give his consent if the transmission has not been legitimized by a legal provision under the BDSG or otherwise.

One law that falls within this category and is particularly important to financial institutions is Section 44a of the Act Regulating Banking and Credit Business (Kreditwesengesetz—KWG).[42] Under this requirement, institutions with at least 20 percent of their shares held by a company domiciled abroad must pass on to this company all data required for fulfilling the provisions in the recipient country relating to bank supervision.[43] In addition to global figures, this may include data on borrowers, for example, notification of individual loans of one million or more Deutschmarks. Otherwise, the persons involved must give their consent if transmission is not legitimized. In international data transactions, however, this will often be the case, since executing a transfer or other noncash transaction is part of the purpose of the contract with the customer, so that reference can be made to Section 28, Paragraph 1, Number 1 of the BDSG.

Within the European payments system these transactions will be processed by Gesellschaft für Zahlungssysteme (GZS) (Eurocheques, Euro/Mastercard, and Visacard). To the best of my knowledge, there is no special data-protection or data-security policy for either this organization or for the SWIFT system; if data transfer is needed in order to fulfill the terms of a contract, additional admissibility conditions do not need to be observed.

However, the situation is different if the data transfer is only indirectly linked to the customer, for instance, if a bank uses a service center in another country. Although the cost savings that can be achieved through this may be of indirect benefit to the customer, ultimately the bank is acting here in its own interests and is required under Section 28 of the BDSG to weigh these interests against the affected customer's need for protection. This may mean a reasonable standard of protection needs to be defined at the outset.

Although a uniform internal market will have been created once the EU Directive on Data Protection has been implemented, the situation will remain unchanged as far as nonmember states are concerned. In other words, providers of financial services may only transfer data to countries demonstrating a reasonable level of protection. In the absence of such a level of protection, an exception will be needed. The same questions arise here as for all companies participating in international data transactions.[44] For this reason I will not enter into any greater detail here on the "third countries discussion."[45]

IX. ADDITIONAL OBLIGATIONS OF FINANCIAL INSTITUTIONS AS DATA CONTROLLERS, AND THE RIGHTS OF INDIVIDUALS

In addition to the requirements discussed, all data controllers must require employees involved in processing personal data to observe data secrecy, that is, to ensure confidentiality. Moreover, the clearly specified requirements of data security set out by the BDSG must be guaranteed by both the controller and the contractor by deploying suitable technical and organizational measures.

In the interests of effective data protection, the BDSG guarantees affected individuals various rights. Individuals' rights to access gives them the right to find out about data stored regarding them. If the data are incorrect or outdated, the individual may require correction under Section 35 of the BDSG. If storage of individuals' data is impermissible or no longer permissible,[46] or if there is a dispute about the data's accuracy, individuals may require deletion or blocking. Attention has already been drawn to the right to object to direct marketing.

Asserting these individual rights assumes the affected party is aware of the use of data in question. For this reason the law requires notification of affected parties in cases where the individual does not know his data were being processed. In the loans business, for instance, notification may be unnecessary since processing of data can be regarded as normal practice in the industry.

Access to data must be requested by the person affected, and this person is required by law to specify what his request applies to. The right to access does not have the same scope as the right of freedom of information. The right to access affects the following information: the purpose of storage, the origin of data, and, possibly, the recipient of data, if regular transmissions are made to this recipient. If the right of access is used in a malevolent or troublemaking fashion, it may in exceptional cases be refused.[47] Information is provided free of charge. If the information is not provided within a reasonable period of time or not provided accurately, the claim may be asserted in a civil court.

In the event of contraventions of data-protection obligations, the BDSG provides for criminal penalties and fines, and eases requirements on the provision of evidence for affected parties when they assert their compensation claims in court.

A number of new requirements will be included in the new BDSG. In this respect, the new provisions on mobile storage media (chip cards) will be particularly relevant to banks. According to the EU Directive on Data Protection, chip cards must be submitted to prior data-protection checks by the corporate data-protection officer. In addition, the supervision of premises open to the public using optical-electronic installations will also be regulated by law for the first time.[48]

X. DISTRIBUTION OF FINANCIAL SERVICES VIA NEW MEDIA

Financial institutions are turning increasingly to new media to rationalize existing business processes and open up new financial-services markets. The legal conditions under which this may be done are governed in Germany by the IuKDG.[49] A significant element in this act is the Teleservices Act (Teledienstegesetz— TDG), covering, in particular, the issue of freedom of entry, providers' obligation to identify clients' and providers' responsibilities, as well as defining the concept of teleservices. The data-protection requirements imposed upon providers of teleservices are laid down in the TDDSG, whose provisions take precedence over the more general BDSG. Finally, the Digital Signature Act (Signaturgesetz) should be mentioned. This creates the conditions that ensure safe use of digital signatures in legal and business transactions. It is worth noting that the opportunities opened up by the law have been little used to date.

The relevance of these relatively new laws is not limited to home banking in its narrow sense, extending to all financial services offered through the Internet, as long as they are "teleservices." With respect to financial-service providers, the TDG defines as teleservices information and communications opportunities offered by financial institutions in which digital data can be used by consumers in electronic online dialogue with the aid of their computers.[50]

The main requirements laid down in the Teleservices Data Protection Act are as follows:

- legal authorization or consent is needed;
- the purpose-binding principle, that information not be used for

purposes other than those for which it was collected, must be respected;

- the principle of user autonomy must be respected;
- the principle of data thrift must be respected;
- the principle of notification before consent must respected;
- electronic consent is introduced.

Data-protection obligations on the part of teleservices providers to be stressed are:

- to facilitate anonymous use and use based on a pseudonym if economically reasonable;
- to secure data protection using information technology;
- not to create user profiles related to individuals;
- to observe regulation with regard to the use of contract, connecting, and billing data;
- to provide a right of access that can be electronically requested and granted.

The law formulates special data-protection regulations based on the specific features of teleservices. A key feature here is the ban on creating user profiles.

Irrespective of the requirements defined by law, increasing awareness of data protection and security matters amongst customers, especially with respect to use of the Internet, has created a customer need for safer financial services designed in a manner that complies better with data protection. In particular, plans for safeguarding authenticity, integrity, and confidentiality are essential, in view of the high potential losses linked with financial transactions, and the potential threats from the use of electronic and networked communications media. With this need in mind, the national industry-standard Home Banking Computer Interface (HBCI) was introduced under the leadership of the Central Credit Committee (Zentraler Kreditausschuss).[51] In this way, bank customers can communicate with the bank computer using their computers to obtain information or conduct transactions such as fund transfers. Security is achieved by encoding the contents of the message and initialing it with the customer's personal code.

XI. DATA PROTECTION SUPERVISION AND THE CORPORATE DATA-PROTECTION OFFICER

Under the BDSG, compliance with the data-protection requirements by private industry is monitored by the supervisory authorities of the different Bundesländer. The field of telecommunications is an exception, falling within the jurisdiction of the Federal Commissioner for Data Protection. This federal commissioner also shall observe developments in the field of teleservices and comment on these in his report on his activities.

Government supervision distinguishes between supervision based on particular incidents (*e.g.* after a complaint has been received by a person affected) and official supervision. This has the following consequences: Private financial-services providers are checked if there is sufficient indication of an infringement against data-protection regulations. But enterprises that store personal data for the purpose of transmission as part of their operations, or that process them under contract, are officially monitored; in other words, a check can be carried out by the authority without the need for a specific incident. The same applies to the providers of teleservices. In implementing the EU Directive on Data Protection, the non-incident-related form of supervision will be introduced generally for all enterprises.[52] As part of its supervisory process, the authority may utilize its rights of inspection and examination, as well as its rights of direction and intervention.

A corporate data-protection officer must be appointed by all financial institutions with at least five employees constantly working on automated processing of personal data. This position is the interface between the company and data-protection supervision and may be described as a legally legitimized organ of self-regulation. The law requires the data-protection commissioner to report directly to company management, that he can operate without instructions and can carry out his duties independently. To do so he should be allocated sufficient personnel and resources. A person with the requisite professional knowledge and personal reliability may be appointed data-protection officer.

Independent companies within a group must appoint their own officers, although prevailing opinion holds that the same officer may be appointed for all or some of the companies if this does not give rise to any conflict of interest. At a minimum, the corporate data-protection officer must safeguard data-protection principles and data security in the enterprise, monitor data-processing programs by random sampling, and train staff involved in the processing of personal data.

XII. DATA PROTECTION AS A SELF-REGULATION TASK AND AS A CHALLENGE FOR GLOBAL COMPANIES

Because economic globalization is occurring in the context of different international legislative regimes in the field of data protection, global companies are likely to adopt self-regulation measures to establish unified data-protection policies, thereby creating or specifying an appropriate framework for their own business processes. The position of the corporate data-protection officer offers the opportunity to develop plans that go beyond the simple fulfillment of the legal requirements, taking in the business significance of data protection and data security as quality and competition features,[53] particularly in the field of financial services. Approaches of this kind are already available if we read the privacy statements issued by Citibank or American Express.

DaimlerChrysler has also begun developing a group-wide self-regulation plan that would set unified worldwide standards for relevant issues of data protection and data security. In order to define a data-protection standard that is as uniform as possible and can be implemented throughout the group, a Privacy Code of Conduct has been developed, and is now in the approval phase. Initially, this code is limited to customer and supplier data. The aim is to create a uniform philosophy with regard to the management and implementation of data protection and data security in customers' relationships with the group.

DaimlerChrysler has selected a mixture of centralized and decentralized elements for organizing its data protection. The Chief Corporate Data Protection Officer for the Group is empowered to issue guidelines and is supported by decentralized data-protection coordinators in the individual regions and companies of the group. In this respect the Chief Corporate Data Protection Officer for the Group and his staff function as the Competence Center. The independent position of the corporate data-protection officer is intended to guarantee compliance with the self-created system. A uniform Privacy Statement has already been implemented.

The increasing importance of the Internet as the infrastructure for e-commerce is making it necessary for a company like DaimlerChrysler to design its business-to-customer relationships as well as its business-to-business relationships in a data-protection-compliant manner. Privacy enhancing technologies (*e.g.* self-protection measures such as encoding) must be based on infrastructures that inspire trust to maintain or gain the confidence of customers and other communications partners. At the same time, internal processes—*e.g.* for data-warehouse and data-mining applications—need to be organized in a manner that secures optimal information processing with respect for the private sphere. Companies that have undertaken to provide their customers with first-class service must conceive their customer-relationship management in its full dimension as an essential element in the value-added chain to promote long-term acceptance for electronic commerce.

Notes

[1] Danish Public Authorities Registers Act.

[2] Danish Private Registers Act.

[3] Nominal Data (Automatic Processing) Act.

[4] Act providing rules for the Protection of Privacy in Connection with Personal Data Files.

[5] Federal Act on Personal Data.

[6] Federal Act on Protection of Personal Data with the Decree of June 14, 1993.

[7] Law on the Regulation of the Automatic Processing of Personal Data.

[8] Law concerning the Protection of Personal Privacy in Relation to the Processing of Personal Data.

[9] Personal Data Protection Act.

[10] Personal Data File Act and Personal Data File Decree.

[11] Law No. 78-17.

[12] Law on the Protection of Individuals with Regard to the Processing of Personal Data.

[13] Data Protection Act.

[14] Ibid.

[15] Protection of Individuals and other Subjects with Regard to the Processing of Personal Data.

[16] Act on Personal Data Registers.

[17] Law of August 29, 1997, on the Protection of Personal Data.

[18] Law for the Protection of Personal Data with Regard to Automatic Processing.

[19] Law of the Russian Federation on Information, Informatization and Information Protection, 1995.

[20] Data Act.

[21] Since February, 1998, a new data-protection law has been effective, which closely relies on the EU guideline.

[22] Law on the Protection of Personal Data in Information Systems of April 29, 1992.

[23] Law No. LXIII, 1992, on the Protection of Personal Data and Freedom of Information Act.

[24] Directive of the European Parliament and of the Council on the Processing of Personal Data and on the Protection of the Private Sphere in the Field of Telecommunication.

[25] Directive 1999/93/EG of the European Parliament and Council of December 13, 1999, Regarding Common General Requirements for Electronic Signatures.

[26] Amended Proposal for a Directive of the European Parliament and Council Regarding Distance Marketing of Financial Services to Consumers and the Amendment of Directives 97/7/EG and 98/27/EG, KOM 1999-385 endg. 98/0245—COD.

[27] In this connection, the Discussion Regarding the Effects of the European Data Protection Directive on Financial Services in the USA is being referenced, *e.g.* Peter Swire, "Effects of the European Privacy Directive on Financial Services," available at http://www.osu.edu/units/law/swire.htm.

[28] See Thorwald Hellner and Stephan Steuer, *Bankrecht und Bankpraxis*, vol. 6 (Köln: Bank-Verlag, 1999), Section 17. "Datenschutz," RN 14.

[29] This restriction is not required: The Austrian Data Protection Law includes legal persons (Section 4, Number 3 DS G2000). According to Italian Law (Article 26), data of legal persons are protected on a restricted basis.

[30] Reference Draft of the Federal Ministry of the Interior Regarding the New Draft of the BDSG.

[31] According to the reference draft, an establishment is presented when the financial-service provider constantly uses an established, continuous, or regularly recurrent space which is used by him for the operation of his business.

[32] See the exhaustive *Bankrecht und Bankpraxis*, vol. 6, 17/36.

[33] Schutzgemeinschaft für allgemeine Kreditsicherung.

[34] See Section 28, Paragraph 4 of the new BDSG draft (Federal Ministry, Stand 6, July 1999).

[35] See *Bankrecht und Bankpraxis*, vol. 6, 17/136. More detailed information in Alfred Büllesbach, "Datenschutz bei Data Warehouse und Data Mining," in *Computer und Recht* (2000), p. 11.

[36] See *Bankrecht und Bankpraxis*, vol. 6, 17/150.

[37] See the 17 Tätigkeitsbericht des Bundesbeauftragten für den Datenschutz (1997-98), p. 503 f.

[38] See Section 28, Paragraph 1, Record 1, Number 2 or Section 28, Paragraph 2, Record 1a of the BDSG.

[39] See the 17 Tätigkeitsbericht des Bundesbeauftragten für den Datenschutz (1997-98), p. 501 ff.

[40] Correspondingly formulated according to Section 3, Paragraph 8, Record 3 of the new BDSG draft: "Third parties are not the concerned party as well as those persons or locations, which acquire, process or use personal data domestically or in the area of application of legal regulations regarding the protection of personal data of the Member States of the EU."

[41] See Simitis in Simitis/Dammann/Geiger/Mallmann/Walz, BDSG, 4th ed. (April 1998), Section 28/8.1.

[42] Section 44a of the KWG is based on the EC Directive of June 13, 1983, on supervision of credit institutions on a consolidated basis (EC file no. L 193 dated July 18, 1983).

[43] See *Bankrecht und Bankpraxis*, vol. 6, 17/238.

[44] Barbara Wellbury, "The U.S. Side of Data Protection Policy," in Alfred Büllesbach, ed., *Datenverkehr ohne Datenschutz?—Eine globale Herausforderung* (Dr. Otto Schmidt Verlag, 1999).

[45] Schwartz/Reidenberg, *Data Privacy Law* (Michie Law Publishers, 1996) provides a summarised comparison of the EU requirements and US data-protection legislation, including aspects relating to the finance industry. An up-to-date worldwide comparison is given by EPIC and Privacy International, *Privacy & Human Rights, An International Survey of Privacy Laws and Developments*, 1999.

[46] For instance, a credit-protection organisation must observe the ban on utilisation contained in Section 51 of the Federal Central Register Act (Bundeszentralregistergesetz) or in Section 153, Paragraph 5 of the Trading Regulations (Gewerbeordnung), whereby data deleted from these registers on

the basis of statutory deletion dates may not be kept in other legal handlings, or used to the detriment of the affected party.

[47] *Bankrecht und Bankpraxis*, vol. 6, 17/280.

[48] See consideration (14) in the EU Directive on Data Protection.

[49] Information and Communication Services Act dated August 1, 1997, Federal Gazette (BGBl.), vol. 1.

[50] See *Bankrecht und Bankpraxis*, vol. 6, 17/390.

[51] The most important central associations in the German loans industry work together in the Central Credit Committee (Zentraler Kreditauschuß).

[52] See Section 38, Paragraph 1 of the draft amendment of the BDSG.

[53] For more details on this see Alfred Büllesbach, "Innovative and Technology-Shaping Data Protection—Social and Commercial Requirements," in *Multilateral Security in Communications*, vol. 3, Günter Müller, Kai Rannenberg (Addison-Wesley, 1999), p. 61.

Contributors

Marty Abrams is vice president for information policy and privacy for Experian Inc., a leading provider of information solutions. Prior to joining Experian, Mr. Abrams was assistant vice president and community affairs officer for the Federal Reserve Bank of Cleveland, administering the Community Reinvestment Act of 1977 and coordinating analysis of consumer issues.

Robert R. Belair is a partner in the Washington, DC, law firm of Mullenholz, Brimsek & Belair and, with Dr. Alan F. Westin, he is the editor of *Privacy and American Business*. Mr. Belair's government service includes work at the Federal Trade Commission on privacy matters and service as deputy counsel of the White House Privacy Committee.

Franz A. Blankart is former state secretary for foreign economic affairs of Switzerland. Prior to that he served in the banking industry, and as Swiss ambassador to international bodies such as the GATT and the United Nations Economic Commission for Europe.

Jean A. Bonna is managing partner in Lombard Odier & CIE, a private bank located in Geneva, Switzerland. He is a member of the board of the Association of Geneva Private Bankers, as well as a member of both the board and the committee of the Swiss Banker's Association.

Dr. Alfred Büllesbach is chief data protection officer for DaimlerChrysler AG and all its subsidiary companies worldwide. Previously he served as commissioner for data protection for the German state of Bremen. He is also a professor of applied computer and legal information service at the University of Bremen.

Fred H. Cate is a professor of law and director of the Information Law and Commerce Institute at the Indiana University

School of Law-Bloomington, as well as senior counsel for information law in the Indianapolis law firm of Ice Miller Donadio & Ryan. Professor Cate is the author of several books, including *Privacy in the Information Age* (Brookings Institute Press, 1997). He also chairs the drafting committee of the United Nations Working Group on Emergency Telecommunications. Professor Cate gratefully acknowledges the research assistance of Jean Walker and Melissa Luftig in preparing his chapter.

Kevin Coy is an associate at Mullenholz, Brimsek & Belair, specializing in health, financial, criminal justice, and consumer privacy issues.

Michel Y. Dérobert is secretary general of the Swiss Private Bankers Association and managing director of the Geneva Private Bankers Association.

Peter Gray is chairman and cofounder of the Internet Consumers Organization (ICO), a nonprofit organization that provides government and business policymakers, the media, and other interested parties with impartial analysis of important issues that affect consumer users of the Internet and providers of online products and services. Prior to forming the ICO, Mr. Gray was director of government relations for Citicorp.

Daniel B. Klein is an associate professor of economics at Santa Clara University in California. Professor Klein is the co-author of *Curb Rights: A Foundation for Free Enterprise in Urban Transit*, editor of *Reputation: Studies in the Voluntary Elicitation of Good Conduct*, and editor of *What Do Economists Contribute?*

Lawrence B. Lindsey is managing director of Economic Strategies, Inc. He is also a resident scholar and holder of the Arthur F. Burns chair at the American Enterprise Institute in

Washington, DC. Dr. Lindsey served as a member of the Board of Governors of the Federal Reserve System for five years from November, 1991, to February, 1997.

Julius L. ("Jerry") Loeser is senior vice president and deputy general counsel for Comerica Bank. He served previously as the Federal Reserve Board's senior counsel in the areas of bank holding company regulation, the Glass-Steagall Act, and various securities laws. Mr. Loeser has also specialized in bank regulation for several law firms, as well as for First Interstate Bancorp.

Duncan A. MacDonald is a writer and consultant to various business organizations on such topics as Y2K, privacy and data protection, ADR, bankruptcy reform, and plain-language writing. He retired as general counsel of Citibank's Card Products division for Europe and North America in 1997.

Dr. Richard W. Rahn is chairman of Novecon Financial, Ltd. He was the former vice president and chief economist of the US Chamber of Commerce, and has served as an economic advisor to senior government officials in the US and foreign countries. He holds a Ph.D. from Columbia University and is the author of *The End of Money and the Struggle for Financial Privacy.*

Solveig Singleton is director of information studies at the Cato Institute, where she specializes in privacy policy, encryption, and telecommunications law. Ms. Singleton also serves as vice chairman of publications for the Telecommunications and Electronic Media Practice Group of the Federalist Society for Law & Public Policy Studies.

Fred L. Smith, Jr., is the founder and president of the Competitive Enterprise Institute. Mr. Smith is coeditor of *Environmental Politics: Public Costs, Private Rewards*, and has contributed chapters to over one dozen books, including *The True State of the Planet, Market Liberalism: A Paradigm for the 21st Century*, and *Assessing the Reagan Years.*

Eugene Volokh teaches free speech law, copyright law, the law of government and religion, and the law of firearms regulation at UCLA Law School. Before joining the faculty at UCLA, he clerked for Justice Sandra Day O'Connor on the US Supreme Court and for Judge Alex Kozinski on the US Court of Appeals for the 9th Circuit. Professor Volokh also worked for 12 years as a computer programmer, and is still partner in a small software company which sells HP 3000 software that he wrote.